125+ secret coves, wreck sites, abandoned armaments, and other off-the-beaten-path destinations

Hidden Nova Scotia

Scott Osmond

BOULDER
BOOKS

Library and Archives Canada Cataloguing in Publication

Title: Hidden Nova Scotia : 125+ secret coves, wreck sites, abandoned armaments, and other
   off-the-beaten-path destinations / Scott Osmond.
Names: Osmond, Scott, author.
Description: Includes bibliographical references and index.
Identifiers: Canadiana 20230163718 | ISBN 9781989417676 (softcover)
Subjects: LCSH: Nova Scotia—Description and travel. | LCSH:
Nova Scotia—Guidebooks. | LCSH:
   Curiosities and wonders—Nova Scotia. | LCGFT: Guidebooks.
Classification: LCC FC2317.6 .O86 2023 | DDC 917.1604/5—dc23

© 2023 Scott Osmond

Published by Boulder Books
Portugal Cove-St. Philip's, Newfoundland and Labrador
www.boulderbooks.ca

Design and layout: Tanya Montini
Editor: Stephanie Porter
Copy editor: Iona Bulgin

Printed in Canada

We acknowledge the financial support of the Government of Newfoundland and Labrador through the Department of Tourism, Culture, Arts and Recreation.

Funded by the Government of Canada   Financé par le gouvernement du Canada   Canada

125+ secret coves, wreck sites,
abandoned armaments, and other
off-the-beaten-path destinations

Hidden
Nova Scotia

Table of Contents

CUMBERLAND & COLCHESTER COUNTIES

1. LONDONDERRY IRON MINES
2. BERLIN WALL
3. CFS DEBERT & THE DIEFENBUNKER
4. ECONOMY'S BOMBING OBSERVATION TOWER
5. TUNNELS OF WENTWORTH VALLEY
6. WATERFALLS OF THE COBEQUID HILLS
7. PARRSBORO DAM
8. MV KIPAWO
9. WARDS FALLS & THE DILIGENT RIVER SLOT CANYON
10. EATONVILLE
11. CHIGNECTO MARINE TRANSPORT RAILWAY
12. SLADE LAKE & OXFORD'S KARST TOPOGRAPHY

EAST ANNAPOLIS VALLEY TO THE SHUBENACADIE RIVER

1. BAXTERS HARBOUR & BLACK HOLE FALLS
2. PADDYS ISLAND & THE MEDFORD ROCK FORMATIONS
3. NOVA SCOTIA TEXTILE LIMITED MILL
4. WINDSOR AND HANTSPORT RAILWAY
5. FALMOUTH STATION'S APPLE WAREHOUSE & GREENHOUSES
6. BRAMBER FLOWER POT ROCK
7. WALTON GYPSUM & BARITE MINE
8. SOUTH MAITLAND RAILWAY BRIDGE

WESTERN NOVA SCOTIA & LOWER ANNAPOLIS VALLEY

1. MCMASTER MILL
2. NICTAUX RIVER FALLS & HYDRO FACILITY
3. BRITEX FACTORY
4. UPPER CLEMENTS PARK
5. RUSSEL BROTHERS WINCH BOAT & FORGOTTEN LOGGING CAMPS
6. MOOSE RIVER STONE TUNNEL
7. PETER ISLAND LIGHTHOUSE
8. TOWN OF NEW FRANCE, THE ELECTRIC CITY
9. ÉGLISE SAINTE-MARIE
10. BANGOR SAWMILL

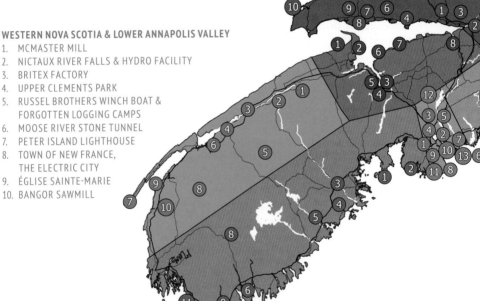

ST. MARGARET'S BAY AND THE SOUTHERN SHORE

1. BLANDFORD WHALING STATION
2. POLLY'S COVE FOUNDATIONS
3. ABANDONED SHIPS OF THE LEHAVE RIVER
4. BRIDGEWATERS PUBLIC SERVICE COMMISSION HYDROELECTRIC DAM
5. NOVA SCOTIA WOOD PULP AND PAPER COMPANY MILL
6. CFS SHELBURNE
7. MCNUTTS ISLAND
8. INDIAN FIELDS AIRFIELD
9. REMAINS OF CLYDE RIVER'S FORESTRY INDUSTRY
10. BARRINGTON AIR STATION
11. HISPON CREEK STONE ARCH

CAPE BRETON
1. RELICS OF THE CAPE
   ST. LAWRENCE LIGHTHOUSES
2. CAPE NORTH LIGHTHOUSES
3. WRECK OF THE MV CARITA
4. CHÉTICAMP GYPSUM MINE POND
5. PORT HOOD ISLAND'S
   LOST CAUSEWAY
6. RIVER DENYS MOUNTAIN
7. DIOGENES CAVE
8. MARBLE MOUNTAIN
9. CAPE BRETON'S
   CENTRAL RAILWAY
10. PLASTER PONDS
11. ST. PETERS CANAL
12. MINDAMAR MINE
13. ARCH CAVE

SYDNEY AND LOUISBOURG
1. KLUSKAP'S CAVE
2. ST. ALPHONSUS CHURCH
3. OXFORD BATTERY
4. CRANBERRY POINT BATTERY
5. CHAPEL POINT BATTERY
6. STUBBERT'S POINT BATTERY
7. POINT EDWARD SEARCHLIGHT
   EMPLACEMENTS
8. HMCS PROTECTOR II: POINT
   EDWARD NAVAL BASE
9. CFS SYDNEY
10. SOUTH BAR BATTERY
11. FORT PETRIE
12. FORT LINGAN
13. BROUGHTON
14. LOUISBOURG RAILWAY TUNNEL

CENTRAL NOVA SCOTIA & THE EASTERN SHORE
1. MILLSTREAM BROOK FOUNDATIONS
2. HART ISLAND LIGHTHOUSE
3. HULBERT'S SAWMILL AND GRISTMILL
4. HAZEL HILL COMMERCIAL CABLE STATION
5. RCAF NO. 5 RADAR SITE: COLE HARBOUR
6. DOLLIVER MINE COMPANY'S POWERHOUSE
7. GOLDENVILLE GOLD DISTRICT
8. SHIPWRECK OF THE FURY
9. DERELICT SHIPS OF MARIE JOSEPH
10. SHEET HARBOUR LUMBER AND PULP MILL REMAINS

HALIFAX REGION
1. BAYERS LAKE MYSTERY WALLS
2. SS DAISY & THE FORMER J.P.
   PORTER SCRAPYARD
3. FENERTY LAKE FISH SALVAGE
   PLANT
4. THE STORY OF PAPER MILL LAKE
5. SHUBENACADIE CANAL
6. DEVILS ISLAND
7. DEVILS POINT BATTERY
8. FORT CHEBUCTO
9. CONNAUGHT BATTERY
10. POINT PLEASANT PARK
11. YORK REDOUBT & YORK SHORE
    BATTERY
12. RCAF STATION BEAVERBANK
13. MCNABS ISLAND

Introduction

About This Guide

Nova Scotia's social, political, and cultural history has long been defined by the movement of people, from the time the Mi'kmaq freely roamed their land to colonization, when Nova Scotia became the gateway for settlers in Canada and North America. This mix of cultural values and practices have shaped the province's political, cultural, and physical landscapes. Each year thousands of people visit Canada's ocean playground, hoping to experience a slice of that east coast lifestyle made famous by this province.

From the beautiful Cape Breton Highlands National Park to historic Halifax, from the Peggy's Cove lighthouse to the picturesque Southern Shore and the rich soils of the Annapolis Valley, Nova Scotia has no shortage of iconic destinations. Even though visiting these sites and others found in tourism guides is an excellent way to see the province, Nova Scotia's diverse landscape offers so much more to explore.

With its small geographic size and widespread population, it may seem like it would be difficult to find *hidden* or *lost* destinations in Nova Scotia. While it's true that you are never too far from a community, Nova Scotia contains a world of hidden stories, curious places, and off-the-beaten path destinations. Relics, each representing a significant period in the province's development, are found everywhere. Throughout the centuries, mining operations, sawmills, railways, and military fortifications have come and gone, leaving unique places to explore. Nova Scotia's physical landscape also contains world-class geology and geographic sites, including cave systems, sea arches, waterfalls, and hidden wonders made by the world's highest tides, in the Bay of Fundy.

This guide is for explorers—novice and experienced, local and tourist, off-the-beaten-path hikers and armchair voyagers—who wish to see more of Nova Scotia and experience places that have been lost or forgotten or are yet to be found.

This guide has three main goals:

Introduce new places to visit and explore

The selection of destinations has not been influenced by ease of access, politics, or economic value. Just because a place does not meet the economic or political viability of many tourism sites does not mean that it is not worth sharing. In many cases, these places outshine more popular destinations.

Promote Nova Scotia's incredible built and natural heritage

Each location represents a piece of Nova Scotia's history and development. I hope to raise awareness of cultural, historic, and geologic preservation while also sharing forgotten stories.

Show that exploring is for everyone

Whether you wish to explore the wonders of Nova Scotia from a car or are looking for a new hiking destination, this guide is for you. And if you're an armchair explorer, I hope this book brings these places alive and inspires wonder for you, wherever you are.

USING THIS GUIDE

Assumption of Risk

Many of the places in this guide are abandoned and/or unmarked, and therefore risky to visit. This guide provides general information about each place, its history, and its location. Proper caution and safety must be taken at all times.

This guide does not encourage illegal, illicit, or dangerous activities. Those who visit the described locations do so at their own risk, and proper safety precautions must be taken.

To ensure a safe adventure:

- Research and understand the potential risks before you go.
- Use caution around cliffs, steep hillsides, and the ocean.
- Never enter an unmaintained or abandoned building/structure. Falling debris, risk of collapse, and other hidden dangers are extremely likely. Obtain permission to enter all structures and properties.
- Take out what you take in and leave the area as it was when you arrived.

This guide shares some of Nova Scotia's obscure attractions and provides general information about the location and condition of each place at the time of writing. It is the sole responsibility of the explorer to determine if it is safe to explore or visit any of the places listed here.

Land Acknowledgement

We must first respectfully acknowledge that we are in Mi'kma'ki, the ancestral, unceded, and current territory of the Mi'kmaq. This territory is covered by the "Treaties of Peace and Friendship" which the Mi'kmaq first signed with the British Crown in 1725. The treaties did not deal with the surrender of lands and resources but recognized Mi'kmaw title and established the rules for what would be an ongoing relationship between nations. We also acknowledge the rich histories, ongoing contributions, and legacies of African Nova Scotians and their communities over the last 400 years. We are all treaty people, and we have responsibilities to each other and this land and I would invite you to reflect on these relationships as you learn more about and explore Mi'kma'ki.

The Origins of Nova Scotia's Lost Wonders

The hidden wonders and places throughout this province fall into several categories, each with its own history and significance toward Nova Scotia's development. Each site represents a piece of a larger story. Below are the general themes of which each of these stories are a part.

MILITARY

Nova Scotia's history is inundated with war and military fortifications. When European settlers first arrived in North America, they brought their European wars. For centuries, fighting between France, Britain, and the US have influenced settlement patterns in this province. Annapolis, Louisbourg, and Halifax can trace their origins, in part, to their strategic military positions. But this was just the beginning of how military operations would shape the province. From the time Europeans first settled on the land, dozens of military outpost and fortifications were built along Nova Scotia's coast. Some of these sites have been restored, such as Citadel Hill in Halifax or Fort Louisbourg in Cape Breton. But to capture the scale of how war shaped the province and its people, we need to look beyond tourist destinations to the hundreds of coastal batteries, airfields, bunkers, bases, and radar sites built over the last 150 years. Each one exemplifies the government's and the people's fear of being attacked by an opposing nation.

While many of these historic sites predate the American Civil War, most of what remains from Nova Scotia's military history was built after the mid-19th century. This war sparked fear in the British government of another invasion into what would become Canada. Because of this, beginning during the war and continuing until the turn of the century, many new fortifications were constructed across the province with a focus on Halifax and Sydney, both of which had become busy shipping and commercial ports. After confederation in 1867, the British Army maintained control over Halifax's defences until 1906, when all of its fortifications were controlled by the Canadian government. Shortly after, the Government of Canada built its first coastal defence battery in the harbour (Connaught Battery, page 202).

World War I brought many changes. Halifax became the departure point for Canadian troops and supplies heading to Europe, and Halifax's and Sydney's industrial and commercial importance as seaports made their protection crucial. The result was the construction of a meticulously designed, province-wide system of coastal defence batteries, lookout stations, minefields, anti-submarine nets, and training facilities. As the province became a staging location for ship convoys en route to Europe, protecting Allied ships from the threat of the German Navy and its U-boats became a top priority.

Following the war, many of the province's defence systems were placed in reserve or decommissioned. In 1936, the political situation deteriorated again in Europe and, with war looming, Canada's Department of Defence commissioned Major B.D.C. Treatt to investigate the country's coastal defences. The Treatt Report outlined the condition of current defences and how to properly protect the country's waters.

After declaring war on Germany in September 1939, Canada took the threat to its harbours and ports seriously, particularly those on the east coast, which were deemed most vulnerable. As Halifax and Sydney would again become one of the main ports for shipping supplies, ammunition, and troops to Europe, additional defences would be required. This launched an unprecedented effort, with coastal defence facilities, training bases, airfields, and operations centres being constructed for Navy, Army, and Air Force use. Seemingly overnight, the province became a heavily defended fortress. As radar was an emerging technology, radar sites were established all along the province's eastern coast.

Following the war, the government disarmed many of the forts and defences, placing guns, equipment, and supplies in reserve. This decision was briefly reversed a few years later due to the threat of war in Korea and the slowly building Cold War. By the mid-1950s, however, almost all of the province's forts and batteries were decommissioned and abandoned. The Cold War continued into the early 1990s and led to the construction of several advanced radar sites, in an effort to track potential threats that might approach North America by flying over the Atlantic or Arctic oceans. In 2023, Nova Scotia plays an important role with the Canadian military, with several sites still operational.

As a result of a long turbulent history, pieces of Nova Scotia's military are now found in almost every town. Some of these structures have been preserved and transformed into accessible, tourist-friendly destinations; others have been abandoned or forgotten. In addition to these being sites to explore, they also reflect the effects of war on Nova Scotians and the lengths governments went through to ensure their protection.

MINING

Mineral extraction has long been one of Nova Scotia's most important industries. Rich reserves of gold, iron, copper, gypsum, and coal have been found. This industry began as small, isolated operations to take minerals from exposed rock outcrops and coastal cliffs. Over time, these endeavours and the demand for minerals increased, as did the effort to discover new reserves. Mining remains an important industry in Nova Scotia in 2023, but due to shifting global economies, depletion of resources, and more accessible minerals elsewhere, it is only a fraction of its former self.

Perhaps no mineral has had a longer-lasting effect on Nova Scotia than coal, an industry launched with the invention of steam-powered machinery during the Industrial Revolution. By the mid- to late 19th century, major operations were under way in Pictou County, Springhill, and throughout Cape Breton. At the same time, another major mineral was gaining popularity: iron, mined and smelted in Nova Scotia since the late 18th century, experienced a major increase in operations by the mid-1800s with the establishment of the Londonderry iron mines and

works in 1848 (Londonderry Iron Mines, page 366).

By the end of the century, the opening of new iron mines led to the next major industry, steel making. Steel manufacturing was energy intensive, and coal, or its derivative coke, was needed in large supply, leading to the establishment of steel manufacturing plants in the coal towns of Pictou County and Cape Breton. In 1870, Canada's first steel was produced in Nova Scotia. Provincial iron mining would decrease into the 20th century, but its steel manufacturing would soon become one of the most important in Canada. A declining market, shipping problems, and new technologies precipitated the end of the steel industry; Nova Scotia's last major plant closed in 2001.

Gold has also left its impact on Nova Scotia. Beginning around 1850, most of the province's gold mining occurred along the Eastern Shore. Discovery of gold at Tangier River in Mooseland in 1858 marked the first of three gold rushes; several towns were established, some of which remain (Goldenville Gold District, page 151). Gold mining operations were typically small in scale and, even with the introduction of new processing methods, remained relatively small, isolated operations compared to other types of mining.

Gypsum has been extracted since the 1770s. At the time, gypsum had little use but with its introduction as a construction material,

the demand for it spiked. By the 1950s, dozens of gypsum mines stretched from Windsor to northern Cape Breton. Nova Scotia continues to provide a significant amount of Canada's gypsum and boasts the largest gypsum mine in North America, at Milford (Windsor & Hantsport Railway, page 341).

Copper, zinc, and lead have also been regularly mined. Often confined to smaller operations except when processing plants were also installed, these mines have each impacted local communities and environments (Mindamar Mine, page 82). Discussing mining in Nova Scotia would not be complete without mentioning the historic barite mining near Walton, which is said to contain the world's largest single ore body of barite (Walton Gypsum & Barite Mine, page 353).

The remnants of these operations are found in every nook and cranny of the province. Each site tells the story of the miners and their families, but it also demonstrates the widespread effects of these mines on the environment. In addition to tunnels, foundations, and deteriorated buildings, many of these sites are accompanied by the harsh realities of abandoned tailings ponds and pollution. While some mining sites are relatively safe to visit, others are plagued with open holes, crumbling structures, toxic gases, contaminated soil, and other associated risks to those who live in the vicinity.

NATURAL WONDERS

Nova Scotia has a complex and diverse geology and physical geography. From the mountains of northern Cape Breton to the fertile land of the Annapolis Valley, Nova Scotia's geology and physical geography is a story that is over 1 billion years old. The spectacular scenery of Canada's ocean playground results from millions of years of geological processes. Sea stacks, caves, dramatic seascapes, and miles of lakes and rivers all trace their origin to supercontinents and glaciation episodes. No collection of Nova Scotia's hidden wonders would be complete without the inclusion of some of these landforms and geologic wonders.

The geologic formation of Nova Scotia is generally divided into two distinct regions. The first, in the north, is comprised of Cape Breton, Antigonish, and the Chignecto Isthmus. This former microcontinent, known as the Avalon Zone, was formed from a volcanic arc, on the predecessor of the Atlantic Ocean known as the Iapetus Ocean during the Cambrian Period (600 million to 400 million years ago). To the south, encompassing the southern portion, is the Meguma Zone. Formed at the edge of the supercontinent Gondwana, sediment deposited from turbidity currents slowly accumulated until a massive layer of earth formed. When the supercontinent Pangea formed approximately 200 million years ago, the two geologic regions were forced together along an east-to-west running fault system known as the Cobequid-Chedabucto Fault or Minas Fault Zone. After the breakup of Pangea, the Atlantic Ocean began to form, separating the two microcontinents from similar rocks which can now be found throughout Europe and Africa. In the millions of years since, plate tectonics have twisted the rock layers, with intrusions, leaving a conglomerate of igneous, metamorphic, and sedimentary rocks. These processes led to the accumulation of the many minerals mined throughout the province.

While over 1 billion years of geologic evolution laid the foundations for modern Nova Scotia, the last 2 million years carved the province into its current diverse landscape. A succession of glaciations and ice ages modified the rocks and the landscape. During these ice ages, glaciers covered the earth's surface, reaching thicknesses of more than 300 metres. This moving ice sheet gouged and eroded the land, leaving barrens, mountains, valleys, and deposits of glacial till. At the end of the last ice age, approximately 12,000 years ago, melting glaciers carved new rivers, created new lakes, and irrevocably changed the province's hydrology.

Within this time, the province's most intriguing geologic formations were created: caves, sinkholes, disappearing streams, and other features due to the erosion of weak carbonate and evaporite rocks, known as karst topography. Thanks to the carboniferous era geologic formation known as the Windsor group, layers of gypsum, limestone, and sandstone have created spectacular sites from the Annapolis Valley to northern Cape Breton. Similarly, the sedimentary and igneous layers of rock along the shores of the Minas Basin and Bay of Fundy have produced spectacular waterfalls, slot canyons, sea stacks, and caves. Many fossils preserved in rocks throughout Cape Breton have helped scientists describe the evolution of life on the planet.

Nova Scotia is known worldwide for its scenery—but there are still many unexplored secrets and hidden wonders. Tracing these hidden wonders allows explorers to understand the fascinating, complex history of Nova Scotia's geology.

FORESTRY AND LOGGING

From the time the forests were first used by the Mi'kmaq to the first sawmills introduced during the early years of colonization to today's large pulp and paper mills, Nova Scotia's forestry industry has had a turbulent history. Since the beginning of large-scale operations in the late 1700s, the industry has been susceptible to change caused by both domestic and foreign political situations, to which it is not immune even in the 21st century.

The use of the forest as a resource started small, with harvested logs being used locally to construct houses, buildings, wharves, and sheds. The first sawmill was established in the Annapolis Valley in 1630. One hundred years later, the number of sawmills increased greatly as more people settled in Nova Scotia.

In the 19th century, the forestry industry entered a new era of productivity due to the requirements of shipbuilders in coastal settlements and the growing demand for timber across North America and Europe. A similar industry took shape in 1819 when the Acadian Paper Mill, Nova Scotia's first paper mill, was established. While that mill made its paper from rags and cloths, Upper Sackville resident Charles Fenerty was inspired by the process and, after years of experimenting, became one of the first people to make pulp from wood, in 1844. This ignited the pulp and paper industry; large mills were established in

Bedford, Milton, Halifax, and on the Sissiboo River.

Later in the 19th century, the province's interior opened up with the establishment of regional roads and railways. Sawmills had been concentrated along the coast but, soon, depleted forestry resources and overcrowded harbours caused many to migrate inland to take advantage of inland forest reserves and rivers. At the same time, shipbuilding was reaching its peak and was a major user of logged timber.

The 20th century experienced another shift in the use of the province's forests. A growing population meant that little was left of accessible forests and new, much-needed forestry management legalization and policy narrowed the market on who could establish a sawmill. Nova Scotia's shipbuilding industry was declining due to the growing popularity of steel ships, and the market for timber, pulp, and paper was now heavily dictated by international markets. Sawmills were forced to close and soon the forestry industry was comprised solely of large-scale sawmills or pulp and paper mills.

In 2023, remnants of Nova Scotia's historic logging and forestry operations are found in every corner. Relics of logging operations are still visible and stone or concrete foundations are found on nearly every river.

MARITIME HISTORY

Few would challenge the importance of maritime history to the development of Nova Scotia. For millennia, humans traversed the waters surrounding Nova Scotia as a means of fishing, transporting goods, and travelling. From fishing history to the Mi'kmaq crossing the Cabot Strait in canoes to the mega ships that still use the port of Halifax, the province's maritime history is filled with stories of incredible accomplishments, adventure, and tragedy.

The province's exposed position in the Atlantic Ocean combined with its jagged, rocky coastlines has long made it a danger to those sailing in its waters. Since the time of colonization, ships have run aground and sunk off the coast, claiming the lives of thousands.

With the arrival of more settlers, the importance of maritime navigation aids became apparent. Historically, nautical charts and natural landmarks guided ships, but the establishment of the province's first lighthouse at Louisbourg in 1734 initiated safer maritime practices. Lighthouses popped up on every dangerous stretch of coastline frequently visited by ships. Every major island, headland, and shoal had some form of light, warning sailors and providing guidance. These lighthouses evolved, and their remains, along with their associated structures, are still visible.

Nova Scotia's treacherous waters have claimed countless ships and lives, with Sable Island and St. Paul Island having notoriously high death tolls. The turbulent waters and rocky shores that caused many of these wrecks are also why so few are seen along the shores today. Most of the debris has been washed away; however, tangible evidence offers a solemn reminder of the dangers that sailors faced and represent an important part of Nova Scotia's maritime history.

TRANSPORTATION

The first Europeans to arrive in Nova Scotia settled along the coastline where they could use boats to fish and travel between communities, avoiding the need to traverse the difficult terrain of the interior. For centuries, boats were the primary means of transportation. Slowly small road networks connected more communities, opening up new land to cultivate. By the mid-1800s, a network of well-travelled roads connected many larger communities across Nova Scotia.

The mid-1850s brought a growing demand for a railway to connect the far reaches of the province to the rest of British North America. Before this time, the province's railways were small, locally owned, and often associated with a mine (such as Nova Scotia's first railway at Albion Mines in Stellarton). In 1853, a charter was received to begin construction on a railway line from Halifax to Pictou County and a second line from Halifax to the community of Digby via Windsor and the Annapolis Valley. Both lines opened in 1858. In 1872, the completed Intercolonial Railway connected the railway lines to New Brunswick and the rest of Canada. Following this, railways spread across the province, eventually connecting Cape Breton and Yarmouth to the rest of the province. Nova Scotia's railways allowed greater access to the interior as well as to new markets.

Many railway lines have been abandoned or transformed into popular recreation trails, while others seem to have been forgotten. Either way, the province's past railway infrastructure hides many incredible places to explore, each showcasing the extent and importance of these transportation networks.

Another transportation network in Nova Scotia is canals. Similar to railways, canals opened up the interior, speeding the transportation of goods. As sailing was the primary means of transporting supplies and cargo between communities in the early 1800s, business owners and governments looked to canals, as well as the railway, to access inland communities. In the case of the Shubenacadie Canal that transported small boats between Halifax harbour and the Minas Basin, the endeavour was short-lived, as other networks quickly made it obsolete. In contrast, the canal at St. Peters is still being used for recreation and the occasional commercial vessel.

AGRICULTURE AND MANUFACTURING

The last, but certainly not the least, reason for some of the hidden wonders in this book is changing regional economies. Nova Scotia has long been associated with agriculture, as small farms provided food and income for families. Throughout the 18th century, the government encouraged land clearing for farming by providing subsidies to farmers. This paved the way for increased transportation networks in the 19th century, as goods were shipped to markets across Canada. Farming remains an important industry to Nova Scotians.

Similarly, manufacturing drastically changed the industrial landscape of Nova Scotia when it became mainstream following the Industrial Revolution. By the mid-1800s, an array of new manufacturing jobs provided employment for thousands. Factories producing textiles, processing produce, and building furniture popped up in small communities. Manufacturing was diverse but each factory and mill became an important hub to its community. While manufacturing remains evident, many factories have come and gone, leaving behind some of Nova Scotia's most astonishing built heritage.

Exploring Nova Scotia Safely

Exploring comes with risk but, with common sense, proper preparation, and research, you can greatly minimize any risks. Always take out what you take in, leaving every place in the same condition as you found it—leave nothing behind but footsteps.

CLIMATE

Despite its location in the North Atlantic Ocean, Nova Scotia has favourable weather for outdoor exploring. Located halfway between the North Pole and the Equator, Nova Scotia's climate is more continental than the expected maritime climate. The Gulf Stream brings warm air to its shorelines from the south. Along the coast, air temperatures are temperate, cooling in the summer and warming in the winter. Fog is a regular occurrence along the southern and eastern shores. Cape Breton receives the most snow, due to its higher latitudes; in the south, Yarmouth's warmer climate means that it receives far less. In the west, the Annapolis Valley's hot humid summers make it a popular tourist destination for both residents and visitors.

While Nova Scotia's weather is favourable for hikers and explorers throughout the year, it is important to monitor the forecast and always plan for quick weather changes, especially when exploring near the coast.

ABANDONED BUILDINGS AND DETERIORATED STRUCTURES

Do not enter the neglected, deteriorated, or abandoned buildings and structures described in this book. In addition to concerns about falling debris, collapsing structures, and mould or other airborne bacteria or chemicals, many places remain under private or government ownership and exploring them is considered trespassing. Almost all the places described here can and should be experienced from a safe distance. With some preparation and foresight, they can still be exciting and safe places to visit.

Always be respectful of private property. Look for signs of regular use and abide by all posted signs. Check with local landowners and consult online resources to determine site access. Land ownership and land use can change quickly.

ENVIRONMENTAL CONDITIONS

Heights and Loose Rocks

Many hiking trails and lookouts take you to the vicinity of cliffs or other steep slopes. Always wear proper footwear, maintain a safe distance from the edge, and use caution when deteriorating weather or water has caused slippery conditions. Avoid going too close to rock cuts and cliffs, as falling rock is extremely dangerous. Watch for fractured rocks and areas that look prone to collapse.

Ocean Hazards and Tides

Never turn your back on the ocean. Be aware of waves, tides, and changing weather conditions. Slippery rocks and quickly changing sea conditions pose extreme hazards. Caution should be taken when exploring the shores and estuaries of the Bay of Fundy, where the world's highest tides can be up to 15 metres. Best practices when hiking along the sea floor during low tide: plan ahead—keep track of high- and low-tide times—and always have a reliable way off an intertidal zone.

Cape Breton

Scenic Cape Breton Island is an irregularly shaped island with large rivers, mountains, and, of course, the Bras d'Or Lake, a large inland sea found at the centre of the island. In the north, the Cape Breton Highlands are a collection of forested mountains, deep valleys, and dramatic coastlines that, despite leaving most of the area uninhabitable, attract thousands of tourists and outdoor enthusiasts each year. The coastal plateaus and low-lying coastlines have long made the island's west home to fishing and farming villages such as Cheticamp, Inverness, and Mabou. Bras d'Or Lake's many protected harbours, coves, and inlets make it a world-famous sailing destination. To the east, rolling hills give way to rocky coastlines that are regularly draped in a blanket of fog. In the south, the Strait of Canso separates Cape Breton from the rest of Nova Scotia. Although it is geographically an island, since 1955 Cape Breton has been connected to the rest of the province by the Canso Causeway.

Cape Breton's people, culture, and heritage make the area an incredible place to visit. The province's indigenous people, the Mi'kmaq, have long held a spiritual connection to the land and continue to live in the area. Following European colonization of the island, English, French, and perhaps most notably Scottish immigrants established communities defined by a mix of cultures and architecture that can still be seen. Each group prospered from the bountiful fishing grounds and forest reserves found across the island. Cape Breton's separation from

the rest of the province fostered a strong sense of identity and island pride which still persist.

In the 18th, 19th, and 20th centuries, mines were established to take advantage of the bountiful reserves of coal, limestone, and gypsum. Mining established new communities and provided additional sources of employment for others.

The first settlements of Cape Breton were isolated and scattered along the coast, and just as the island remained separated from the rest of Canada, so too were communities disconnected from one another. Because of this, the history of Cape Breton's transportation networks is a defining chapter in the island's history—from the struggle to conquer the Strait of Canso, to the establishment of railway lines and finally its road network.

While the island is dotted with small paved and gravel roads, from the southern end of the island at Port Hawkesbury three main highways

can be taken. Crossing the causeway and continuing north along the TCH (Highway 105) brings visitors alongside Bras d'Or Lake, passing through the forested interior of Cape Breton before Whycocomagh, Baddeck, and finally the Newfoundland and Labrador ferry terminal in North Sydney. From Port Hawkesbury and following the western shore, Highway 19 leads through the coastal communities of Port Hood, Mabou, and Inverness; following Highway 4 east passes through the community of St. Peters before turning north and following the eastern shore of Bras d'Or Lake. The most popular and scenic route in Cape Breton, however, is the Cabot Trail (Highway 30), which leaves the community of St. Anns and heads north, following the mountainous coastline to Cape Breton Highlands National Park. From here, the highway circles the north tip of Cape Breton before returning south, on the west coast of the island.

1. Relics of the Cape St. Lawrence Lighthouses

Lowland Cove, Northwest Cape Breton

The lighthouses of Cape North (page 41) are some of the most isolated in Nova Scotia. The only competition for the title is the series of lighthouses constructed at Cape St. Lawrence on Cape Breton's northwest coast. All that remains are several foundations, but the area's beautiful coastal plains and rolling hills make an adventure to the isolated coastline well worth it.

The first lighthouse at Cape St. Lawrence was constructed by Thomas O'Neil in 1888. It was a white square wooden tower, with an attached dwelling for the lighthouse keeper and his family. The 17-metre-high tower housed two fixed white lights: one near its base, the other in a lantern room at the top. Inside the lantern room, a kerosene lantern created a powerful beacon that could be seen 27 kilometres away. The lighthouse was commissioned on June 1, 1889, and Alexander McLennan was appointed its first lighthouse keeper.

As with every lighthouse, its story is found both in the building and the families that operated it. The lighthouse's location on exposed land on Cape Breton's western shore meant that it bore the brunt of frequent storms. With no running water, no electricity, and the nearest town miles away, life was challenging on that coast. This was exemplified by a December gale that struck in 1890, heavily damaging the lighthouse and knocking it temporarily out of commission. It was replaced by two temporary lights until repairs could be made.

This was only the start. In 1893, Charles Jamieson was appointed the new lighthouse keeper; with his wife, Christina, he established a family there. In 1901, their three children died in a diphtheria outbreak. The couple remained at the lighthouse and raised seven more children.

A more powerful light was installed in 1909 and the lower light was decommissioned. After this, activity stagnated until 1952, when a new

lighthouse and residence were built. Thirteen years later, the light was automated and the lighthouse keeper and his family abandoned their seaside home. Over time, the lighthouse and dwelling fell into disrepair. The light was removed from the wooden structure and placed on a mast installed at the point. Over the next 30 years, the two buildings collapsed, leaving only their foundations. The current navigation aid is a skeletal steel tower that displays a flashing white light warning ships to avoid the dangerous shoreline.

The area hosts horses and cattle which seasonally graze the grassy fields void of fences or restraints. Cape Breton's western shore is defined by rolling mountains that transition into grassy meadows that stretch along the coast. Contained within the stone foundations of the former lighthouses and lighthouse keepers' dwellings are hundreds of relics, including fragments of equipment and chimneys. The beauty of the peaceful windswept meadows contrasts dramatically with the relentless swells of the Gulf of St. Lawrence.

 RELICS OF THE CAPE ST. LAWRENCE LIGHTHOUSES:
N 47.041038, W 60.598138
The trailhead is located at the northern tip of Cape Breton, in the community of Meat Cove, at the end of Meat Cove Road (N 47.025503, W 60.561331). A moderate, 5.4-kilometre hike is required to reach the site of the former lighthouses. The area is isolated and proper preparation is required to safely reach the destination.

2. Cape North Lighthouses

Money Point, Victoria County

The establishment of navigation aids along Cape Breton's north coast was nearly impossible due to the area's isolation and dangerous waters. Eventually, however, need outweighed difficulty, and a small lighthouse was established on a plot of grassy land at the base of towering mountains in the late 1800s. Since then, three lighthouses have come and gone, leaving artifacts along the shoreline that reflect the cape's cultural and historic significance to maritime travel in the Cabot Strait.

HISTORY

The decision to build a lighthouse at Cape North was made in 1874. Local contractor Jacob Bowser built the tower on an isolated grassy field 1 kilometre south of Money Point. Bowser and his crew travelled to and from the site by boat and hauled all the materials for a square wooden building and attached tower over the coastal embankment.

Built on a stone foundation, the structure—including the lighthouse and a single dwelling for the lighthouse keeper—was made entirely of wood except for the 9-foot-diameter lantern room on top of the tower, which was comprised of a steel frame enclosed by 12 glass panes. Inside the lantern room, three flat wick lanterns accompanied by 22-inch reflectors created a revolving red light that could be seen from far out at sea. The lighthouse was built a short distance from the coast, on a raised plot, giving the light an elevation of 23 metres above sea level and projecting it up to 24 kilometres. An oil storage shed housed fuel for the lighthouse's lanterns.

In 1876, John McKinnon was appointed the first lighthouse keeper. Although the area offers some of the most spectacular scenery in Nova Scotia, life for the lighthouse keeper and his family was lonely. With no road down the steep 400-metre mountain, the only connections to the outside world would have been when supplies were brought in by boat

or by the occasional passing ship en route to Sydney, Halifax, or beyond.

The light's location at the base of the mountain facing west was adequate for visual purposes, but in 1906 an air diaphone fog alarm was installed 1 kilometre north, at Money Point, so that the mountain would not prohibit the sound from propagating to the west. The wooden building measured 16 metres long and 9 metres wide. Completed in 1907, it housed a 3-inch diaphone powered by a boiler within the structure, which obtained its water from a large storage tank beneath the building.

A new dwelling was built to house both the lighthouse keeper and the engineer required to operate the fog alarm. At this time, a new lighthouse was being constructed at Cape Race, Newfoundland, and its old, cast-iron tower was transported to Money Point. The tower was constructed of 32 rounded plates held together by 800 bolts. Originally cast in England, it had provided navigation aid to ships rounding Cape Race since 1856, until it was dissasembled, shipped, and installed at Money Point in 1909. The checkered red-and-white tower provided a wider range of view than its predecessor, with a flashing white light perched 34 metres above the frigid waters of the Cabot Strait. The

lighthouse, operational in 1911, was distinguished by its unique white light flashing every 5 seconds.

For a short period, six buildings occupied the point: the lighthouse; a two-storey dwelling for the lighthouse keeper, engineer, and their families; and storage sheds and outhouses. In 1912, a fire destroyed the fog-alarm building and a replacement building was constructed quickly. By then, a road to the isolated point provided comfort and sense of safety to those living there.

The lighthouse operated for almost 70 years before the Canadian Coast Guard announced a replacement. Little had changed on the site to that time, except that electricity had been provided in 1973. Lighthouses are often discarded, purposely burned, or torn down—or in the case of the original lighthouse, left to deteriorate. This was the fate of the Money Point lighthouse until Dr. David Baird of the National Museum of Science and Technology in Ottawa heard of the Coast Guard's intention. Baird was looking for an historic lighthouse that could be easily transported to become a display. The Money Point lighthouse fit that mandate.

Construction of the lighthouse began in July 1980, while the older light was still active. In October, a temporary light was installed and, on October

14, the cast-iron lighthouse was disassembled and, using a bulldozer and truck, towed up the narrow roadway, four sections at a time. After being refurbished in Dartmouth, the light was transported to Ottawa, where it resides outside the National Museum of Science and Technology.

The new lighthouse at Money Point was commissioned shortly after, and, in September 1987, the facility was automated. At this time, nearby residents petitioned the government to preserve the lighthouse and the buildings as an historic site. This was not done and, shortly after the site was automated, many of the buildings were burned down. After more than 100 years of operating, lighthouses at that location had helped ships navigate the difficult waters.

In 2010, the Coast Guard replaced the lighthouse and tower with a skeletal steel tower equipped with a modern-day beacon.

ABOUT THE AREA

The isolated coastline offers spectacular views of Cabot Strait and the mountains of Cape Breton. Barren, grassy fields wind along the base of the mountains, seemingly void of any human-built structure. Despite the loss of many historic buildings, many signs of the landscape's significance to Nova Scotia's maritime history remain. An ATV trail tracks north along the coastal edge. At the base of the mountain, a stone foundation filled with debris, fragments of a former chimney, and rusted metal are all that are left of the first lighthouse at the point.

Following the ATV trail north leads to Money Point, where foundations mark the locations of the fog-alarm building, storage sheds, and the lighthouse keeper and fog-alarm engineer's residence. Relics of the site's history come alive as you explore the area. Scattered along the rocky shoreline are pieces of corroded iron and rusting steel that likely once belonged to the many ships that ran aground there. Maritime history is Nova Scotia history and while little has been done to preserve this at Cape North, the signatures of what was left behind continue to tell their story.

 FIRST LIGHTHOUSE: N 47.029214, W 60.391931
SECOND AND THIRD LIGHTHOUSES: N 47.019221, W 60.387982
Drive approximately 6.5 kilometres north of Aspy Bay on Bay St. Lawrence Road and turn east onto a gravel road (6014 Road). The rough road is driveable for most vehicles for approximately 7 kilometres. Park beside the road and then continue on foot, being sure to stay on the main road/trail. As the trail descends the mountain, it becomes strenuous for 1.6 kilometres until the base of the mountain. Cape North can be reached by continuing to hike north. The area is isolated and proper preparation and knowledge of the area is required to safely reach the destination.

3. Wreck of the MV *Carita*

Money Point, Victoria County

The Cabot Strait between the island of Newfoundland and Cape Breton can be treacherous. As the Gulf of St. Lawrence opens to the North Atlantic Ocean, it is not uncommon for weather to change quickly, putting ships and lives at risk. Few safe ports exist along this stretch. In December 1975, the crew of the Swedish cargo ship MV *Carita* learned this the hard way when the ship experienced engine trouble in a strong windstorm. Although the crew survived, the ship broke up on the isolated northern tip of Cape Breton. Pieces of its steel hull are still visible and the debris field is a reminder of the dangerousness of Nova Scotian waters.

The steel MV *Carita*, built in 1966 by Oy Wärtsilä A/B of Turku, Finland, with its three sister ships *Tilia Gorthon*, *Nils Gorthon*, and *Margit Gorthon*, measured 102 metres long and 15.8 metres wide and had a depth of 9.1 metres with a gross tonnage of 3,676 tonnes. Beneath the deck, the ship housed a single 4,000-horsepower diesel engine which turned a single propeller, giving it a cruising speed of 28 kilometres (15 knots) per hour.

Launched in 1966, it was delivered to Rederi Ab Gylfe in Helsingborg. Christened the MV *Ingrid Gorthon*, it carried a variety of cargo across the Atlantic Ocean for nine years. In late 1975, it was sold to the Swedish shipping company Dag Engström, and, on September 2, the ship sailed as the MV *Carita*.

On December 18, 1975, on a voyage from Thunder Bay, Ontario, to Port of Spain, Trinidad and Tobago, the ship experienced engine troubles and was left helpless in the waters north of Cape Breton. At the time, a strong winter storm, producing gusts of up to 100 kilometres an hour, made rescue efforts dangerous. After drifting for almost two days, the ship ran aground several kilometres south of Money Point. All crew members made it to shore safely, likely finding refuge at a nearby lighthouse.

Over the winter, pounding surf and repeated storms caused the ship to break up, eliminating any potential salvage operations. Almost 50 years later, a debris field of rusted metal now lines the coast. Several large pieces have been pushed inshore and, closer to the water, lie portholes, engine vents, and other artifacts. The area is difficult to access, but visitors will not be disappointed. The jagged rusting metal stands out against the grassy hillsides and towering mountains of Money Point.

WRECK OF THE MV *CARITA*: N 47.013469, W 60.389938

Drive approximately 6.5 kilometres north of Aspy Bay on Bay St. Lawrence Road and turn east onto a gravel road (6014 Road). The rough road is driveable for most vehicles for approximately 7.0 kilometres. Park along the road and continue hiking along the road, being sure to stay on the main trail. The hike is considered easy for the first 2 kilometres; however, as the trail descends the mountain, it becomes strenuous for 1.6 kilometres until it reaches the base of the mountain. There, the shipwreck lies to the south, along the rocky beach. The area is very isolated and proper preparation and knowledge of the area is required to safely reach the destination.

4. Chéticamp Gypsum Mine Pond

Chéticamp, Inverness County

It has been described as Cape Breton's own little Lake Louise, and although that may be an exaggeration, the Chéticamp Gypsum Mine Pond is a flooded gypsum quarry nestled in forested hills near Cape Breton National Park. The mine was once an important employer in the small town; after its closure, it became a hidden gem. The secret has slowly come to light and now more people complete the short hike to the quarry, where they are treated with not only the beautiful views of the small pond but also of neighbouring Chéticamp.

Before the 20th century, residents of the seaside Chéticamp relied almost entirely on the fishery for employment. This changed in 1897, when New Glasgow prospector M.W. Grandin discovered a large quantity of high-grade gypsum in the hills behind the town. Having seen the success of mining in other towns in Cape Breton and Nova Scotia, the area's residents were elated by this potential source of employment.

In 1907, local parish priest Father Pierre Fiset and his nephew Louis Fiset established the Great Northern Mining Company Limited to extract the gypsum. To fund the operation, Fiset sold 5 cent shares to investors in Quebec and the Chéticamp area. The money was used to construct storage sheds, blacksmith shops, and a calcination mill. The gypsum was to be mined from a quarry approximately 3 kilometres from the town and mill, with ore being transported by horse and cart. Fiset also purchased the 5,000-ton *Amethyst* to deliver the ore to overseas markets.

Gypsum was shipped to the mill on August 20, 1908. Its high quality resulted from little overburden or soil to contaminate the rock as it was being removed from the ground. Hand augers drilled holes, which were filled with explosives, and the ore was placed on horse-drawn carts and towed to the mill. After being processed, the ore was loaded onto a ship via a nearby wharf and sent to markets in New York and Portsmouth.

In December 18, 1909, Pierre Fiset died, leaving the company to his

nephew. Work continued and, after two years of operations, the company wanted to expand and upgrade the mill and quarry. In 1910, it borrowed $100,000 from Montreal merchant P.M. O'Neil to build a new wharf and a 3-kilometre-long railroad capable of transporting 20-ton side-dumping ore cars between the quarry and mill via a steam locomotive, which became known as La Vielle Louise or Old Louise.

In 1912, a second processing unit was added and a power plant built nearby to supply it with reliable power. This enabled the processing of up to 90 tonnes per day and employed 65 people. In 1914, the operation was sold to Montrealer James Brodie, who continued mining operations before falling behind on paying his workers; after facing a class action lawsuit, he abandoned the operation. The company was transferred to P.M. O'Neil, who had funded railway upgrades several years earlier. O'Neil paid wages, but work was halted at the quarry until 1923.

The next era of mining began in 1926 when the Atlantic Gypsum Mining Company upgraded the mill, storage sheds, and loading dock. These upgrades increased the quarry's daily production rates and the company could give back to the community, including a $5,000 donation to the construction of a new hospital.

The mine's days were limited. In 1932, the Atlantic Gypsum Mining Company opened another mine in Dingwall, resulting in less activity at the Chéticamp mine; the latter was purchased by the National Gypsum Company in 1936, but the outbreak of World War II reduced both the demand for gypsum and worker availability, and the mine was closed and the quarry eventually filled with water.

ABOUT THE AREA

In 2010, the mine properties were transferred to the Highland Trail Groomers Association. Working with a team of volunteers, the trail was revitalized and is now a popular swimming and hiking location. In 2021, the Gypsum Mine Trial committee was awarded the Mobius Award for environmental excellence. Many trails now wind through the white cliff quarry and offer unique scenery. While nothing remains of the Chéticamp processing facilities, the railway line can be traced through the forest and surrounding land, part of which makes up the current trail into the quarry.

⊕ **CHÉTICAMP GYPSUM MINE POND: N 46.627985, W 60.968229**
Pass through the community of Chéticamp on the Cabot Trail and continue driving north and turn onto Chéticamp Back Road. Drive south for 1.7 kilometres to the trailhead (N 46.629889, W 60.980604). Follow the signs and hike for approximately 1.3 kilometres.

5. Port Hood Island's Lost Causeway

Port Hood, Inverness County

On the southwest coast of Cape Breton Island is the historic Port Hood, a long-established fishing outport that boomed with the discovery of bountiful coal deposits nearby. The fishery has been replaced with tourism as a key industry, and thousands flock there each summer to enjoy its beautiful beaches. Seeing the town's sandy beaches makes it easy to understand its claims as the beach capital of Cape Breton. But near the base of Court Street, the sandy stretch of beach is interrupted by a linear pile of large boulders that extends perpendicular to the shoreline toward Port Hood Island. To assume that the structure is a former breakwater or a measure to prevent beach erosion is not wrong—but the bar has an interesting history, one that established Port Hood and nearby Port Hood Island as the region's fishing centre.

The Mi'kmaq are believed to have called Port Hood *Kagweamkek* or "sandbar," as Port Hood Island was connected to the rest of Cape Breton by a natural sandbar. Appearing on early European survey charts, the 1.2-kilometre-long isthmus allowed people to walk freely to and from the island. The first Europeans to settle in the area used the low-lying sandbar as a place to establish fishing stages, sheds, and wharves. The beach provided an accessible place for fishers to store gear and land their ships, and it protected the harbour from ocean swells and storms.

As more people used the beach, it became increasingly susceptible to coastal erosion. In April 1819, a strong storm washed away part of the sandbar, creating a gap that could be traversed only at low tide and left part of the inner harbour vulnerable to storms. This began a 150-year battle to preserve and retain its best line of protection.

Throughout the 19th century, Port Hood and Port Hood Island became the region's largest fishery outpost. Taking advantage of the harbour's natural defences and the many miles of coastal property, fishers, sailors, and seafarers safely stored their boats and equipment

while remaining close to the Gulf of St. Lawrence fishing grounds. By the end of the century, the harbour held several fish plants and lobster canneries as well as being a port for shipping coal that was mined nearby. By this time, the former land bridge to Port Hood Island was severely compromised, putting at risk many ships and the buildings constructed along the waterfront.

Recognizing this risk, residents of Port Hood and Port Hood Island signed a petition that expressed their concern about the deteriorating breakwater. In 1904, the Canadian Department of Public Works responded with plans to rebuild the breakwater and restore the causeway. Work commenced shortly after, with horse-pulled carts transporting large rocks

and fill to the end of the breakwater where it was placed using hand tools and manual labour. The project was abandoned before it could be finished due to exorbitant costs and recurring erosion.

A second attempt was made in 1937; this time a mix of armour stone and vertical wooden piles was used to secure the breakwater and limit erosion. This attempt was short-lived, due to the cost and labour required to construct the 1,200-metre-long causeway.

One more attempt was made to reconnect Port Hood Island to the rest of Cape Breton. In March 1958, Port Hood Island native and minister of External Affairs Sidney Earl Smith advocated for reconstruction of the breakwater. Smith received the necessary support and a causeway was completed by October 1960. This causeway would enable cars and trucks to traverse the gap, providing a connection to those on Port Hood Island and protection for nearby fishing facilities.

But nature always wins. Not long after the Port Hood Island causeway opened, a powerful storm destroyed it. No further attempts have been made to reconnect Port Hood Island to Cape Breton.

What began as 1-kilometre-long natural land bridge became an unconquerable engineering challenge. Port Hood and Port Hood Island have long been important fishing communities, established because of the harbour's protection from the unforgiving storms that plague the Gulf of St. Lawrence. The causeway's remains are still visible in the line of boulders and rocks that extend beneath the waves, all the way to Port Hood Island.

PORT HOOD ISLAND'S LOST CAUSEWAY: N 46.020475, W 61.540159 The former road can be viewed from Port Hood Beach located at the ends of Water Street and Court Street in the community.

6. River Denys Mountain

Inverness County

Among the forested hills of Cape Breton, a lonely white Roman Catholic church marks the last remaining building in the Scottish pioneering settlement of River Denys Mountain. Few remnants remain, yet the community-run church serves the people of the surrounding communities and is a symbol of Scottish immigration in Cape Breton. While little is left of the settlement, the history and culture represented by the church along with the beautiful scenery along the backroads of Cape Breton make River Denys Mountain worth the trip.

In 1833, settlers arrived at River Denys Mountain from the western Scottish Highlands after being evicted from their homes and land during the Highland Clearances. Approximately 30 Gaelic families arrived in Cape Breton hoping to find land and build a new home together. However, as most of the desirable land in Cape Breton had already been claimed, the families were forced into the hills above the community of Judique, where the climate and soil were less suited to growing crops. The families cleared the land for subsistence farming, used the forest's supply of wood to construct houses and workshops, and formed the community of River Denys Mountain.

Until the 1840s, the people of River Denys Mountain travelled to Judique to attend mass but, in 1841, encouraged by Judique's Father Alexander MacDonnell, the community banded together to construct their own church. Made of all locally sourced timber, the church was named St. Margaret of Scotland, likely after the original St. Margaret's Chapel in Edinburgh, Scotland. In the fall of 1841, it held its first mass, but MacDonnell had died the previous year and never saw the completed church.

As the town grew, care of the church passed from Judique to the closer Glendale. In 1899, Father Donald MacIsaac added a large rectangular room to the church's eastern side, hoping to attract new parishioners and accommodate the town's growing population.

The shorter growing season and harsher winters of Cape Breton versus Scotland pressured residents to relocate. As well, nearby Sydney offered a growing number of high-paying jobs at the coal mine; soon many residents moved from River Denys Mountain.

By the early 1950s, the last of the town's families had left. Many of the houses were already abandoned and the church was falling into disrepair. One hundred years after its humble beginnings, the settlement had become a ghost town.

Although many of the wooden houses and buildings were torn down or left to rot, the church remained standing. In 1963, under the supervision of Father Angus Rankin, members of surrounding communities, many of whom had ties to River Denys Mountain, restored the church, cemetery, and surrounding grounds. This preservation paid off—the church is the last symbol of the community and the oldest surviving church building in Inverness County. In 1967, changes in the Catholic church system allowed the church to host the first Gaelic mass in North America.

The church, registered as a municipal heritage structure, is an example of an early era simplified, Gothic-designed church. It is used on special occasions, including weddings, hosted and attended by those from surrounding communities.

⊕ **RIVER DENYS MOUNTAIN: N 45.866825, W 61.314104**
From the intersection of Northside River Denys Road and the TCH (N 45.873295, W 61.259544), drive south on the TCH for 400 metres and turn onto a gravel road named River Denys Road. Continue along the rough road for approximately 5.2 kilometres to the church.

7. Diogenes Cave

River Denys Mountain, Inverness County

Diogenes Cave (also known as River Denys Cave or Glen Brook Cave) is in the backcountry of Inverness County. Originating near the lost community of River Denys Mountain, Glen Brook (formerly Diogenes Brook) winds through the forest to a tall rock face, plunging beneath it.

The cave was formed from the gradual erosion of a bed of weak limestone overlaid by the more resistant rock syenite (similar to granite). Pieces of limestone lie at the bottom of the cave, but syenite, which dominates in the area, composes most of the steep cliff at the cave's entrance. The stream penetrated the rock through a small fissure between the two rock layers. Over time, the weak layers of rock dissolved and were transported downstream, leaving behind the cave.

In 1974, the Nova Scotia Speleological Society mapped the cave: the 170-metre-long cave is predominantly air filled and passable by the average human; however, at several points, the passageway is flooded by the stream (known as sumps) and is only passable by divers. The cave ends by re-emerging into Glen Brook. During an early expedition to the cave, a population of depigmented trout were recorded, possibly the first of its kind in Canada.

The cave is visible at the end of a short trail near River Denys Mountain. A small passage twists its way into the cave, but signs of past collapses should deter anyone from entering it. In the forest to the northeast, sinkholes have formed along the cave's path and its re-emergence point is also visible.

 DIOGENES CAVE: N 45.874753, W 61.317629

From the intersection of Northside River Denys Road and the TCH (N 45.873295, W 61.259544), drive south on the TCH for 400 metres and turn onto River Denys Road. Drive 5.3 kilometres, then keep right for another 500 metres. Markers note the trailhead; walk 100 metres.

8. Marble Mountain

Marble Mountain, Bras d'Or Lake

On the shores of Bras d'Or Lake is the small town of Marble Mountain, named for the large quantities of marble found in the area. Limestone and marble mining not only established the town but transformed it into a bustling boom town. No mining occurs in the area, but visitors to this lonely part of Cape Breton Island are greeted with crystal clear waters and a bright white lake bottom, both the result of the mining industry. On the waterfront at the site of the mine's former shipping facilities, a park tells the story of the industry that birthed the town. The surrounding forest and hillside are now littered with relics from the historic operations.

HISTORY

In September 1868, when Nicholas James Brown visited the Bras d'Or Lake area, he noticed an outcrop of high-quality marble on the face of North Mountain. Looking for a new business venture, Brown spent the next several months acquiring land rights to the mountain—almost 6,000 acres. After being awarded mineral rights to the mountain, Brown established the N.J. Brown and Company, and started quarrying in 1869.

The company mined two areas. The first was a lower quarry where limestone was extracted to produce white lime, commonly used in agriculture or construction. The blasted rock was loaded onto rail cars and towed by horse to a nearby kiln where the limestone was heated and calcium oxide or lime extracted; it was then placed in barrels and bags and stored until it could be shipped.

The second quarry, located higher on the mountain, was accompanied by two underground horizontal shafts. Marble was carefully cut using drills and wedges, which split the rock into large slabs. It was then placed on sleds and lowered down the hill to a wharf, where it was cut into more manageable slabs before being shipped to market. The North

Mountain marble, coveted for its high quality and few imperfections, made it an ideal building material.

The start-up cost for the operation was higher than Brown had expected, and the company quickly experienced financial difficulties. Brown eventually found several Halifax businesspeople interested in investing in the company. In December 1870, Brown signed over all of his assets at Marble Mountain to the new investors and, on April 4, 1871, the Cape Breton Marble Company was incorporated, with Brown owning a partial share.

A post office was established nearby and, on May 1, 1871, the town of Marble Mountain was established. Its name may have been chosen as a sales tactic to make the business and the area's marble more appealing to investors and potential buyers. The mine did attract people from all over the region, and workers built homes in the nearby settlement.

Production slowed in 1873 as the company's financial troubles continued. Only lime had been sold—slabs of marble had been cut and readied for shipment, but the company could not find any potential buyers. In one of his last searches for buyers, Brown sent marble samples to the 1876 Centennial Exposition in Philadelphia. Although

the marble was admired for its purity and texture, it failed to attract the attention Brown desired.

Brown died suddenly on January 25, 1880, from an apparent stroke, which was said to have been brought on by heartache from the continually struggling quarry. In 1885, the Sheriff's Office auctioned the land and mineral rights.

With the financial backing of wealthy Halifax builder Henry Sanders and accountant George Hattie, the land and mineral rights were purchased by Dugald MacLachlan. MacLachlan, along with his financial backers, incorporated the Bras d'Or Lime and Marble Company,

which restarted production at the quarry on July 17, 1886. The original quarries established by Brown 17 years earlier were abandoned and a much larger quarry excavated higher on the hill. The company planned to create a monopoly on local marble supplies by purchasing small quarries in the area that also mined high-grade marble.

With the confidence that they controlled the local market, the company installed an elaborate system of conveyor belts and pulley systems to allow large slabs of marble to be efficiently cut and moved to shipping facilities along the water's edge. Two modern, 8.5-metre-high vertical draw kilns were installed near the wharf to more efficiently

transform the quarry's limestone into lime. The company thrived for several years; in 1895, an estimated 4,500 tonnes of limestone and 320 tonnes of marble were quarried and 1,800 barrels of lime produced.

The company sold the mine in July 1900 to the Dominion Iron and Steel Company, which was looking for a new source of lime (the lime would increase the fluidity of iron being produced in their Sydney steel plant, which opened in 1901). The company installed a system of railway lines and overhead cranes/pulleys to transport the ore from the quarry to the shipping facilities. This cable and pan system consisted of two large towers on each side of the quarry with a pulley line running between them that could lift and move the ore after it was excavated by explosives and steam shovels. Near the wharf, a large rock crusher, hopper, and series of conveyor belts expedited the loading of ore onto ships.

At this time, the mine employed over 1,000 people. The town contained two churches, seven stores, a Royal Bank of Canada, and its own power station to produce electricity for the mine and town streetlights. The town's size and population remained relatively stable until 1921, when the Dominion Iron and Steel Company shut it down in favour of a new source of limestone at the Aguathuna Quarry on the Port au Port Peninsula, Newfoundland. After this, many families moved away in search of new employment.

In 1961, Marble Mountain Quarries Limited reopened the mine for a brief period, but these relatively small operations were abandoned after 20 years.

It has been estimated that approximately 2.7 million tonnes of high-grade marble remain at the Marble Mountain site.

ABOUT THE AREA

The area in the vicinity of the old loading docks has been transformed into a small community park with several information panels telling the history of Marble Mountain. The nearby waters of Bras d'Or Lake are now crystal clear. Once dissolved in water, carbonate rocks such as limestone and marble purify the water, making it appear bright blue.

In the forests and hills near the wharf, large piles of limestone, marble, and waste rock slowly erode. Several large concrete foundations are visible along the water's edge and in the hillsides. The most eye-catching are the concrete walls of the wharf's hopper, which controlled the amount of ore placed on each ship. The enormous structure was once supported by central steel beams but, like most of the quarry's remaining equipment and materials, these were scrapped for metal during World War II. Nearby, a shallow concrete tunnel protruding into the hillside is believed to have been a former entrance to the adjacent hopper structure.

Although many buildings still exist, such as MacLachlan and Sanders' Store at the beginning of the road leading to the park, many were torn down or removed when people moved from the area in the 1920s. Another legacy of the quarry is the many buildings and houses that were constructed from Marble Mountain marble: Halifax's Wright Building or Marble Building on Barrington Street and the Oland Castle residence on Young Avenue.

 MARBLE MOUNTAIN: N 45.822370, W 61.038421

Located 37 kilometres north of Port Hawkesbury is the community of Marble Mountain. Follow the main road through the town and turn onto William MacInnis Lane, a gravel road that brings you to a small day park near the site of the former wharf. A small fee, which can be placed in a box along the side of the road, is required to use the park.

9. Cape Breton's Central Railway

Strait of Canso to Sydney, Cape Breton

Winding through the interior of Cape Breton from the Canso Causeway to Iona, across the Barra Strait at Grand Narrows, and on to North Sydney is the abandoned Cape Breton and Central Nova Scotia Railway. The railway dates to the late 19th century, when most of Cape Breton was inaccessible except by boat or, in some cases, primitive roads. From the time it was announced, the line was celebrated by the people and politicians of Cape Breton, who knew that it would mean big things for the island. The line was not easy to construct, as it would have to cross wetlands, river valleys, and the Barra Strait. The completed railway contained many spectacular structures cleverly and aesthetically designed to aid in the uninterrupted route from the Strait of Canso to the industrial centre of Sydney. In 2014, operations were halted on the line, leaving to deteriorate numerous engineering marvels hidden in the backcountry of beautiful Cape Breton Island.

EARLY HISTORY

Before 1886, the communities of Cape Breton, especially those located inland or along Bras d'Or Lake, were isolated. Except for a network of small gravel roads, the only means of bringing in supplies was a steamship service that made regular trips between communities on the large inland lake. This changed in 1876, when the Halifax and Cape Breton Railway and Coal Company was incorporated. Without investors or funders, plans to extend the provincial railway network from its terminus in New Glasgow to the Strait of Canso were in jeopardy—until the idea captured the attention of the Government of Canada, which, after confederation, looked at plans to create an uninterrupted railway route (the Intercolonial Railway) from Windsor, Ontario, to Sydney, Cape Breton. The federal government took over the company and, in June 1886, approved the funds to construct a railway to Sydney. The railway would not only enable the delivery of supplies, cargo, and passengers to and from Cape Breton Island but also connect the rest of the country with the bountiful coal deposits being discovered in the Sydney area. As well, railways were used as a political promotion.

In 1886, surveys determined possible railway routes. A ferry terminal would be established at Mulgrave on the western shore of the Strait of Canso where barges and ferries would transport rail cars to a similar terminal at Point Tupper. From there, the railway had two options for the remaining trip to Sydney: either travel north along the eastern side of Bras d'Or Lake, passing through Richmond County and the town of St. Peters, or a more direct route north along the western side of Bras d'Or Lake, crossing the lake at Barra Strait and continuing north to Sydney. It is believed that the western route via the Barra Strait was selected prior to the February 1887 election, using the logic that the western route would come within the proximity of twice as many people as that of the eastern route. Whatever the case, the decision was made to construct the railway line along the western side of Bras d'Or Lake, crossing the lake at the Barra Strait and continuing north to Sydney.

Construction began in 1887 with the ferry terminal at Mulgrave, followed by the railway line north to Iona and the Barra Strait. This western section was the most difficult to construct. Along the way, narrow river valleys would have to be traversed, the bogs and wetland of interior Cape Breton crossed, and the 0.5-kilometre-wide Barra Strait traversed.

Big Brook Culverts & Stone Tunnels

West Bay Road to River Denys

Railway construction immediately proved difficult due to the many ponds and wetlands that the line had to cross between Point Tupper and Orangedale. Additional backfill was required and, to reduce the chances of flooding, elaborate culverts were constructed on each of the line's rivers. The best examples are on a stretch of road between the settlements of West Bay Road and Big Brook; these culverts were architecturally designed tunnels rather than contemporary utilitarian corrugated steel culverts. The tunnels, constructed of carefully cut stone cemented together to create

beautiful archways ranging from 1 to 3.5 metres tall, offered sufficient room for water to freely pass beneath the railway line.

The risk posed by the region's high water table was tested shortly after the line opened, when a train encountered a section that had sunk beneath the surface of a bog, likely due to ground subsidence from erosion; more fill was added to prevent further disaster.

Many stone culverts and tunnels are evident along the railway. While some have collapsed from years of neglect, others, such as that found on a small tributary of Big Brook, remain remarkably intact, considering that they were built over 130 years ago. Each stone tunnel holds architectural value and is a reminder of the time, money, and effort designers and labourers put into constructing the Cape Breton Railway.

⊕ BIG BROOK TRIBUTARY TUNNEL: **N 45.769872, W 61.229660**
The tunnels are along Big Brook Road between the communities of West Bay Road and River Denys.

Ottawa Brook Viaducts

Ottawa Brook

The wetlands and rivers of interior Cape Breton were not the only obstacle engineers needed to overcome while constructing the western route of the Cape Breton Railway. As the proposed line approached the Barra Strait, it encountered two river valleys that were too large to be filled in: Ottawa Brook and Walkers Brook. To traverse the narrow valleys, two tall steel bridges were constructed: approximately 160 metres across the Ottawa Brook Valley and 150 metres across Walkers Brook. The rusting steel structures spanning the river valleys still capture the interest of those who glimpse them as they drive along Highway 223.

 OTTAWA BROOK VIADUCT: N 45.934046, W 60.944783
WALKER BROOK VIADUCT: N 45.940563, W 60.921438

Both viaducts can be seen along Highway 223 near the community of Ottawa Brook.

Grand Narrows Bridge

Iona, Barra Strait

The greatest engineering challenge faced by designers of the Cape Breton Railway was the Barra Strait, a 500-metre section of lake that would have to be traversed near the community of Iona. The length of the gap, combined with water depths of more than 20 metres, meant that building a bridge would be expensive—but it avoided the slowdowns and construction requirements of establishing another ferry and two terminals. The bridge had to accommodate the passage of large cargo ships transporting lumber, coal, gypsum, and marble from the mines and sawmills scattered around the lake. Engineers agreed to construct seven steel arch trusses: six static, and the seventh, on the eastern side, a swing span capable of rotating 90 degrees to allow the passage of ships.

Isbester and Reid were awarded the contract to construct the bridge's piers and foundations. Robert G. Reid was a Scottish railway contractor with a background in building bridges across the Niagara Gorge and in Montreal. Following the completion of the Cape Breton Railway, Reid took over, completed, and operated the Newfoundland Railway.

Work on the bridge started in 1887, with wooden cofferdams constructed at the site of each pier. Water was pumped out of the holes to allow workers to access the bedrock normally submerged in up to 28 metres of water. After drilling anchor bolts to the rock, large blocks of cut stone were lowered into the hole and placed one on top of the other. The stone pillars were cemented together and piled until they reached 2 metres above the high-water mark.

Quebec firm Dominion Bridge Company was hired to construct the steel truss spans. Steel, rivets, and equipment were prefabricated and shipped to the site. Each span was assembled along the shore of the harbour, placed on a barge, floated into position, and slowly lowered onto the stone piers.

This 500-metre-long engineering marvel was one of the longest bridges in Nova Scotia and supported a single railway line. Governor General Frederick Stanley officially opened the bridge in 1890.

The bridge was expensive, but the feat of engineering was a sense of pride and accomplishment for politicians and Cape Bretoners. It represented the scale of the railway project and was a symbol of the new connectivity between communities and the rest of Canada. The bridge has fallen into disrepair, its swing section left open to allow the passage of ships, and grass has overgrown the tracks traversing the bridge.

PARKING LOT AND VIEWPOINT: N 45.957494, W 60.794260
The Grand Narrows bridge is approximately 53 kilometres south of Highway 125 near North Sydney on Highway 223. A viewing platform and interpretive signs are located near Grand Narrows Drive on the east side of the strait.

OPENING OF THE RAILWAY

The Cape Breton Railway opened as sections were completed; despite financial setbacks, it was operational by summer 1891 and once-isolated interior communities were now connected to the outside world. The railway encouraged new development and industry throughout Cape Breton and is believed to have been a major driver in the industrialization of Sydney, as more people, equipment, and supplies could be quickly shipped there.

CLOSURE

In the early 2010s, the railway and its infrastructure (now known as the Cape Breton and Central Nova Scotia Railway) was owned by the Connecticut-based railroad company Genesee and Wyoming. The railway, more than 120 years old, was increasingly expensive to repair. As operations slowed, the company closed the railway in 2014 and scrapped the line and its bridges. In 2017, the provincial government still saw potential value in the railway line and entered a payment plan with Genesee and Wyoming to delay scrapping the line. With plans to establish a container port in Sydney, closing the line was seen as detrimental. In 2018, the Port of Sydney Development Corporation commissioned an engineering study; it determined the cost of restoring the railway to be just over $100 million.

Since then, the railway and all its bridges have remained dormant. But while its future is uncertain, the historic significance of its past is well known. The line helped establish Sydney as an industrial hub and has encouraged the development of mines, mills, and other industries across Cape Breton. The impressive Grand Narrows Bridge, the steel viaducts across the river in Ottawa Brook, and the beautifully crafted stone culverts that regularly intersect it are hidden wonders left after the railway's abandonment.

10. Plaster Ponds

Cains Mountain, Ottawa Brook

Tucked away in the forested rolling hills of central Cape Breton is a curious line of ponds, surrounded by steep white cliffs, known as Plaster Ponds. They are easy to miss when travelling along one of the area's gravel roads but venturing closer or viewing them from the air reveals a distinct group of symmetrical oval and circular lakes seemingly in a north-to-south line.

Plaster Ponds could easily be confused with a reclaimed mine or quarry because of the near perfect vertical cliffs, circular shapes, and its distinctness from the surrounding landscape. But the line of ponds was formed by natural processes. The area's geology is dominated by the Windsor Formation, a grouping of primarily weak carbonate rocks such as limestone and gypsum. In the area of Plaster Ponds, both surface and ground water likely seeped into the underlying gypsum, slowly eroding it through dissolution. Eventually water collected in the depressions left on the surface, forming today's lakes. Such features are often known as karst topography and, as with other karst landscapes, the surrounding areas are populated with disappearing streams, sinkholes, and cave systems.

The Plaster Ponds karst landforms have created a beautiful landscape and a one-of-a-kind ecosystem comprised of more than a dozen rare plants. The erosion of rocks with a high carbonate content, such as gypsum, often causes nearby water to have above-average acidity and environments with a high calcium content. This uncommon occurrence welcomes flora and fauna that thrive in these environments. The area is one of the few places in Nova Scotia unaffected by logging and mining and, as such, contains some of its last old-age Acadian forests. The Plaster Ponds ecosystem is not unique to Nova Scotia but occurs in most of North America.

These qualities made the area an important candidate for conservation. A portion of land was donated by owners David and Pam

Newtown to the Nature Conservancy of Canada. This parcel, in addition to other generous donations, forms the Cains Mountain Nature Reserve. Announced in October 2017, the 162-hectare area has now been fully protected from mining and logging development, helping preserve the spectacular area for future generations.

 PLASTER PONDS: N 45.956814, W 60.930808
From the community of Iona, travel 10.5 kilometres west on Highway 223 and turn onto a gravel road named Highland Road. Continuing along the road for 2 kilometres brings you to the beginning of the conservation area.

11. St. Peters Canal

St. Peters, Richmond County

Bras d'Or Lake, a large inland lake in the centre of Cape Breton, is approximately 1,100 square kilometres in area, stretching from the Gulf of St. Lawrence in the north to its southern extremity at St. Peters, only 30 kilometres from the bottom of Cape Breton. For millennia, the inland lake comprised of salt and fresh water has been used as a transportation route, first by the Mi'kmaq and later by European settlers. Throughout its history, the lakeshores have been dotted with settlements, sawmills, and mines, each taking advantage of the lake's abundant resources and the ability to transport goods and materials.

The lake, however, is surrounded by rolling hills and dense forest, making the only access point to the ocean in the north. At the lake's southern end, an 800-metre-wide, 20-metre-high ridge in the modern community of St. Peters is the only barrier that prohibits ships from entering the lake from the sea. The Mi'kmaq first used the ridge as a portage point, regularly carrying their boats over it to access the ocean. The first Europeans to settle in the area are believed to have been fur traders and trappers who, recognizing the gateway to the inland lake, established a trading post at what was then known as Port Toulouse.

After the British gained control of Cape Breton in the 1700s, the settlement was renamed St. Peters and a road was established to aid in portaging canoes and boats across the narrow plot of land. As shipping and ferry services expanded on Bras d'Or Lake throughout the late 18th and early 19th centuries, a new means of transporting ships across the ridge was considered. In 1825, the British government commissioned an investigation into the feasibility of excavating a canal.

After the study's completion, the government spent years debating the viability of such a project. It would require excavating the 20-metre-high bedrock ridge, constructing a canal with a lock system to deal with differing tidal heights on either side of the canal, and building a bridge over the canal

to allow people and carts to travel without impeding ships passing through the canal. Almost 30 years after the completion of the feasibility study, the government approved the project, and construction began in 1854.

Excavating the ridge was achieved by drilling and blasting. Waste rock was hand-loaded into carts and carried away. The process took nearly 15 years to complete. The cut had an average width of 30 metres and a maximum height of 20 metres. At the base of the cut, a rectangular canal was carved into the rock.

To accommodate different tidal levels (which could be as high as 1.5 metres from one side to the other), a lock system was constructed. Each side of the lock had two V-shaped gates which could swing independently, allowing water levels to equalize to either side of the lock and the safe passage of ships. The lock measurements dictated the maximum size of ships that could use the canal: the lock was 91.4 metres long, 14.5 metres wide, and 4.9 metres deep.

The canal officially opened in 1869. Soon small steamships and sailing vessels made regular passages, taking advantage of the much shorter route to the south end of Bras d'Or Lake. The region experienced a boost in industry as sawmills and mines were established, using the new

means to get lumber and ore to market. One of these mining endeavours was the marble quarry at Marble Mountain (page 62), which shipped blocks of marble and lime to market via the St. Peters Canal.

As the number of ships using the canal grew, Department of Public Works engineer Henry F. Perley oversaw renovating and expanding it. Work began in 1876 to deepen the canal and construct a two-storey wooden building to be used by the lockmaster. This building is one of the oldest in the region. The construction project was the first of many to expand the canal's capacity.

By the end of the 19th century, the canal was a critical transportation route for commercial vessels, a status it retained into the 20th century. In 1929, the canal was designated a National Historic Site. In World War II, a large influx of coal barges from Sydney used the canal as a safer alternative than traversing the U-boat-infested waters of the Cabot Strait.

As the commercial importance of the St. Peters Canal dwindled, it and its adjacent property was given to Parks Canada in 1972. In 1985, another major renovation turned the area into a tourism location. The canal, operated by Parks Canada, allows the passage of hundreds of personal watercrafts each operating season. In 2017, a new swing bridge became the fifth to span the gap.

Although the canal remains a National Historic Site and is noted in many tourism brochures, it remains an often-overlooked gem. Its cultural and industrial importance to the development of St. Peters and the lower half of Bras d'Or Lake is unforgettable. The best time to visit is during the annual Swim the Canal event, when hundreds of people swim the 800-metre route from the Atlantic Ocean to Bras d'Or Lake.

 ST. PETERS CANAL: N 45.652154, W 60.870401

The community of St. Peters is approximately 43 kilometres east of Port Hawkesbury. Continue through the community on Highway 4, then follow the signs for Battery Provincial Park. The canal can be viewed from many different locations: the most popular is the day-use area of Battery Provincial Park.

12. Mindamar Mine

Stirling, Richmond County

Hidden in the backcountry of western Cape Breton are the remains of Nova Scotia's largest base metal mine, the Mindamar Mine. For the first half of the 20th century, the mine brought employment opportunities to the area, with a new town being established nearby to support its workers. After it was shut down, the site was abandoned, leaving intricate concrete foundations, mineshafts, and an eerie dead forest produced from the careless disposal of waste.

The first ore to be found in the area was in 1885 at Copper Brook (later renamed Strachan Brook), where zinc, lead, and copper sulfides were discovered. The prospectors who made the discovery were looking for copper; however, the ore's low copper grade and the complex metallurgical techniques required to separate the mineral from the rock meant that extracting the ore would not be feasible. In 1904, a short-lived mine extracted the ore through a small, open pit. After determining that the ore grade was too low, the mine was abandoned.

In 1915, Barytes Limited began prospecting the site through trenching. They found that the area contained large quantities of zinc-lead-copper sulphides, but the cost of extracting the minerals from its parent rock was too expensive to make the ore worth mining. Nonetheless, Barytes Limited continued exploring the area by drilling and later opening a small underground shaft to better examine the ore.

The area and its potential for mineral extraction were not forgotten. Between 1916 and 1924, five companies explored the area by trenching, stripping, and drilling. In 1925, the Stirling Zinc Company completed a detailed area survey which involved excavating a mine shaft to a depth of 122 metres. The exploration turned up little of value, and, even though operations were abandoned, it caught the attention of the British Metals Corporation, who obtained the property in 1927. Working under the name Stirling Mines Limited, the company deepened the existing shaft to 240 metres below the surface and installed a 250-tonne-per-day processing mill that extracted the minerals from its surrounding rock by flotation. As the rock was processed through the mill, zinc, lead, copper, and even trace amounts of silver and gold were extracted.

In 1930, the processing mill was upgraded to allow it to process 300

tonnes per day. Later that year, because of dropping metal prices, the mine shut down once again.

In 1935, Stirling Mines Limited resumed operations for three years, until low zinc prices and labour shortages forced the mine's closure in 1938. By then, the company had extracted over 178,000 tonnes of ore.

After World War II, the Nova Scotia Department of Mines began additional surveying and exploratory drilling, and determined that the former mine site contained large quantities of ore.

In 1949, Mindamar Metals Corporation investigated the former mine site through advanced geophysical surveys, underground explorations, and additional drilling. After two years of surveying, Mindamar Metals optioned the mine to Dome Explorations Limited, who took over operations in 1951 and installed a new mill capable of processing 500 tonnes of ore per day; in 1952, the first zinc-lead-copper ore concentrates were shipped. In 1954, a new mine shaft was sunk to a depth of 358 metres on the north side of Strachan Brook and, to process the additional ore, the mill was upgraded to allow it to process 650 tonnes per day.

The mine operated until April 1956, when it was shut down for the last time. This latest era of mining had produced approximately 776,800 tonnes of ore with mineral grades of 5.5 per cent zinc, 1.3 per cent lead, and 0.7 per cent copper, plus trace amounts of gold and silver. At the time of its closure, it was the largest base metal ore mine in Nova Scotia.

Additional surveying, drilling, and surface prospecting continued throughout the 20th century, but no mining has occurred since its closure.

ABOUT THE AREA

After the mine closed, its processing mill, operation buildings, and mining equipment were removed. South of Strachan Brook the concrete foundations of the first processing mill built in the 1920s and 1930s can be found, along with dumpsites, a tailings pond, and closer to the brook, the first shaft. Operations in the early 1950s were concentrated on the north side of the brook; the enormous foundations of the second processing mill lie alongside foundations for the ore crusher, shaft structure, and several underground rooms which provided better access to the second and largest mine shaft, which is gated.

Two shafts were excavated: one south and adjacent to Strachan Brook, the other approximately 150 metres north, near the main road to the site. For many years, the two open shafts and an accompanying ventilation shaft posed a danger to people using the area. In 1996, the provincial government used the site as a demonstration project on capping open and abandoned mine shafts and a large metal grate and concrete coverings were placed over the holes.

To the east of the mine site is a tailings pond, where waste from the processing mill was disposed. Early mining had little regard for the waste rock and chemicals used to extract the minerals and it was piled into the wetland and riparian areas surrounding Strachan Brook. This area, approximately 600 metres long and 200 metres wide, contains a fine grain sediment that averages about 4 metres in depth. Sizeable quantities of barium, cadmium, lead, and manganese are believed to be contained in the sediment; Strachan Brook continues to flow through the tailings, and these metals can also be detected much farther downstream. Because of this, the area contains no vegetation except for the forest of dead trees that still partly stand near the middle of the former tailings pond.

Throughout the area are many relics and foundations, including the original exploratory open pits, which are now two small ponds in the centre of the site. The remains of barracks, houses, and roads are also visible. Although its operation was periodic and short-lived, the mine was a major employer during its years of operation.

MINDAMAR MINE: N 45.729304, W 60.436758

From the community of Framboise, turn onto Stirling Road and travel on the gravel road for approximately 6.1 kilometres. Then turn right onto a gravel road and continue for approximately 400 metres.

13. Arch Cave

Baddeck, Victoria County

In the forest near the town of Baddeck is one of the largest known cave systems in Nova Scotia, Arch Cave. This cave has been explored and surveyed for at least 520 metres, though it likely extends well beyond this. Arch Cave, named for a natural arch at one of its largest entrances, was formed by the gradual erosion of gypsum from groundwater and a small stream flowing through it. One of the cave's most spectacular (and difficult to access) features is the "Skylight," a collapsed section which creates a stunning sinkhole in the cave.

Arch Cave is part of the larger landscape comprised of karst topography, landforms that have been carved and formed by the dissolution or erosion of such soluble rocks as gypsum or limestone. That karst landforms are rarely isolated is demonstrated in the landscape surrounding this cave.

Hidden among the thick forest and chaotic terrain surrounding the cave is a collection of strange landforms including hundreds of deep, small-diameter depressions in the forest floor, sharp pointed rock features, and surface cracks. These landforms contribute to the area's beauty and geologic significance but also produce a dangerous landscape that should be explored sparingly. New and existing sinkholes exist throughout the area (some up to 24 metres deep), with many likely hidden by the forested overburden. Similarly, surface cracks and depressions pose a potential falling risk to those traversing above.

While not particularly far off the beaten path, due to its dangerous and difficult-to-traverse landscape Arch Cave is one of the more dangerous sites in this book. Exploring the area should be done only with experts who know the terrain well.

 CAVE ENTRANCE: **N 46.136498, W 60.634495**

No trail system exists to the cave and proper knowledge of the area and

cave is needed before visiting. The closest paved access road is Highway 205, east of Baddeck. Turn onto Old Big Harbour Road (N46.135334, W60.689163), drive for 1 kilometre before keeping right and continuing for another 450 metres. Keep right and turn onto Plaister Mines Road. Drive 4 kilometres to the relative vicinity of the cave.

Point Aconi

New Waterford

Englishtown

Glace Bay

North Sydney

Dominion

Port Morien

Sydney

Sydney River

Louisbourg

Sydney & Louisbourg

This region covers the northeast area of Cape Breton Island, spanning from the natural inlet into the Bras d'Or Lake in the west to the low-lying coastline in Louisbourg in the east. This diverse landscape of rugged coastlines, rolling hills, and protected harbours helped establish the area as a centre for the region. The Mi'kmaq, who have long held a deep spiritual connection with this region, regularly used its bountiful fishing and hunting grounds to provide a rich life. Later these traits attracted European settlers who established settlements and forts along the coast which were based around fishing and forestry. For many years, both France and England competed for ownership of the land; the area finally came under British control.

But the bountiful coal reserves solidified this area as Cape Breton's economic centre. Throughout the 19th and 20th centuries, coal mines sprang up in every corner of the region, with thousands migrating to the area for well-paying jobs. The region's coal, shipped around the world, encouraged the establishment of new industries such as steel making, as well as complex networks of military defences to ensure the protection of ships using the Sydney and Louisbourg harbours. People from around the world immigrated to the area, bringing with them their culture, traditions, and architecture.

Dozens of communities popped up around the region's mines. Railway networks were added to transport coal and people to the communities, and the area became home to many new technological

achievements such as the first transatlantic telegraph message. Over time, coal reserves—as well as demand—declined, as did the area's population. While Sydney, Louisbourg, and New Waterford boast healthy tourism, the area holds relics from its industrial past.

Most of the area is characterized by rural communities and neighbourhoods. As the region's industry declined, many moved to the larger centres of Sydney Mines, Sydney, New Waterford, and Glace Bay which spread across the north coast of the area. The most popular access route is the TCH (Highway 105), which has a terminus at the

Newfoundland and Labrador Ferry terminal in North Sydney. From the terminus, Highway 125 encircles historic Sydney harbour, ending at the region's largest community and hub, Sydney. From here, the highways disperse outward, with Highways 28 and 225 following the north coast through the former mining communities of Victoria Mines, New Waterford, Dominion, and Glace Bay. Additionally, the southbound Highway 4 provides access to Bras d'Or Lake, while Highway 22 traverses the interior, from Sydney to Louisbourg.

1. Kluskap's Cave

Cape Dauphin

Climbing down a near-vertical cliff into the Big Brook ravine and tracing the stream to the ocean's edge brings you to a small cove at the northern reaches of Kluskap's Mountain (known as Kelly's Mountain). Scaling the steep rocks to the right of the cove brings you to Kluskap's Cave (commonly called Glooscap's Cave or Fairy Hole).

The picturesque hole in the side of the mountain appears, at first glance, to be a sea cave. But its origins are likely from surface water seeping into the cave and eroding it. The Mi'kmaq believe that the cave was the original home of Kluskap, a legendary figure who created much of Atlantic Canada's landscapes.

In 2012, the site was nominated a National Historic Site. Instead, in 2016, Kluskap's Cave and the northern section of Kluskap's Mountain was designated the Kluskap Wilderness Area because of its cultural and spiritual importance to the Mi'kmaq. In early 2023, it became Nova Scotia's first Indigenous Protected and Conserved Area (IPCA), co-managed by the Unama'ki Institute of Natural Resources and the Province of Nova Scotia.

The cave's large, circular entrance is located at sea level; the cave's

interior rises in elevation as you continue through it. A small, saltwater pool at its entrance is partially protected by three distinctive rocks. The circular tunnel continues for at least 60 metres. As the cave extends deeper into the hillside, the tunnel size decreases until human passage is prohibited.

From a geologic perspective, the cave is likely a phreatic cave: it was carved over time by water seeping through the rocks and slowly eroding the weak limestone layer. The end of the cave is believed to be marked by a fault line where the limestone meets an overlying body of hard granite.

The site is considered one of the most sacred places to the Mi'kmaq. Several versions of the story of Kluskap Cave exist, but the most widely accepted is that when Kluskap was sent to protect the Mi'kmaq, he lived in this cave. One day a group of women approached him after seeing that his canoe had broken into two pieces (represented by Bird Island located nearby). Kluskap then transformed the women into rocks which now protect the cave opening. The silhouette of one woman is seen on the opposite wall of the cave. Many believe that Kluskap will return to his cave, and great efforts are being made to preserve this location.

While the hike to the cave is only 1.5 kilometres long, its location at the base of an almost-vertical climb requires ropes, and the hazards of the ocean make the cave inaccessible to most. For those able to make it to the beach but not the final walk or swim to the cave itself, a small side porthole provides a glimpse inside the cave. Those who venture to the rocky shore at the mouth of Big Brook are treated with spectacular views and scenery. Offshore, Bird Island, believed to be Kluskap's broken canoe, is still visible.

⊕ KLUSKAP'S CAVE: N 46.344329, W 60.434511

From the TCH, approximately 2.6 kilometres east of the Seal Island Bridge, turn onto New Campbellton Road. Drive 13 kilometres to the end of the road to the trailhead (N 46.342366, W 60.420537). A 1.4-kilometre hike leads to the cove. While the trail is relatively easy, to access the cove a steep descent using a system of ropes is required. The cave is located to the east of the cove. As the area is considered sacred to many, treat it with respect.

2. St. Alphonsus Church
Victoria Mines

St. Alphonsus Roman Catholic Church exemplifies the efforts people go through to restore life to abandoned and forgotten structures. Built in 1916 on the site of its predecessor, the concrete church's twin spires made it a local landmark. Surrounded by a graveyard dating to the 1850s, the church is referred to as the Stone Church. It was constructed in a manner common to many fishing communities in Nova Scotia, that is, it is perched on a hilltop overlooking the nearby community and ocean. For over a century, the steeples of St. Alphonsus welcomed returning sailors into the harbour, providing them with an easily distinguishable monument to guide them home. This was especially true at a time when navigation systems were uncommon and seafarers relied almost entirely on coastal landmarks to determine their locations. The local Atlantic Pilotage Authority contributed funds to rebuild one of the spires because of its importance as a navigation aid.

In the second half of the 20th century, the region's once-prosperous coal and steel industry declined. As a result, the area's population dwindled—as did the number of churchgoers. By the early 2000s, the church experienced maintenance and structural issues. The controlling diocese determined that the cost of repairs would exceed $600,000; deciding that this price tag was too high, it officially closed the church in 2007.

By 2014, the church's broken bell tower windows allowed water to seep in, and the stone exterior had begun to crumble. With the building now posing a safety hazard, in February 2014 the diocese issued a tender for its demolition. News of the demolition spurred residents into action: a group of dedicated volunteers formed the Stone Church Restoration Society to restore and preserve the historic and cultural landmark. It submitted a last-minute proposal to the diocese for temporary postponement of the demolition until the organization could raise the funds to purchase it. The diocese agreed.

The Stone Church Restoration Society aimed to raise $43,000 to purchase the church and another $300,000 to repair it. In 2017, the urgency of the society's work increased: the roof had begun to leak. The Canadian Armed Forces agreed to repair the roof as a training exercise for its Army engineers and troops.

By 2018, the group had purchased the church, signing the deed in December and obtaining full ownership in March 2019. After a COVID-19 interruption, fundraising efforts resumed in 2022. The group plans to transform the church into a tourism site, with a museum and rental space for weddings and special occasions. The church's ultimate fate is still unknown but, thanks to the collaborative efforts of the Stone Church Restoration Society and its contributors, it still has a chance to be restored.

St. Alphonsus Church towers over the Sydney harbour entrance, serving as a navigation aid. The church remains a historic and cultural landmark and is an example of what can be done to save such landmarks.

◎ ST. ALPHONSUS CHURCH: **N 46.233562, W 60.174441**
The church is located at 39 Arthur Drive in the community of Victoria Mines.

3. Oxford Battery
Little Pond

As the Battle of the Atlantic raged during World War II, Sydney's importance to the supply lines and war efforts in Europe grew. Although Sydney harbour was heavily defended, it was still vulnerable to a potential long-range attack from German warships entering the outer reaches of the harbour. To address this, the Oxford Battery (also known as Fort Oxford), a long-range counter-bombardment battery, was constructed. It was one of the largest single military construction projects in Sydney, but its late arrival meant that it was never fully operational before it was no longer needed. Now deteriorated and overgrown, the concrete structure testifies to the harbour's military history.

HISTORY

The Oxford Battery was originally slated to be located near the coast at Oxford Point (giving it its name) but, before construction began, it was decided that the battery should be moved to a more defensible position farther inland. Excavation at the No. 1 gun site began in August 1943, and first concrete was poured within a month. The site's layout consisted of three concrete gun emplacements, each spaced almost 150 metres from the next. Behind each emplacement, a series of underground concrete rooms and structures housed the gun's operating equipment, ammunition, and crew. Therefore, each self-contained gun could operate independently.

The coastal battery was constructed late in the war relative to others in North America. This meant that it had to be built as quickly and economically as possible, and any materials or design features deemed unnecessary to the battery's performance were eliminated. This included concrete walls and parapets which typically protected the guns and operations buildings in similar batteries along the North American coast.

The Oxford Battery was a long-range counter-bombardment battery. Should an enemy warship approach the harbour, the battery, in joint effort with a similar battery at Fort Lingan, could return fire and prevent an attack. The Oxford Battery was armed with three 9.2-inch Mark 15 guns which were encased in an armoured housing, unique for guns of this type. Each gun weighed approximately 28,000 kilograms and was capable of firing projectiles up to 26.5 kilometres. The first two guns were test-fired in March 1946, the third in May 1948 (some sources state that the third gun was never installed due to the war ending in 1945). The fort also housed a 20-millimetre anti-aircraft gun.

Behind the battery, a series of underground buildings and tunnels protected the battery's ammunition and personnel. Farther to the southwest, wooden barracks and accommodations were camouflaged as a small village to deter attack. Nearby, a communications tower equipped with long-range radar detected ships approaching the harbour.

As with many coastal defence batteries, a fire control tower was constructed 350 metres away on a small hill, giving it sweeping views of the surrounding landscape. This four-storey reinforced-concrete tower located targets. It then relayed this information to the battery's operating crew, who could fire at the target if necessary.

The battery was not completed by the end of the war, but construction continued until the end of 1947, when crews were ordered to halt construction. In 1948, the battery's guns and equipment were dismantled and placed in reserve. They remained there until August 1953, when the guns and equipment were transported to Portugal as part of a NATO aid mission. Oxford Battery was officially deactivated.

ABOUT THE AREA

Even though this was one of the largest and last batteries constructed in Sydney, no preservation efforts were ever undertaken. The battery and its gun emplacements have fallen into disrepair but remain visible. Behind the gun emplacements, the four-storey fire control tower stands high above the surrounding forest, a marker of the community and its contributions to the harbour's military history. The battery has been extensively researched since World War II, preserving the story of Sydney's last wartime coastal defence project.

OXFORD BATTERY: **N 46.288254, W 60.273749**
FIRE CONTROL TOWER: **N 46.285295, W 60.276564**
The trailhead (N 46.285343, W 60.275260) to access the Fire Control Tower is located at the end of Boutiliers Lane in the community of Little Pond. From here, a 100-metre hike on an ATV trail is required to reach the site.

4. Cranberry Point Battery

Sydney Mines

Connected to the rest of the Cape Breton by a jagged, narrow ridge, Cranberry Point extends into Sydney harbour. The small, grassy peninsula is the location of the Cranberry Point Battery, a World War I fortification designed to protect the harbour's western extremity. In June 1917, Sydney was selected as an assembly point for convoys sailing to the war in Europe. This put the harbour at great risk of being attacked; to ensure the safety of both the harbour's facilities and ships entering and leaving it, a small defence battery was constructed at Cranberry Point. The concrete structures were armed with two 4.7-inch quick-firing guns, with a third installed in August 1918. Several concrete buildings were constructed nearby, including ammunition and equipment storage and a fire control observation tower. During World War I, the battery denoted the harbour's outer line of defence. It worked with the harbour's examination vessels, which identified and inspected every ship entering the harbour. If a ship refused to identify itself, the Cranberry Point Battery responded. After the war, the battery was placed in reserve.

The Cranberry Point Battery was reactivated during World War II as a fire control observation post for surrounding gun emplacements. Additionally, two coastal artillery searchlights were installed to illuminate the outer reaches of the harbour. After the war, the battery was decommissioned, and eventually abandoned. Its location on a small, isolated peninsula has made it inaccessible. Nearly 75 years of storms and coastal erosion has destroyed the narrow path to the island, leaving an impassable, jagged ridge connecting the peninsula to the mainland. Coastal erosion has also eroded the small block of land, causing portions of the battery to fall into the sea. While the remains of the fire control tower, concrete barracks, and gun emplacements continue to stand, the battery will likely slowly fall victim to the sea.

CRANBERRY POINT BATTERY: **N 46.262184, W 60.207066**

The best viewing point of the Cranberry Point Battery is at the end of Peck Street in the community of Sydney Mines. Much of the land in the area is private property and permission is required to get closer to the site.

5. Chapel Point Battery

Sydney Mines

Chapel Point has been a vital military outpost since at least 1862, when fears that the American Civil War could lead to a Canadian invasion led the British government to build a multiple gun fortification. Although the stone and brick battery was praised for its size and abilities, it was abandoned and dismantled in 1865. The location was not used again until August 1914, when the outbreak of World War I again raised the fear of attack. To protect the harbour, a temporary battery was constructed approximately 700 metres from the coastline and armed with two 4.7-inch field guns. Once a defence plan was produced for the harbour, both guns were removed in November 1915—to be replaced by a single 4.7-inch gun in October 1916 to support the nearby examination battery at Cranberry Point. This was soon considered a redundant system and in May 1917 the gun was relocated to the Cranberry Point Battery, and Chapel Point was abandoned.

In 1939, World War II led the Department of Defence to revaluate Sydney harbour's defences. One outcome was the decision to construct a large gun emplacement at Chapel Point, near the site of the former two military installations. Montreal construction firm E.G.M. Cape and Company demolished the World War I battery remnants and constructed what would be the harbour's primary examination battery. Working with Fort Petrie across the harbour, the battery's primary objective was to protect the naval and merchant marine vessels stationed in the harbour.

To do this, two 4.7-inch Mark 7 quick-firing guns were installed on large concrete foundations overlooking the harbour. In 1944, these were replaced with two 4-inch twin-barreled Mark 16 guns. The gun emplacements were protected from attack by 4.5 metres of concrete poured at the front of each gun and then backfilled to blend them into the hillside. The battery contained an extensive underground tunnel system to protect ammunition, operating equipment, and gun crews. Below the battery, three searchlights were installed in separate concrete bunkers, each able to light up a significant portion of the inner harbour.

In addition, a four-storey, concrete fire control and observation tower was constructed immediately behind the gun emplacement to detect and report the location and direction of ships approaching the inner harbour. The tower's design resembled that of a church to deter an attack. The building's main section was used for storage and personnel accommodations; the tower's large window openings provided panoramic views of the harbour.

The battery remained active until 1948, when it was decommissioned. In 1991, concerned citizens noticed the structure's disrepair and expressed their support for the town to preserve it as an historic site. A study to determine what would be needed to restore the aging structure was completed that same year, but the town's amalgamation with surrounding communities temporarily halted preservation efforts.

Fast forward to the late 2010s and renewed government and public interest in preserving the site. In 2018, funding from private fundraisers and the federal and provincial governments was awarded to the not-for-profit Atlantic Memorial Park Society, and the first tangible preservation efforts began. In spring 2019, restoration work began. Plans are for the site to become a public park that incorporates the restored World War II battery plus a Mi'kmaw cultural site, walking trails, and a family park.

 CHAPEL POINT BATTERY: N 46.244253, W 60.211494

The entrance to Chapel Point Battery is at the end of Amber Drive. As the site is within Atlantic Memorial Park, check the park's hours of operation before visiting.

6. Stubbert's Point Battery

Sydney Mines

Stubbert's Point Battery is located immediately along the side of Shore Road in Sydney Mines. This compact battery hosts several underground rooms surrounding a single concrete gun emplacement. During both world wars, the site was the western terminus of the harbour's anti-submarine nets that stretched to the South Bar Battery across the harbour. The anti-submarine nets, installed during World War I, were made of

5-centimetre-diameter steel cables woven together in 3.6-metre sections. Each section, suspended from a float, created a protective barrier to ward off torpedoes and German U-boats. During the war, the nets were only in place from August 1917 to the early winter of 1919, after the war ended.

With the outbreak of World War II, the point of land was again commissioned as the western terminus of the harbour's anti-submarine and boom defences. While little was done to the site during World War I, the War Department contracted local construction company M.R. Chappell to construct a compact concrete battery with a single gun emplacement, crew accommodations, a fire control tower, and an underground ammunition magazine. At the edge of the coastal cliffs to the north, three concrete searchlight emplacements would light up the harbour's anti-submarine nets. Although the battery's primary purpose was to secure and maintain the nets, it was armed with a twin 6-pounder Hotchkiss gun that was moved from the South Bar Battery in April 1941. Stubbert's Point Battery continued to operate in some capacity until 1951, when the gun and equipment were relocated to nearby Fort Petrie and Kilkenny Barracks and placed in reserve.

The concrete foundation of the abandoned battery has fallen into ruin. The fortifications perched at the edge of the harbour puts the battery at great risk of collapsing into the sea. From Stubbert's Point, it is possible to see the now-inaccessible concrete searchlight emplacements below the cliff face; many have since collapsed into the sea. Several underground rooms, narrow passages, and the gun emplacement itself remain at the site. A pillar that once belonged to the observation tower marks the battery's location.

 STUBBERT'S POINT BATTERY: N 46.224114, W 60.227565
The site is on Shore Road, approximately 2 kilometres north of the Marine Atlantic Ferry Terminal.

7. Point Edward Searchlight Emplacements

Edwardsville

Point Edward, which lies halfway between North Sydney and Sydney, is a large peninsula that splits Sydney harbour into northwest and south arms. From the rocky shoreline at its tip, visitors have a spectacular 270-degree view of the harbour; it is one of the few places in the southern harbour from which to see the ocean. This is what made Point Edward an ideal place to install two concrete searchlights in World War II. Originally, the site was the temporary location of a 4.7-inch quick-firing Mark 4 gun, but it was later relocated to batteries nearby. The searchlight emplacement was operated only during the summer months of the war and provided the primary lights for the inner harbour. Their purpose: to supply aid to any ships moving in the harbour at night and to identify and detect smaller, fast-moving ships that might attempt to break through the harbour's defences.

Following the war, the site was abandoned, leaving the two-searchlight emplacements still visible from across the water in North Sydney. While this site holds little significance to the war efforts, this off-the-beaten path location provides some of the best panoramic views of the harbour.

 POINT EDWARD SEARCHLIGHT EMPLACEMENTS: N 46.187417, W 60.228623

In the community of Edwardsville, continue down Point Edward Highway (Route 239) and turn onto Hospital Road. Travel approximately 1.2 kilometres and park at the trailhead (N 46.179318, W 60.229701). Walk down the short path to Keating Cove. Head left (north) and continue walking along the water's edge for approximately 1.2 kilometres.

8. HMCS Protector II: Point Edward Naval Base

Point Edward

During World War II, Sydney harbour became one of the most important harbours on North America's east coast after it was chosen as a rallying point for Atlantic convoys. As a result, the harbour became overcrowded with merchant and naval ships loading cargo, supplies, and troops and in need of repairs or retrofits.

In June 1940, the Royal Canadian Navy established a base, HMCS Protector, on the east side of the harbour to alleviate crowding, but, by 1942 it, too, had become congested. HMCS Protector's location in Sydney meant that it could not expand, and a second base was built across the harbour on Point Edward.

The new base, HMCS Protector II, opened on March 15, 1943. Resembling a small town, it held workshops, repair shops, and storage facilities. Wharves were built along the water and a railway spur line connected the base to the province's main railway line. Offices, living quarters, a drill hall, and a hospital allowed the base to accommodate almost 500 people. The base also housed the naval recruitment centre until later in 1943 when it was transferred to HMCS Cornwallis in Deep Brook.

Following the war, the base served as a supply depot, storing surplus vessels, equipment, and ammunition for the Navy. The base was relatively quiet until May 1956, when the HMCS Acadia Summer Training Centre was established. Only eight years later, the Navy no longer required the base, and in 1964 it was closed.

Part of the former base became the new home of the Canadian Coast Guard College, until 1981, when a new facility was built nearby, which remains in operation. The areas of the base not used by the Coast Guard were retransferred to local governments and in 1969 became the Sydport Industrial Park. Many former base buildings have been repurposed into warehouses, workshops, and storage yards. The former railway line still winds through the base, abandoned and overgrown. This, along with fire hydrants on empty plots of land, deteriorated structures, and traces of fences and equipment scattered throughout the area, gives the site an empty, eerie feel.

 POINT EDWARD NAVAL BASE: N 46.156216, W 60.219494
From Highway 125, take Exit 5 onto the Sydport Access Road. Drive 3.8 kilometres to the Sydport Industrial Park.

No Trespassing
By Order MND

Accès interdit
Par ordre / MDN

9. CFS Sydney
Sydney

Given the importance of Sydney's coal mines and steel industry, its harbour was fortified with gun emplacements and forts, starting in the mid-19th century—until the end of World War II, when the area's military activity dwindled and nearly all of its fortifications were demolished. This was not the case for a small plot of land high on a hill overlooking the town. There, a new type of defence was constructed: a radar station. Instead of defending against naval ships or U-boats, it was part of a network of radar sites designed to warn of a potential nuclear attack. The radar is still in use. Although much of the land has been purchased by private developers, it remains one of the most intact sites of its kind in Eastern Canada.

As fear of a Soviet Union attack on North America grew in the early 1950s, Canada and the US devised a plan to warn of such an attack: a series of sites concentrated around similar degrees of latitude that would use the relatively new concept of radar to locate and detect aircraft flying over the Arctic and Atlantic oceans. The most northern of these lines, the Distant Early Warning Line, loosely followed the Arctic Circle. Below this was the Mid-Canada Line, at approximately 55 degrees latitude. Finally, at approximately 50 degrees latitude was the Pinetree Line. Operated jointly by the US Air Force and Royal Canadian Air Force, the bases eventually were placed under NORAD command.

Sydney's history as a military centre, along with its location in northeastern Nova Scotia, made it an obvious choice for a radar site. Planning and construction happened quickly, with work beginning in 1951. The Sydney site was designed to be completely self-sufficient, with its own power source, water supply, and personnel provisions. Accompanying these facilities was a mess hall, motor pool, gymnasium, and the main operations buildings. As was standard on the Pinetree Line sites, three towers supported the early warning radar systems.

Completed in March 1953, the radar site was operated by the No. 221 Aircraft Control and Warning Squadron and complemented similar radar sites nearby, providing coverage over the Cabot Strait and the south coast of Newfoundland. If an aircraft was detected, the radar system would track its direction and speed, which would be relayed to Canadian and American intercept fighter jets in Chatham, New Brunswick, or Stephenville, Newfoundland.

By the early 1960s, the radar systems at the Pinetree Line sites had become obsolete. While some sites were shut down, others, such as that in Sydney, were upgraded with the advanced computer and networking system Semi-Automatic Ground Environment (SAGE). This system automated many of the facilities' existing equipment, capable of relaying information to a command centre at Topsham Air Force Base. When the system was decommissioned in late 1962, many of the site's personnel were redeployed or laid off and two of its radar towers were torn down.

As the site was now entirely operated by the Royal Canadian Air Force, in February 1968 it was redesignated CFS Sydney. Throughout the early 1980s, the remaining Pinetree Line sites had again become obsolete. Most were decommissioned, except CFS Sydney, which continued to track aircraft over the Atlantic. Eventually this site too

became obsolete, and radar operations ended on January 17, 1991. The site was officially decommissioned in 1992.

ABOUT THE AREA

Following the site's closure, the Government of Canada transferred the land to the County of Cape Breton, where it was sold to New Dawn Enterprises and transformed into residential housing and an assisted-living community, including a retirement home for seniors. Named Pine Tree Park Estates, the development has reutilized many of the former base's buildings, helping to preserve them and the site's history. A small portion of the site's radar facilities, including a former tower and radar dome, was transferred to the Canadian Coast Guard to provide support for tracking ships and search and rescue efforts. Throughout the area, many relics of this former Cold War-era radar station can still be found, each symbolizing the fear of an attack by the Soviet Union just 60 years ago.

 CFS SYDNEY: N 46.168404, W 60.166211

From the community of Sydney, drive north on Lingan Road and turn onto Military Road. The road marks the beginning of the former site. As many of the remaining buildings are still in use, respect private property when visiting.

10. South Bar Battery
South Bar

Located immediately across the harbour from Stubbert's Battery, the South Bar Battery was the eastern terminus of the harbour's antisubmarine and boom defences during World Wars I and II. The site was chosen because South Bar, a natural spit that extends into the harbour, creates a bottleneck where ships have only a narrow clearance. During the wars, this gave the military more control over ships entering the harbour.

As was the case with Stubbert's Point Battery (page 104), at the beginning of World War II the South Bar Battery was equipped with twin 6-pounder Hotchkiss guns on timber or wooden mounts embedded in the hillside. To support the gun, a small concrete structure nearby housed an ammunition magazine, crew shelter, and an engine house. Searchlight emplacements were also built. The South Bar Battery had a slightly better vantage point than its complementary battery across the harbour; in 1943, the Hotchkiss guns were replaced with a more advanced, 6-pounder quick-firing gun. The new gun protected the harbour's anti-submarine nets and provided support for the anti-aircraft battery nearby.

In 1944, the barracks burned down and in February 1954—several months before Germany surrendered—the battery was declared surplus, and deactivated. As part of the decommissioning and disarmament of Sydney harbour's defence network in the 1950s, any remaining equipment at the site was removed in 1953 and 1954.

A few remnants of the old battery still exist, though much has been lost to coastal erosion. The last pieces of intact concrete of the former battery are visible near the shoreline. On South Bar are a string of wooden cribs and piers; originally used to tie up ships, they now mitigate erosion of the bar. Visitors should be cautious: at high tide, the bar can become partly cut off from the nearby land, potentially stranding anyone who wishes not to get wet on their return.

SOUTH BAR BATTERY: **N 46.211062, W 60.198022**

Approximately 5 kilometres north of Sydney on New Waterford Highway, turn onto a small gravel road (N 46.209408, W 60.195536) and follow it to its end. From here a short walk to the water brings you to the site.

11. Fort Petrie

New Victoria

Located on a point of flat land on the western shore of Sydney harbour is Fort Petrie, the harbour's last active military defence fortification. Unlike its sister battery, Chapel Point (page 102), with which it shares an almost identical layout, Fort Petrie's significance was recognized early. In 1990, when it was slated for demolition, the fort was restored as a museum and memorial to those who served in the harbour. While the defence outpost may not be considered hidden, it is often overlooked and is an excellent place to safely explore one of the harbour's most important World War II defence batteries.

Although a military blockhouse is believed to have been situated on site in the mid- to late 1800s, the first significant military activity happened during World War I. In 1914, two 4.7-inch field guns were installed on concrete mounts, followed by a third, near the end of the war. The battery's objective was to protect the increasing number of cargo ships transporting coal and steel from Sydney. Throughout the war, the fortification's importance grew as the harbour became a starting point for transatlantic shipping convoys carrying food, supplies, and personnel to Europe. Immediately following the war, Fort Petrie was abandoned, and most of the equipment placed in reserve.

The site was reactivated at the outbreak of World War II. This time, the Canadian War Department contracted the construction company E.G.M. Cape and Company to construct a two-gun, concrete battery at the site.

When completed, the battery contained two gun emplacements, a three-storey battery observation tower, and a radar and communications tower.

Ammunition was stored in underground rooms between the guns. A system of elevators, whose openings are still visible, were used to move the ammunition. Behind the guns, a three-storey concrete observation tower was built. Similar to the battery at Chapel Point, the tower's pointed roof disguised it as a church.

Beneath the battery along the cliff, two coastal artillery searchlights were installed in concrete structures. Each structure had a self-contained, underground diesel powerhouse which allowed the lights to illuminate the outer harbour even in the event of a power failure at the nearby battery. The searchlight emplacements were used as a Naval Signal Station and to illuminate potential targets for the guns above.

Two 6-inch Mark 2 quick-firing naval guns were installed on temporary mounts at Fort Petrie in 1939. Shortly afterward, concrete foundations were constructed; these are still visible. In 1943, the battery was used as the harbour's examination battery and, as a result, a 6-pounder Hotchkiss gun was installed nearby. The battery became

redundant when construction was completed on Fort Oxford on the harbour's eastern side. The guns were replaced with two 4-inch twin-barrelled quick-firing Mark 14 guns in 1944. Following the end of World War II in 1945, the battery was placed in reserve. Between 1947 and 1948, the equipment and guns were removed, but reinstalled in 1951. In 1956, the guns were removed again, and the fort was maintained as a reserve battery until it was officially decommissioned in 1968. At that time, it was the last active military fortification in the harbour.

In 1990, the battery was slated for demolition but, with the support of residents, an injunction was filed, and the battery was saved. In 1991, it was purchased by the Sydney Harbour Fortification Society, who, in 1998, transformed the battery into an interpretation site, and its observation tower now houses a museum.

⊕ FORT PETRIE: N 46.249815, W 60.152861

Fort Petrie is on the side of New Waterford Highway in the community of Victoria Mines.

12. Fort Lingan
New Waterford

As you drive along the scenic coastal road connecting the communities of Lingan and New Waterford, it is easy to dismiss the passing empty grassy fields. If you take a closer look, however, you will find one of Sydney's most important World War II defences, Fort Lingan, Sydney's first counter-bombardment battery constructed during the war. Designed to be the first to respond to a long-range naval attack by German ships, the battery was armed with three evenly spaced 6-inch quick-firing guns and supported by a nearby anti-aircraft battery. Each gun was installed on a large concrete foundation and, nearby, ammunition storage bunkers and an operations building were constructed. A series of concrete buildings were constructed nearby: a fire control tower, a range-finder building, and an operations building, all designed to resemble one- to two-storey buildings.

Construction, which began in 1940 by local contractor J.P. Porter and Sons, was completed in spring 1941. Over 80 personnel were stationed at the battery, most of whom were housed in nearby wooden barracks. In addition to its primary purpose as a counter-bombardment defence, the fort protected the New Waterford shoreline, where hundreds of ships and convoys regularly sailed.

The fort operated until 1947, when most of its equipment and ammunition were placed in storage at Fort Petrie. A few components of the fort's guns were kept in place, in case they would have to be reactivated, but soon fell into disrepair. In the early 1950s, these too were disassembled and shipped to Europe as part of a NATO agreement.

The fort's concrete foundations have been neglected and many of the surrounding support structures have been demolished. The exception: one of Fort Lingan's fire control towers on a point of land north of the Lingan Generating Station. As for the gun emplacements, when the road was built between Lingan and New Waterford, part of the road was built on top of a former foundation; the other two are partly buried and

overgrown by vegetation. With some exploring in the tall grass, it is still possible to see them. Visiting the area makes one curious about all the other facilities and accompanying underground storage rooms that are buried beneath the ground.

 FORT LINGAN: N 46.249786, W 60.057316
The site is located east of the community of New Waterford along the side of Hinchey Avenue. While there are no established trails to the site, it is possible to see remnants of the site from the road when vegetation is low in the spring and fall.

13. Broughton

Birch Grove

As you drive along forested Broughton Road, signs indicate the mining town that once existed there. But venture farther into the forest and you will see house foundations, buildings, and roads in what was considered Canada's first planned community. Broughton began as a mining town, designed to reflect the modernity of the Cape Breton Coal, Iron and Railway Company and showcase a new-age coal mining town. Although it flourished for a short time, what is left of the town is slowly being reclaimed by nature.

The story of Broughton began in 1897 when Sydney lawyer Edgar T. Mosely hired Alex Maclean to prospect the area around Loon Lake, about 10 kilometres south of Glace Bay. Maclean hired four men who worked for the Cape Breton Coal, Iron and Railway Company; they quickly

discovered a 6-foot coal seam, later known as the Broughton or Mosely Seam. Under Mosely's supervision, the company sank a mine shaft to a depth of 36.5 metres to investigate further and extract its coal.

Progress at the mine was slow. In 1902, the pace picked up when the operation caught the attention of British mining engineer Thomas Lancaster and his partner George Jacques, who purchased the charter for the Cape Breton Coal, Iron and Railway Company. The first (and continuing) problem with the isolated Broughton mine was finding a method to transport the coal to a shipping port. Lancaster approached the Dominion Securities Company and proposed a partnership: the Dominion Securities Company owned the railway line from Canso to St. Peters, which could theoretically be extended and then used to transport coal to a shipping port. However, the company showed little interest. Lancaster then made a similar pitch to the Dominion Coal Company, but, similarly, they saw little value in the joint venture.

In need of financial support, in 1904 Lancaster partnered with businessperson Colonel Horace Mayhew, who, along with investors in England and Montreal, purchased the charter and leases from the Cape Breton Coal, Iron and Railway Company. Instead of establishing a single mining project, Mayhew aspired to develop an innovative town. The company hired architect William Harris to design a town that could support 10,000 to 12,000 people. Using the investors' money originally intended for the mining operation, Mayhew constructed streets, houses, and extravagant buildings with the expectation that the town would attract further investment in the project. A railway spur line connecting the community to the Sydney and Louisburg Railway would allow for the delivery of materials and equipment. Mayhew named the town Broughton after the estate he had purchased in Hawarden, England.

Its thoughtful design labelled Broughton one of the first planned towns in Canada. At peak, 400 workers were engaged in construction. Harris planned nearly 20 kilometres of streets which, once completed, allowed workers to build the town's first buildings, including mining offices, churches, stores, and schools. The town was also equipped with electric lights, running water, a sewer system, and telephone lines. Forty-three houses housed the mine's workers, and several larger houses provided accommodations for its managers.

The most notable buildings were the Crown Hotel and the Broughton Arms Hotel. The Crown Hotel, intended to provide temporary accommodations for the mine's workers, was less luxurious than the Broughton Arms Hotel. The Broughton Arms Hotel, a lavishly designed three-storey wooden building intended to host investors, managers, and other notable figures, was equipped with electric lights, a telephone system between rooms, and the first revolving door installed in a hotel in North America. These features, along with its rounded towers and spacious interior, allowed the owners to promote the hotel as the finest lakeside resort east of Montreal.

As the town and mine grew, Mosely's challenges also grew. Broughton was located inland, away from shipping supports or suitable railways

capable of transporting coal cars. Mayhew considered building a railway line to a nearby port such as Mira Bay, Louisbourg, or Sydney but all were too expensive, given the rising cost of the town's construction. In desperation, Mayhew and Lancaster again approached the Dominion Coal Company, which operated the nearby Sydney and Louisburg Railway to work out a deal to transport coal along its railway. The Dominion Coal Company, one of the area's largest operations at the time, feared that the Broughton Mine would be unnecessary competition and denied the request to build a connecting railway to Broughton. It was reported that Dominion Coal even purchased parcels of land near Broughton, prohibiting the mine from expanding.

Financial problems grew as money was put into the town instead of the mining operation. In March 1906, Lancaster resigned as general manager, while Mayhew searched for more investment money. Later that year, Mayhew returned to England to find investment opportunities, leaving his son, Horace Mayhew Jr., to oversee the town and mine; however, Mayhew's son died on a hunting trip in August 1906.

The following year, the Cape Breton Coal, Iron and Railroad Company went bankrupt, and the mine was closed. Although he did not return to the town after his son's death, Mayhew remained optimistic about Broughton's mining potential. His outlook seemed to be accurate for a short time—the mine reopened between 1912 and 1915. In 1914, a new school was built to accommodate the children. Once the mine closed, due to continuing shipping problems, the town's population quickly dwindled.

Broughton experienced a brief period of activity during World War I when 1,200 soldiers of the 185th Cape Breton Highlanders established a training camp and headquarters there. The soldiers stayed in the buildings, including the Broughton Arms Hotel. In 1916, a fire destroyed the once-grand hotel. In the weeks, months, and years after the mine's closure, the town's buildings were progressively dismantled or burned by vandals.

No mining endeavour was pursued again at Broughton until 1948, when the Bras d'Or Company pumped out the flooded site and established the Four Star Mine and a second mine, Beaver Mine, farther to the northwest. The two mines were considered the most modern of their time and, unlike previous endeavours, new roads through the area allowed the company to transport coal to shipping facilities via trucks. While the coal seam at Broughton was once considered of high value, impurities detected in the coal made the ventures less economically viable. The Beaver Mine closed in 1961, and in 1967 the Cape Breton Development Corporation took over all mining operations throughout Cape Breton. Broughton's Four Star Mine was permanently closed in February 1970.

ABOUT THE AREA

Few reminders exist of the once-booming town. Many of its buildings, including the miners' wooden houses, were removed after the town's decline. The two hotels and managers' houses had large concrete basements and foundations which can still be explored throughout the area. While many of the largest remnants are concentrated near Loon Lake, concrete foundations throughout the area have been marked with Falling Hazard signs, which make them easy to identify.

Despite the impact of the industry on the area, little research exists on Broughton. But the town has not gone completely unnoticed: many local residents have worked diligently to preserve the site, installing homemade signs to guide visitors around the complex system of former roads. Broughton and its overgrown roads and foundations offer a window into the region's coal mining history.

 BROUGHTON: N 46.080645, W 59.972964

Approximately 6 kilometres south of Glace Bay is the community of Birch Grove. From the community, drive west on the unpaved Broughton Road for 7.5 kilometres to the trailhead (N 46.082580, W 59.971988). From here, accessible walking trails take you through the former community.

14. Louisbourg Railway Tunnel
Louisbourg

The historic Sydney and Louisburg Railway has had a long and personal connection to the people of Louisbourg, though few remnants exist. A museum includes the former train station, storage sheds, and several rail cars said to be the last remnants of the railway—but if you explore closer to the water, you may spy another relic. At the base of Aberdeen Street, an unburied concrete tunnel now stores sand and gravel. The tunnel had provided a route for trains travelling the spur line which once ran along Commercial Street and passed beneath the coal shipping piers.

The Sydney and Louisburg Railway was constructed in 1895 to connect the coal mines of Sydney and Glace Bay with the Louisbourg harbour. Once it was completed, the railway's owner, the Dominion Coal Company, built a large coal shipping pier at the railway's terminus. The wooden trestle pier measured 183 metres long and 27.5 metres wide, with an approach of approximately 137 metres, making it one of the largest in the world.

Steam locomotives transported coal cars from the Sydney and Glace Bay mines to the end of the pier. There, the locomotive separated from the cars and was redirected onto a lower set of tracks, where it was refuelled and rewatered. Meanwhile, the coal cars were redirected onto the pier, where the coal was dumped into chutes that moved it onto waiting ships.

In 1950, a spur line was to be added to the railway to run along Commercial Street to access the fish processing plant near the harbour. The challenge: the railway had to intersect the coal pier without disrupting the coal cars and conveyor belts moving overhead. To solve this problem, a section of wooden trestle that constituted the pier's approach was demolished and a square, concrete tunnel built to allow train passage. On September 9, 1950, engine number 42 and a series of cars passed through the tunnel for the first time.

In 1962, maintaining the piers was no longer viable; they were

dismantled and sold for scrap. All that remained were several wooden posts in the harbour for the coal pier and the backfilled approach to the pier, including the Commercial Street spur line's concrete tunnel.

In July 1967, the Sydney and Louisburg Railway line was closed the following year and sold for scrap. To save a piece of the railway's heritage, community volunteers and organizations banded together to restore the Louisburg Railway station, freight shed, and property. On June 26, 1972, the railway station was opened as the Sydney and Louisburg Railway Museum, operated by the Sydney and Louisburg Railway Historical Society.

The museum preserves the history of the railway and its importance to Louisbourg's people. But with the coal piers now demolished, it is difficult to grasp the size of the piers and the scale of the operations. The tunnel, an often-overlooked remnant of the railway, is the last remaining artifact of the piers themselves. The tunnel's size and scale bring to life the effect of the shipping industry on the quiet town of Louisbourg.

⊕ LOUISBOURG RAILWAY TUNNEL: N 45.919200, W 59.971223

The tunnel is best viewed on Aberdeen Street near the Louisbourg Playhouse.

New Glasgow

①

Antigonish

③

Port Hawkesbury

Guysborough

④ ②

⑤

Canso

Sherbrooke

⑥

⑦

⑧

Sheet Harbour

⑨

⑩

Central Nova Scotia & the Eastern Shore

Stretching from Pictou in the north to the Strait of Canso in the east, and then following the rugged Eastern Shore south to Halifax, this historic, isolated region is often overlooked by visitors. The Northumberland Strait coastline transitions from sandy beaches to rocky coastal terraces, interspersed with large natural harbours that have long attracted fishers and seafarers. Along the Eastern Shore, the rocky edges and coastal barrens are sparsely populated, despite its many inlets and coves. Moving inland from the coast, vast forests and wetlands drape over rolling hills and ridges separated by significant rivers. The physical landscape has long defined the region's culture and traditions, which continues to be based around fishing, forestry, and mining.

The first European settlements in the area were established as fishing outports taking advantage of the inshore and offshore fishing grounds. The nearby forest established shipbuilding in the region while also providing land for agriculture and raising livestock. As the population of Nova Scotia grew, immigrants looked for land to live on, with many finding a new home in the province's interior. Here the region's forest and rivers were utilized to power sawmills and gristmills that drove local economies.

But the economies built on fishing and logging were overshadowed when prospectors discovered gold in Mooseland in 1858. They soon launched the first of many gold rushes in Nova Scotia, many of which were confined to the Eastern Shore. In Pictou County, the discovery of

131

large coal seams quickly distinguished the area as one of the largest mining operations in the province. The region's industry and culture are thus as diverse as its landscape. From shipwrecks to abandoned lighthouses, to former mining operations and sawmills, central Nova Scotia and the Eastern Shore hold plenty to explore.

Travellers will find a mix of highways, country roads, and gravel roads. In the north, the TCH (Highway 104) travels between the large centres of New Glasgow and Antigonish and on to the Canso Causeway. On the Eastern Shore, Highway 7 travels from Halifax in the south,

through the communities of Musquodoboit Harbour, Sheet Harbour, and Sherbrooke before turning north inland to Antigonish. To complete the entire Eastern Shore drive, from the historic community of Sherbrooke follow a series of smaller highways east to Highway 316. Intersecting these highways are a series of roads and smaller highways that travel through the sparsely populated interior. Despite this extensive network of roads, many areas are inaccessible by vehicles. Among these are large tracts of forested hills, popular with outdoor enthusiasts; and along the coast, hundreds of small islands and coves are accessible only by boat.

1. Millstream Brook Foundations
Springville

It is difficult to imagine the area around Millstream Brook as ever being a centre of industry. But before the coal mining industry was established, for which Pictou County is best known, the area south of Stellarton was home to recently arrived European immigrants.

In 1773, the first notable Scottish immigrants arrived in Pictou aboard the sailing ship *Hector*. Once ashore, these people scattered, laying claim to land that they soon cultivated. The area around Springville on the banks of the East River of Pictou was one of these areas. Attracted by the freshwater sources, fertile land, and vast timber reserves, they soon called the land home.

James Grant was one of the nearly 200 people who arrived on the *Hector*. After living in the Pictou area for many years, in 1790 he settled near Millstream. By this time, many farmers were producing grain and wheat but had no way to process it for the market. Grant recognized this need, and having spent much of his life in Scotland milling, he established a gristmill on the banks of a small river between Grants Lake and Pictou's East River in 1816. The water-powered mill was one of the earliest of its kind in the province and, along with several other businesses opened by Grant, turned the area into an industrial centre.

The family business grew and, by the mid-1800s, the family operated a gristmill, oat mill, sawmill, and furniture factory, most of which were confined to the 1.2-kilometre stretch of Millstream Brook.

About this time, a member of the Grant family opened a large saw- and lumber mill at the north end of Grants Lake. Known simply as Grant's Mill, the mill used a system of flumes to power the mill's machinery. Logs floated down the river entered the flume, which transported them into the mill where they were cut to the required lengths.

Grant family members maintained, owned, and operated several mills on the river, including Grant's Mill, until well into the 1900s. Throughout

the first part of the century, however, many mills closed, until only the sawmill at the north side of the lake was left. In 1934, Stanley Rogers purchased the aging Grant's Mill from members of the Grant family living nearby. Rogers operated the mill until World War II, when he and his three older sons enlisted. The mill officially shut down in 1944. If the name Stanley Rogers seems familiar, it is because Stanley Rogers was the grandfather of the late well-known Canadian musician Stan Rogers.

The beautiful Millstream Brook lies hidden among the rolling hills and forest of interior Nova Scotia. But hiking along the river reveals moss-covered stone walls and foundations belonging to the once-thriving mills and factories. Similarly, near the outlet of Grants Lake, large stone foundations, pieces of equipment, and the remains of a stone line dam are hidden among the tall grass. These relics represent the work and trades of some of Nova Scotia's first Scottish immigrants, and more specifically of the Grant family, who shaped both the physical and cultural landscapes.

MILLSTREAM BROOK FOUNDATIONS: **N 45.448942, W 62.650494** From Exit 25 on the TCH, drive south on Highway 348 for 13 kilometres to the town of Springville. Drive straight for 650 metres until you cross the East Pictou River Bridge. Turn west onto East River West Side Road and continue 1.5 kilometres before turning onto Millstream 2 Road, which follows the river. Foundations and pieces of machinery are scattered along the length of the river.

2. Hart Island Lighthouse

Canso Islands National Historic Site, Canso Harbour

Across the harbour from the town of Canso a deteriorated church-like white building sits on a small island. The remains of one of the harbour's last lighthouses, contained within the boundaries of the Canso Islands National Historic Site, is a comforting marker to fishing vessels using the harbour.

Canso harbour has been an important European military and fishing outpost since the 1600s. Established because of its proximity to the Grand Banks fishing grounds and its strategic location at the entrance of the Strait of Canso, Canso has a long history in maritime navigation. The first lighthouse on the harbour's nearest island was built in 1872. It was 8.5 metres tall with a square wooden tower which housed four flat-wick lamps fixed to large, mirrored reflectors. The lighthouse, which guided ships entering the harbour's narrow northern entrance, was operated by a lighthouse keeper living in a dwelling attached to the tower.

The light operated until 1928. Over the following year, the lighthouse was removed and a new structure erected. Similar to the original, the new lighthouse was a white square tower with an attached one-storey fog-signal building. The 10-metre-tall tower gave the light more range than its predecessor. After operating for more than 20 years, the light was deactivated in 1960 and replaced by two steel-tower beacons. The lighthouse is owned by the Canadian Coast Guard and managed by Parks Canada.

The lighthouse towers over the grassy island it was built on. Although it can be seen a short distance from the shoreline, it remains accessible only by boat. The harbour is generally well protected from weather and ocean swells, but its proximity to the open ocean can make the journey dangerous for inexperienced paddlers or boaters.

HART ISLAND LIGHTHOUSE: **N 45.343825, W 60.989594**

While it is possible to see the lighthouse from the Canso wharf at the end of Main Street, a short paddle or boat ride to the island is required to get a closer view.

3. Hulbert's Sawmill & Gristmill

Lochaber, Antigonish County

Not long ago, Nova Scotia's farming and forestry industries were run by families instead of large corporations. As coastal forests were logged for timber and shipbuilding, foresters pushed inland to access the province's remaining forest reserves. Because of this, in the early 19th century many Scottish and American Loyalist families called the area along the shores of Lochaber Lake between Antigonish and the Eastern Shore home. One family, the Hulberts, established a small milling operation around 1850 that would continue for almost 100 years. Mill remains are still found at the base of a waterfall on Hulbert's Brook, one of Nova Scotia's most beautiful hidden places. The stone dam and foundations are some of the last relics of the former community of Lochaber and the Hulbert family's milling operations.

The Hulbert family came to Antigonish County from the US after the American Revolutionary War, around 1788. The family, like many others, cleared land to farm around Lochaber Lake, approximately 20 kilometres south of Antigonish. By the mid-19th century, this inland town on the banks of Lochaber Lake was thriving, built on the success of local sawmills, tanneries, gristmills, and blacksmith forges. The mid-19th century brought a push to exploit inland forest, as timber resources closer to the coast had slowly been depleted. Recognizing this, Alexander D. Hulbert purchased the land and timber rights to the south side of the stream; it would become known as Hulbert's Brook.

The piece of flat land purchased by Hulbert was located at the base of a waterfall and stretched along a flat floodplain to Lochaber Lake. Hulbert built a wooden sawmill and gristmill on stone foundations at the base of the waterfall and toward the lake built several wooden structures and storage buildings. At the top of the falls, a stone and concrete dam raised the water level an additional 2 or 3 metres. Water

from the reservoir, redirected through a pipe and fed into both mills, powered the mill's saw and grinding machinery.

By the 1880s, as many as 13 gristmills operated in Antigonish County, including Hulbert's, which ground locally grown wheat and oats into flour, which was then sold at the family's store. The business grew slowly, but the mill's location and abundant power source made it one of the area's largest producers. The sawmill likely operated for two months of the year, the gristmill for seven. Due to low water levels in the river and ice buildup, the mills could not run year-round.

By 1870, two of Alexander Hulbert's children, John Gardiner and William Ralph, had become part owners and continued operating the mill after their father's death in June 1887. By the 1900s, John Gardiner Hulbert's son, Howard John, took over operations. In 1909, a strong November storm extensively damaged the mill when the river flooded the facilities downstream. Driven to keep the mill going, Howard repaired the mill and put it back into operation the following year. While most of the county's gristmills closed in the first half of the 20th century, Hulbert's mill operated until at least the 1950s.

ABOUT THE AREA

The waterfall located next to the former mill is an attraction on its own. At the top, the water falls over the beautiful 19th-century stone dam before cascading over the rocks below, plunging into a deep pool at the base of the cliff. On the north side of the river, a steel pipe protrudes from the dam and travels vertically into a complex of stone walls, formerly the location of the mill's equipment. Across the river, a large stone foundation split in half by a stone wall makes up the largest remains. The craftsmanship is a testament to the care with which the family built the mill at the base of the falls. No wooden structures remain on the property, but by venturing closer to the lakeshore it is possible to imagine the building complex that once thrived there. It is also possible to see the stone foundations of a Presbyterian church constructed in 1867, which burned down in 1950.

The remains of the former sawmill and gristmill represent the hard work of early settlers and a time in Nova Scotia's history when the interior was slowly being encroached upon by Europeans.

⌖ **HULBERT'S SAWMILL AND GRISTMILL: N 45.443812, W 62.013697**
As most of the property is now private property, avoid trespassing. From a bridge on Trunk Highway 7, it is possible to walk along Hulbert's Brook for approximately 300 metres to arrive at the former mill; however, no designated trail exists.

4. Hazel Hill Commercial Cable Station

Canso, Guysborough

For years, the Hazel Hill Commercial Cable Station received and relayed messages from England to the US. After it closed in 1962, it fell into disrepair before the main floors of the historic building were demolished, leaving only the granite block foundation.

In 1888, James G. Bennett and John W. MacKay incorporated the Commercial Cable Company in New York City. Bennett had previously owned the *New York Herald* and McKay owned several successful silver mines in Nevada. Both had worked extensively with telegrams and, after recognizing a lack of competition for established cable companies such as the Anglo-American Telegraph Company, the two decided to establish their own.

Prior to the company's establishment, Bennett and MacKay commissioned the CS *Mackay-Bennett* to lay two submarine telegraph cables from Waterville, Ireland, to Canso, Nova Scotia. Compared to other attempts to lay a transatlantic cable, the endeavour experienced few problems. The cable was brought to shore, where it terminated at the Hazel Hill Commercial Cable Station.

The station was required because messages transmitted from a station in Ireland were too weak after crossing the Atlantic to continue on the same line. Messages were received at Hazel Hill, repeated, and forwarded to operators in New York. Even though several telegraph cables had been established in the years prior to the Commercial Cable Company's line, the technology was considered a major advance in transatlantic communications.

The first repeater station on the site, a small, rectangular wooden building, was constructed in 1884. In 1888, a new station reflected the company's status and importance: a two-and-a-half-storey, neo-classical brick building was constructed on a granite-block foundation. The building was enlarged in 1899, almost doubling its original size and likely making it the largest building on the Canso Peninsula, standing prominently in the landscape.

By the end of the 19th century, the area surrounding the cable station was transformed into a community. Almost a dozen buildings provided accommodations for workers, both temporary and permanent, and for managers. The town layout reflected company seniority, with workers' houses built around superintendents' houses. In addition to workers' housing, a school and church were established. Many tradespeople and workers were hired from the surrounding town.

The operation became an important industry for the area, and local people were proud of the station's importance. Over its history, the cable station received and relayed countless messages, including news of the *Titanic*'s sinking and the 1929 stock market crash. Technology developed throughout the 20th century eventually led to the end of the cable station. In 1927, the Commercial Cable Company was sold to International Telegraph and Telephone, which operated the station until 1962, when the last message was sent.

After the station closed, the building was left to deteriorate. The historic significance of the building was not forgotten, and over the next 40 years, people advocated for it to be saved. On February 14, 2006, the Commercial Cable Building Rehabilitation Society purchased it and began a study to determine restoration requirements. The news was disappointing: it would cost an estimated $1.5 million. The group, however, raised most of the money for the restoration, but a tenant could not be found, which would have made the business endeavour viable. The building was once again abandoned.

In spring 2017, the property was transferred to the municipal government, which did its own engineering assessment: the building had become a hazard and should be torn down. After 10 years of active fighting and more than 40 years of community advocacy to save the building, the upper floors of the brick building were demolished on September 5, 2017.

The building demolition was a significant loss to the region's built heritage. The granite-block foundation is the last reminder of the cable station. Although a fence surrounds the property, it can still be clearly viewed from the surrounding road.

◎ COMMERCIAL CABLE STATION: **N 45.327318, W 61.028863**
The Commercial Cable Station is located near the intersection of Main Street (Highway 16) and Tickle Road in the community of Hazel Hill, approximately 3 kilometres south of Canso.

5. RCAF No. 5 Radar Site: Cole Harbour

Cole Harbour

Situated on a small barren hill above the community of Cole Harbour are the remnants of a World War II-era radar station. The story of the site begins in the early war years when fear that the war would come to the shores of North America was stoked by U-boat attacks in Canadian waters. In response, the Canadian government planned a series of radar and early warning detection sites along the east coast, one of which was a hill near Cole Harbour.

The Canadian government and the Royal Canadian Air Force contracted Storm Construction to build the radar site in May 1942. Over the summer, prefabricated barracks, mess halls, and administration and operations buildings, along with power, water, and sewage systems, were constructed. In August, a team of radar specialists and operators installed the secretive radar.

Given the name No. 5 Radar Unit, Queensport/Cole Harbour, the site's main objective was to monitor aircraft approaching Canadian

airspace and to detect surfaced U-boats if possible. The first personnel arrived in September and the site was commissioned shortly thereafter.

The radar site was equipped with two systems; an Identification Friend or Foe (IFF) tower and a Height-Finding Antenna. Alongside these systems an operations building was also constructed, and the accommodations and barracks were erected approximately 150 metres east.

The site's radar primarily detected and identified incoming aircraft as "friend" or "foe." This information was relayed to Eastern Air Command in Halifax, where an incoming aircraft's position was recorded, plotted, and ready for waiting fighter aircraft to intercept if needed. The radar was believed to be capable of detecting ships and surfaced U-boats; its hourly weather data was also sent to the Halifax command centre.

In May 1945, the end of the war in Europe brought the end of many radar stations along the east coast, including the Cole Harbour No. 5 Radar Site. Operations were phased out completely by June and, over the summer, the site was torn down as quickly as it had been erected.

A gazebo, plaque, and information sign mark the start of the relatively easy hike to the former radar site. No buildings remain at the site, but among the overgrown trees and bushes are the foundations of the administration building and motor pool. Closer to the site of the radar equipment are the foundations that once supported the site's advanced radar systems. A windsock on the hill marks the radar location, and a flagpole and gazebo denote the main base and accommodations. Spectacular views await atop the hill, but relentless wind and ominous offshore fog help visitors understand the hardships that would have been endured by those stationed there.

⊕ RCAF NO. 5 RADAR SITE: **N 45.275903, W 61.269330**
Travelling south along Marine Drive (Highway 316), drive 1.1 kilometres past the intersection of Cole Harbour Village Road and park at the trailhead (N 45.267850, W 61.272671). A 1.1-kilometre hike brings you to the site.

6. Dolliver Mine Company's Powerhouse

Isaacs Harbour

Gold discovered north of Isaacs Harbour in 1896 launched a small mining operation that remained operational until around 1900. In 1910, the Dolliver Mountain Mining and Milling Company was established and soon excavated shafts approximately 400 metres east of the mouth of Isaacs Harbour River. Seemingly overnight, a major mining operation was under way.

Because the mine required large amounts of electricity, the company constructed a hydroelectric facility on the riverbanks. At the top of nearby Isaacs Harbour River Falls, two dams redirected water through a sluice gate and into a channel. It then flowed 1,200 metres along the hillside before entering a conduit and dropping into a powerhouse.

The powerhouse, a wooden structure built at the mouth of the river on stone foundations, more closely resembled a house than a traditional powerplant. Inside the building, the water, which entered from the rear through a small conduit, rotated a 16-inch-diameter turbine before being discharged back into the river. The turbine spun a steel shaft

connected to a generator, capable of producing 250 horsepower, which was then transmitted up the hill to the mine site.

The electricity powered the mine's hoisting systems, and stamp and crushing mills, and provided lighting. This mine was one of the earliest gold mines in the province to use a hydroelectric system to power its machinery.

The operation expanded for several year, but in 1904 it slowed down, and ceased operations in 1905. Although the mine operated only for a short period, at its peak it employed over 90 people and was an important industry for nearby communities.

At the base of the falls, a maze of stone foundations belonging to the former Dolliver Mine Company's powerhouse is still visible. The outer foundations and former water channels, anchor bolts, and rusting equipment are dispersed throughout the surrounding forest. As most of the Dolliver Mountain Mine has been lost to time, the powerhouse's intricate foundations and water channels are the only reminders of this short-lived industry.

POWERHOUSE: N 45.205400, W 61.674121

Follow Marine Drive (Highway 316), and turn onto a small gravel road on the east side of Isaacs Harbour River. Several hiking trails lead to the river and the former powerhouse.

7. Goldenville Gold District

Guysborough County

What remains of the Goldenville Gold District is a small portion of what was once Nova Scotia's most productive gold mine. After gold was discovered in 1862, the area was overwhelmed with prospectors and gold-fevered miners hoping to strike big. The discovery led to the establishment of multiple mines and, to support the miners and their families, the town of Goldenville was born. Unlike the mines, which randomly dotted the landscape, the bustling gold-rush town was almost entirely confined to a single road. At its peak, the town had a population of 3,000—but it is difficult to imagine such a bustling community. The area is littered with mining remnants: tailings piles, large foundations, and even several buildings.

In 1860, gold discovered at Mooseland, southeast of Sheet Harbour, officially marked the beginning of Nova Scotia's first gold rush. As gold fever spread throughout the province, more gold deposits were found. In August 1861, farmer Nelson Nickerson was working in his field near the community of Sherbrooke when he picked up a piece of quartz, took it home, and cut it open. Nickerson, who had completed a prospecting course, immediately identified the flakes of gold inside the rock. Over the next two months, he kept his discovery a secret, slowly collecting rocks and extracting the gold. He had already made a healthy profit when people in the community began noticing. Soon the word was out, and prospectors, geologists, and mining corporations flocked to the area.

Declaring Goldenville a gold district allowed the Nova Scotia government to bring in a survey team to lay out claims and give the government more control over future mining and land ownership.

By 1862, test pits, trenches, and some underground mining had begun and companies imported equipment and supplies that would allow them to mine and process their findings. In March 1862, 69

people submitted applications for mineral leases; this grew to 480 by the end of the year, and a new road and wharf were built to keep up with shipping and importing demands.

Mining continued throughout the 1860s, with 1868 marking the region's most profitable year, with 9,778 ounces of gold produced. By 1869, 19 companies were working in the area and, while many were short-lived endeavours, when one site was abandoned, another company would purchase the mining rights hoping to find something the previous company had missed. The ore was extracted primarily from mine shafts before being sent to a mechanical crusher (or stamp mill), and then separated from the rock by mercury amalgamation.

As more workers immigrated to the area, more houses and accommodations were needed, and the small town of Goldenville was formed. The densely packed town was constructed almost entirely on a single road at the centre of the mining operations. Soon it boasted a

population of 3,000 and a school, a church, houses, hotels, and a post office. In 1900, a Presbyterian church was constructed nearby, which now houses a museum run by the Heritage Goldenville Society.

By 1871, the first Goldenville gold rush ended, with five companies still operating. In 1873, a second gold rush began, but this time company stakes in mineral claims in the area meant that the properties would now be worked by tributers: prospectors and miners paid for the ore that they extracted. This rush did not last and soon poor mining conditions and diminishing investor funding sent the mine into another low production period.

The mine prospered again between 1894 and 1906 with the introduction of new mining and processing methods. The number of companies involved decreased throughout this period and, instead of widespread, sporadic mining as had occurred in the early days of the mine, mining focused on specific deposits. As mining ramped down and gold prices dropped, the population of Goldenville also declined.

The last major mining in the area occurred between 1935 and 1941. The Great Depression precipitated a sudden spike in gold prices, which drew the attention of Guysborough Mines Limited. Although this period was prosperous for the company, labour shortages and difficulty accessing supplies due to the onset of World War II ended the last era of mining at Goldenville.

Exploration work has continued in the area but no further mining has occurred to date. After the war, the provincial government's remediation work ensured that these mine shafts and open pits were filled in and signs warning of dangerous chemicals suspended in the soils, tailings, and waste piles were installed.

The Goldenville Gold District was once the province's largest producers of gold. Between 1862 and 1942, more than 210,000 ounces were mined from over 270 shafts. The area is largely deserted but its legacy and accompanying town will not soon be forgotten.

ABOUT THE AREA

Goldenville Gold District contains many reminders of its rich past. Piles of waste rock, large, cleared lots, and foundations of some of Goldenville's larger building are still visible. Near the centre of operations, visitors can explore the foundations of a former stamp mill and, along the main road into the area, several buildings that once belonged to the community can be seen, including the Goldenville Presbyterian Church operated by the Heritage Goldenville Society as a museum.

Several potentially dangerous tailings piles exist in the area, the largest at the centre of the district along Gegogan Brook. The tailings are now considered to be hardpan, an area of fine-grain, cemented soil that contains potentially dangerous chemicals such as arsenic and sulfide concentrates. Signs line the tailings piles and warn of potential dangers. High chemical concentrations and acidity are detected in surrounding wetlands and downstream in Gegogan Brook. For several

years, the town of Goldenville hosted a Labour Day off-road vehicle rally on the tailings, but the event was shut down in 2006 when the risk of disturbing the dangerous chemicals in the soil was recognized.

⊕ GOLDENVILLE GOLD DISTRICT: N 45.123245, W 62.016377

Travel south on Highway 7 from the community of Sherbrooke for approximately 3 kilometres. Turn right onto Goldenville Road and drive 400 metres to the Heritage Goldenville Society Museum on the right. The town and former mine locations are found throughout the area.

8. Shipwreck of the *Fury*
Cape Gegogan

Pillars of rusted steel rising from the sea off Cape Gegogan are the remains of the freighter *Fury* which ran aground on the rocky shoals 60 years ago and for many years was one of Nova Scotia's largest shipwrecks. The ship has deteriorated over the decades but pieces of rusted metal are still visible on a reef only accessible during low tides.

The steel freighter began its life during World War II when it was officially launched in Hamburg, Germany. Built by Deutsche Werft in 1944, it was placed in the service of the German Merchant Marines. The *Fury* was 92 metres long with a breadth of 13.5 metres and a depth of 5.8 metres.

After the war, the *Fury* was turned over to Canada, where it was owned by the Terra Nova Steamship Company. The ship, registered out of Montreal, transported cargo between Quebec, Halifax, and St. John's.

On November 28, 1964, the *Fury*, commanded by Captain George Pateras and his 17 crew, set sail from Quebec City en route to St. John's with a stop in Halifax. As it neared the community of Canso, a winter storm blew in. The *Fury* continued sailing south but, as it rounded Cape Gegogan, it experienced steering problems. Unable to withstand the waves, it ran aground at Steering Reef.

As the storm subsided and the tide lowered, the captain and his crew walked safely to shore on the narrow bar of land extending to the reef.

A salvage firm was brought in from Halifax to remove equipment and fittings from the ship. The rest of the ship was set on fire to prevent fuel and oil from leaking into the water.

 THE FURY: N 45.020619, W 61.888433

Access the shipwreck via Gegogan Road, approximately 7 kilometres south of Sherbrooke. However, the last section of the road is private property. Alternatively, a 5-kilometre paddle or boat ride is required from nearby Little Liscomb or Sonora; knowledge of the area and ocean is essential.

9. Derelict Ships of Marie Joseph

Marie Joseph, Guysborough County

Often concealed in a blanket of fog, the small fishing village of Marie Joseph on Nova Scotia's eastern shore resembles, at first glance, many other villages in the area. Because of this, many people passing through on Highway 7 opt to bypass via the appropriately named Short Cut Road. But by continuing the path less travelled, visitors see several decommissioned and abandoned ships along the shoreline, ranging from dories and small fishing vessels to a derelict Coast Guard vessel and a former US Army tugboat. While the site will likely eventually be cleaned up, in the meantime it is a ship graveyard worth a visit.

The graveyard is located near the local wharf and Harbour Authority that dozens of fishing ships call home. Over the years, as wooden vessels deteriorated beyond repair, they were placed along the roadside and subsequently forgotten. As well, a small locally owned shipyard on site has historically repaired, refurbished, and scrapped ships; it has also collected several ships, the most impressive being the tugboat *Craig Trans* and the Canadian Coast Guard's *Tupper*. These controversial abandoned ships are described by local residents as eyesores and by the government as an environmental risk.

CCGS *TUPPER*/MV *CARUSO*

The largest of the ships, and likely to be the first to be disposed of, is the Canadian Coast Guard buoy tender *Tupper*. Built in 1959 by Marine Industries in Sorel, Quebec, the 62.4-metre-long, 12.8-metre-wide vessel was designed to manage, repair, and replace navigation aids in the Gulf of St. Lawrence. To navigate the ice floes and dangerous seas, it had an ice-strengthened hull and was powered by a 2,900-horsepower diesel-electric engine driving two stern propellers. The *Tupper* was equipped with a helicopter pad with a telescoping hanger that is still visible at the ship's stern.

The *Tupper* operated in the Gulf of St. Lawrence and Great Lakes region for 38 years before it was retired from service in 1997. It was then brought to the Coast Guard Base in Dartmouth and used temporarily as a training vessel. In 1998, it was sold to a private buyer, who registered it under a Panamanian flag and renamed it MV *Caruso*. The new owner aspired to transform the aging ship into an expedition vessel for tourism and research; however, little came of this endeavour. The ship's fate was sealed when a suspicious fire broke out aboard it on October 11, 2008. The ship continued floating, and in June 2011 it was purchased by the Marie Joseph shipyard, who hoped to scrap the vessel. The owners began the scrapping process but local governments halted the operation due to public safety and environmental concerns.

As of 2023, the ship remains in place, raising concern about its effect on local tourism and the environment. An assessment by the

Environmental Response Branch of the Coast Guard in January 2021 determined that the ship needed to be removed as it is at significant risk of polluting local waters. In September 2022, funding was announced, followed by a call for tenders to dispose of the ship, which will likely occur throughout 2023 and 2024.

LT-648/CRAIG FOSS/CRAIG TRANS

While the *Tupper/Caruso* has become the most impressive and photographed ship in the small harbour, it is not alone. Along its port side is a large tugboat. Built for the US Army in 1944 by the Tampa Marine Corporation in Tampa, Florida, it was named *LT-648*. Measuring 35 metres long and 9 metres wide and having a depth of 5.3 metres, the tugboat was registered out of Seattle, Washington, where it primarily towed barges and equipment between harbours. Fitted with a 3,900-horsepower diesel-electric engine, a 5-ton winch, and a 1.5-ton deck crane, it was delivered in January 1945 and assigned to the US Army Transportation Corps, where it was used on an as-needed basis until it was listed for sale in the early 1960s.

In 1965, the tugboat was purchased by Seattle's Foss Maritime and rebuilt over the following year. Its engine was replaced with two 8-cylinder, 2,500-horsepower diesel engines and a 220-horsepower bow thruster increased its manoeuvrability. The tug, renamed *Craig Foss*, transported materials, goods, and equipment to and from Hawaii, Seattle, and Alaska.

The company operated the tug for 46 years until it was sold in 2011 to Vesta Shipping Lines headquartered in Scotch Plains, New Jersey. Renamed *Craig Trans* under a Bolivian flag, the aging tugboat towed vessels between Canada, the US, and the Caribbean. This career ended in December 2012 while en route to Beuharnois, Quebec, to pick up a ship that was to be scrapped in Mexico. While sailing past Nova Scotia, the ship experienced engine trouble, and to avoid an incoming storm, it took refuge in Halifax harbour. There, the 68-year-old vessel was detained by the City of Halifax due to concerns about its multiple safety defects. The owners abandoned the vessel and its non-Canadian crew. Community

support and donations eventually led to the crew's repatriation to their home countries. The ship was detained and registered under a Canadian flag in 2013. After spending most of its time in Wright's Cove, the ship was auctioned at a Sheriff's auction in 2016; it sold for $1,000 to the Marie Joseph shipyard, where it was towed in June 2017. The ship has remained beached along the shores of the community and, unlike its younger but more deteriorated neighbour, CCGS *Tupper*, *Craig Trans* appears upon first glance to be in relatively good shape.

ABOUT THE AREA

The two ships were still beached along the waterfront in 2022; however, as with many shipwrecks and abandoned ships in Nova Scotia, they

will not be around forever. Although each poses a significant risk to the surrounding environment, they represent some of Nova Scotia's last abandoned or forgotten ships. In addition to unique photograph opportunities, each ship has its own fascinating career history. Even after these vessels are gone, the many deteriorated wooden vessels along Route 7, in contrast with the vibrant fishing community, continues to tell the story of Nova Scotia's changing maritime history and its centuries-long dependence on the sea.

DERELICT SHIPS OF MARIE JOSEPH: N 44.965944, W 62.079713
The ships can be seen alongside Marine Drive (Trunk Highway 7) in the community of Marie Joseph.

10. Sheet Harbour Lumber & Pulp Mill Remains

Sheet Harbour

Sheet Harbour's geography has long made it an ideal harbour for the forestry industry. The deep-water port is well protected from storms and ocean swells and at the far reaches of the harbour are two large rivers that originate in the forested interior of the Eastern Shore. Since the first Europeans settled in the area, sawmills have taken advantage of the area's East and West rivers as a source of power. On the East River banks, a monument marks the location of Canada's first sulphide pulp mill, established in October 1885. While the short-lived endeavour closed in January 1891, the revolutionary mill was the beginning of major logging operations to be established in the community.

But most of the former operations at East River have been lost to time. This is not the case for the West River, where a series of concrete dams, foundations, and wharves tell the 130-year-old story of its lumber and pulp mills. The industrial heritage of Sheet Harbour is often overlooked by the establishment of a new industry sector farther out the harbour, but much remains of Sheet Harbour's history along the banks of West River.

HISTORY

The first major sawmill on West River was likely founded by John Hall in 1841. Established at the base of the turbulent waters near where it meets the ocean, Hall gave the operation to his son-in-law in 1851. The mill operated until 1878, when Havelock McCall Hart purchased the land and timber rights and constructed a new mill there in 1880. Hart's sawmill was a relatively small operation compared to its 20th-century counterpart.

In 1902, Amherst-based entrepreneurs and future politicians Nelson Rhodes and Nathaniel Curry considered the hydropower potential of Sheet Harbour's West River rapids. Recognizing the river's potential,

the men purchased the sawmill and its 60,000-acre timber rights from Hart. Rhodes and Curry expanded the sawmill at the mouth of the river and built several large company stores near the water and named it the Rhodes and Curry Sawmill.

The men also constructed a series of flumes, dams, and reservoirs to improve the mill's efficiency. Above the mill, a large concrete dam formed a reservoir, commonly referred to as Mill Pond. The dam, which raised the water by 5 to 6 metres, increased the amount of power harnessed from the river. From the dam, a wooden flume funnelled water to the mill's water wheel, powering its machinery. A second water chute allowed logs to flow from above the river's rapids to the dam's reservoir where they would be collected and brought into the mill. At the time, logs were cut from the forest upriver before being floated downstream to the mill.

In 1922, the Albany, New York-based American Pulp and Wrapping Paper Co. purchased the Rhodes and Curry Sawmill, wharf, and timber rights. The following year, it began construction on a ground-wood pulp mill where the sawmill and company stores once stood.

Upstream of the mill, a series of trestles supported a log flume that delivered cut logs over the roof of the mill and dumped them into storage bins where they remained until they were needed.

At the mouth of the river, the company also built a wharf and shipping facility to allow larger ships to dock and be loaded with pulp for shipment to New York state. While logging was to still occur upstream, the company established booms as a landing site for logs to be imported to the mill. The first production of pulp at the mill occurred later in 1925 and was shipped to market in Albany, New York.

Although the mill operated for 50 years, it transferred ownership often. In 1933, its name was changed to the Halifax Power and Pulp Company and it was controlled by American businessman Roger Babson. The mill's productivity slowed due to the Great Depression but briefly increased before World War II slowed production. The mill changed hands again in 1944, 1946, 1963, and finally 1964, when it was sold to the Philadelphia-based Scott Paper Company.

Compared to its humble beginnings, the mill had become a huge operation, reportedly employing over 100 people at the mill and up

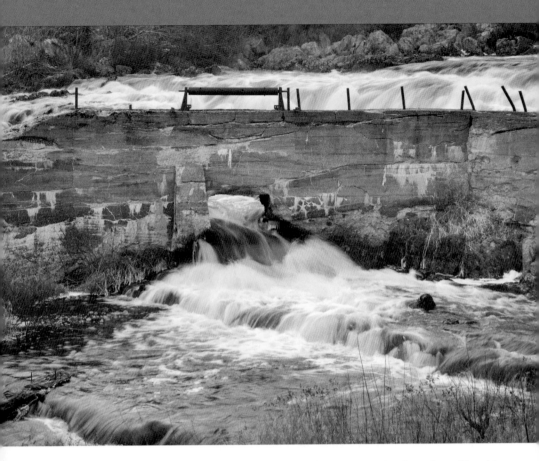

to twice that as seasonal loggers. These unionized and well-paid workers helped the local community prosper. The mill could produce 90 tonnes of groundwood pulp per day, giving it an annual production of approximately 27,000 tonnes. Nearly 27,000 cords of wood were needed each year, with half of that coming from the company's 115,000 acres of forestry land and the rest imported by ship or truck.

From Sheet Harbour's international port, pulp was shipped to markets across the US and Europe.

The long and impactful history of saw-, lumber, and pulp mills built along the banks of the West River ended in August 1971 when Hurricane Beth caused the river's water levels to reach devastating heights. The flooded mill, its wharves, and surrounding support structures were extensively damaged. The market had also taken a plunge and, as a result, the company shut the mill forever.

ABOUT THE AREA

The story of logging on the West River stretches back more than 130 years. During that time, the riverbanks have been home to many large-scale logging operations, each with its own contribution to the success and establishment of Sheet Harbour. When the last mill closed, it was a devastating blow to the town but it was not the last industry to help the local economy.

When looking at the river's turbulent waters today, it is hard to imagine the scale of operations that once existed here. But the concrete dam that once formed the reservoir to which logs were floated before being fed into the mills below catches the eye. Although it no longer retains water, from the dam it is possible to discern the line of vertical foundations that wind down the eastern riverbank, marking the route of the former log flume. Farther downstream, large rectangular foundations delineate the locations of former buildings and along the former wharf and log-landing area, buried cribbing and deteriorated wooden logging booms are visible from the now-forested peninsula.

Although a riverside walking trail safely guides visitors around the site of the former mill operations, much more could be done to recognize the site's significance. Yet the site remains a treasure trove of concrete foundations, dams, and artifacts slowly crumbling to the forces of the powerful West River.

⊕ **LUMBER AND PULP MILL REMAINS: N 44.927493, W 62.544706** In the community of Sheet Harbour, turn onto Elmhurst Drive at the west end of the town. From here, a parking area and several well-maintained trails lead along the river. Remnants of the former mill are found along the river.

Halifax Region

The area surrounding Halifax is one of the most heavily urbanized regions in Atlantic Canada and the social and cultural hub of Nova Scotia. Many large communities, including Cole Harbour, Dartmouth, Bedford, Lower Sackville, and Halifax, are incorporated into this area. Each community has developed around the strategically important Halifax harbour and Bedford Basin. With a landscape that dates to the last ice age, remnants of past glacial features have created many of the strategic military locations that contributed to the harbour's importance: Citadel Hill, Georges Island, its outer islands, and the steep coastline of harbour's western shore.

Halifax harbour was long an important outpost for the Mi'kmaq, who regularly hunted, fished, and travelled the area. After being temporarily occupied by French settlers, the area was controlled by the English, who established Halifax in 1749. As with much of Nova Scotia's history, the story of the Halifax region is defined by the movement of people, both colonizing and immigrating into North America and later through the movement of troops to wars in Europe.

In the 19th and 20th centuries, the area drastically expanded in size and population, with new industries such as pulp mills, shipping and container ports, and oil and gas facilities. Over time, the many small communities that lined the harbour grew and developed unused land or redeveloped other sites for new purposes. Although many important historic sites have been lost, the area's people maintained

their social identities through their culture, heritage, and architecture.

Most of the area is now urbanized, with peninsular Halifax and Dartmouth at its centre. At the mouth of the harbour are several uninhabited islands, and communities such as Eastern Passage and Cole Harbour are on the low-lying land in the east. On the west side, many small coves along the steep shoreline are sparsely populated. The harbour narrows inland between Halifax and Dartmouth. Through the "Narrows," the harbour opens into Bedford Basin. Along its shores is an assortment of residential, commercial, and industrial sites. The community of Bedford is in the north, the first of several strings of communities that loosely follow the highway systems that spread out from the city to Windsor, Truro, and the Southern Shore. Outside the cities are the forests, lakes, and barrens popular with hikers, mountain bikers, and other outdoor enthusiasts.

1. Bayers Lake Mystery Walls
Bayers Lake

Some say that the five-sided stone structure near the Bayers Lake shopping district belonged to pirates or ancient civilizations or that they were created by extraterrestrials, but the truth is likely less dramatic. The Bayers Lake "Mystery Walls" have inspired stories and curiosity for generations, and although historians and archeologists do not know their provenance, they are likely the remnants of a small livestock farm.

Rediscovered in 1990, the five-sided structure is accompanied by a 110-metre-long stone wall, signs of a primitive staircase, and several quarries. Much of what is known about the walls originated from a 2017 archaeological study by Dr. Jonathan Fowler of Saint Mary's University. Funded by the city and the university, Fowler's study concluded that, while there is still no direct evidence of the building's use, it likely raised livestock, because of its resemblance to similar structures throughout England and Scotland.

The site is now protected under Nova Scotia's Special Places Act, which prohibits disturbance to the site or artifact removal. While we may never know exactly what the Bayers Lake Mystery Walls, or BdCv-9 as the site is called in Dr. Fowler's report, are, it is safe to assume that aliens, pirates, or ancient civilizations had little to do with it.

BAYERS LAKE MYSTERY WALLS: **N 44.642981, W 63.660077**
The trailhead (N 44.642158, W 63.660842) is located along Chain Lake Drive. Hike 250 metres; the foundations are in the forest on the right.

2. SS *Daisy* & the Former J.P. Porter Scrapyard

Dartmouth

Halifax harbour holds countless stories of its maritime history that wait to be retold and rediscovered. Perhaps one of the most interesting mysteries is the rediscovery of the SS *Daisy* in the late 2010s. After a diverse career, the 38-metre vessel was towed to Halifax, where it remained inactive for several years before being buried and incorporated into the company's wharf. The rusting hull protruding from the shoreline is still recognizable as a former ship. The last owner, J.P. Porter Company, was responsible for many scuttled ships in the harbour, some of which are still visible. But before it was shut down due to litigation from charges of fraud, the company's marine base in Halifax harbour was a familiar sight to its residents. While the plot of empty land is easily ignored by passersby, the company's history and the ships it operated throughout North America is worth retelling.

SS *DAISY*

SS *Daisy* was built in 1911 by the John Duthie Torry Shipbuilding Company in Aberdeen, Scotland. Launched on February 14, 1911, it measured 38.1 metres long and 7 metres wide and had a depth of 3.7 metres. Constructed of cast iron and steel and powered by a 500-horsepower engine that drove a single propeller, the ship travelled at a speed of 10 knots per hour. Built as a fishing trawler, it was taken over by the British Royal Navy and converted for naval use, receiving the prefix HMS. Fishing trawlers such as the HMS *Daisy* were designed to withstand rough seas and had large working decks, making them ideal candidates for conversion into the naval ships known as Admiralty Trawlers.

At the outbreak of World War I, *Daisy* was assigned to Nore Command in Dover, England, where it operated first as a survey vessel

but was later converted into a minesweeper and then a patrol vessel. In its final war years, it cleared mines and surveyed routes for British attacks in Belgium, including the 1918 raids on Zeebrugge and Ostend.

Following the war, the ship was placed in reserve. Purchased by the Newfoundland government in March 1920, its prefix was changed to SS. Officially owned by the Ministry of Finance and Customs, SS *Daisy* became a revenue cutter stationed in the town of Burin on the island's south coast and tasked with stopping alcohol smugglers from purchasing liquor on the nearby French islands, St. Pierre and Miquelon, and selling it illegally throughout the Atlantic region.

It was for this reason that the SS *Daisy* was docked in Burin on November 18, 1929. That evening a powerful 7.2 earthquake off the Grand Banks

produced a tsunami that devastated communities along Newfoundland's entire south coast. Water levels rose between 13 and 27 metres, killing 28 people and dragging countless houses, sheds, and people out to sea. The *Daisy* survived the wave and provided rescue operations.

Throughout the end of the 1920s and beginning early 1930s, prohibition in Newfoundland and the Maritime provinces ended, eliminating *Daisy*'s use as a revenue cutter. Still in good condition, it was reassigned to transport lawyers, judges, sheriffs, and clerks to and from the many isolated communities along the south coast. It remained in the service of the Newfoundland government until 1945, when it was brought to Halifax harbour and purchased by the J.P. Porter Company, a dredging and general contractor who used the ship as a tugboat.

The ship's working life ended in 1949 when Newfoundland and Labrador joined confederation. At that time, the *Daisy* was registered to the Dominion of Newfoundland, and since the registration was never renewed to reflect its Canadian registry, the company let it sit idle. The *Daisy* remained in place for the next several years, moored to the company's headquarters near the base of the Angus L. MacDonald Bridge. In the early 1950s, instead of scrapping the vessel the company sank it and used it as an extension to its current docking facilities. The rusting hull was filled with rocks, gravel, and debris, and wooden pile stabilizers entombed it in the pier. This was not an unusual practice at the time, as many ships were scuttled for fill.

If ships could talk, the *Daisy* would have endless intriguing stories. After serving as a survey vessel and minesweeper in World War I, thwarting rumrunners off the coast of Newfoundland, and saving lives after the 1929 tsunami, the ship seemingly received a proper burial for its long service history. In Newfoundland, the ship's name has been memorialized in the SS *Daisy* Legal History Committee, a committee of the Law Society of Newfoundland and Labrador.

The *Daisy* protrudes from the former J.P. Porter Company pier in the heart of Halifax harbour. It has deteriorated almost to the point of being unrecognizable; but for those who visit the site, the historic ship inspires wonder and mystery.

J.P. PORTER MARINE BASE

The SS *Daisy*'s last owner was the J.P. Porter Company, a general contracting and dredging company founded by Nova Scotia native J.P. Porter in 1921, which had property and equipment across North America. Shortly after, Porter's sons joined the company, changing the name to J.P. Porter and Sons Ltd. Although the company was headquartered in Montreal, it maintained a prominent marine base in Halifax near the Dartmouth side of the MacDonald Bridge. The company invested little in new ships and equipment, instead purchasing aging ships such as the *Daisy* which was used for a few years before being scrapped or abandoned. (See Ives Cove Shipwreck). Although the company later sold the marine base, the site became a salvage and scrapyard until 1990, when the base was abandoned.

Originally, the facilities consisted of several wharves built on wooden piers. Around the time the *Daisy* was scuttled, the wooden piers were filled in, creating an L-shaped wharf of rock and gravel. Over time, the wharf's middle sections were filled in, creating a rectangular piece of land. The number of ships, barges, and other pieces of equipment used to fill in the former J.P. Porter Marine Base is unknown, but investigating the shores of the former base reveals thousands of pieces of steel, iron, and concrete that once belonged to the prominent waterfront site.

 SS *DAISY*: N 44.666321, W 63.584711

The site is best experienced by boat. From the nearest public boat launch at Alderney Landing in Dartmouth (N 44.665313, W 63.571648), a 1-kilometre-long paddle is required to reach the site. The ship and site can also be viewed from the bike lane of the Angus L. Macdonald Bridge.

3. Fenerty Lake Fish Salvage Plant

Middle Sackville/Beaver Bank

Located along the quiet shores of Fenerty Lake are several abandoned concrete buildings and rusting steel equipment. Debate about who owned the buildings and for how long is ongoing. Once a fish rendering plant that processed fish waste into fertilizer for farms in the Annapolis Valley, it was known by several names. However, it seems likely that its official title was the Scotia Fat Salvage Plant, conveniently constructed at Fenerty Siding along the former Windsor Branch of the Nova Scotia Railway. Fish-plant waste arrived by truck or train and, once processed, was shipped to market via train.

This history is largely unknown and undocumented. The main concrete building and its surrounding concrete platforms are slowly collapsing. Throughout the forest, countless barrels and pieces of rusting machinery are visible. The abandoned railway line nearby contains many relics from its construction in 1858. The area, only visited by recreation vehicles, fishers, and hikers, offers quiet and solitude.

◇ FISH SALVAGE PLANT: **N 44.821267, W 63.708034**

Several trails wind throughout the area, but the quickest route is hiking down a 300-metre trail from nearby Pepperbush Court (trailhead at N 44.819479, W 63.708952). When visiting the area, watch for private property signs: avoid trespassing.

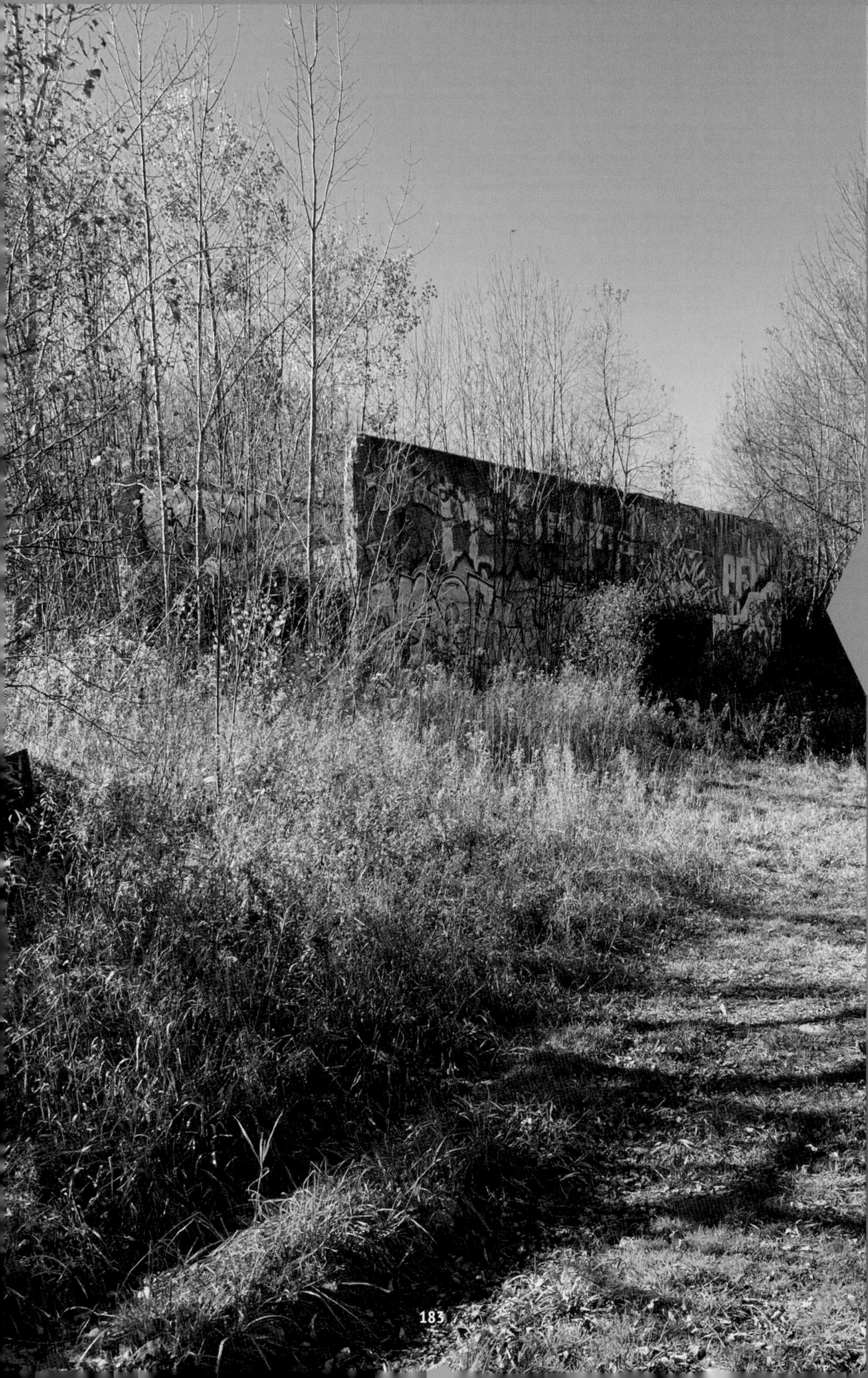

4. The Story of Paper Mill Lake
Bedford

After Halifax was established in 1749, vast resources of timber were required to build forts, stores, houses, wharves, and the infrastructure needed to grow a city. This caused a massive increase in logging, and sawmills were constructed on seemingly every river and brook. One of the earliest was built in 1805 by Christian Schmidt on Nine Mile River in what would become the community of Bedford. The river powered the sawmill's equipment.

Anthony H. Holland, owner of the *Acadian Recorder* newspaper, purchased a large piece of land on the river and built the Acadian Paper Mill in 1819. The mill, which received its power from a dam built on the river, produced paper from clothes and rags; it would be another 25 years until the process of making paper from wood pulp was invented. The mill is immediately east of what is now a swimming location on Lake Drive. The mill was a stone building accompanied by several smaller wooden structures housing a drying area and equipment and material storage. Several dams provided power to the mill, which stretched across the river.

The mill changed ownership several times and once produced rope and twine. Historians are unsure of the precise date, but in the 1850s the Acadian Paper Mill was torn down and a replacement mill constructed farther downstream. The new mill, first owned by Alexander Kissock, was operated by several others before burning down on August 20, 1875.

The next chapter in Paper Mill Lake—in which the lake became a reservoir—came as the result of a small bakery. In 1816, Moirs Limited operated a bakery in nearby Mill Cove. But by the 1870s, bakery owner William Moir enacted his plans to expand the cove's industry beyond his bakery. When land upstream of Mill Cove became available in 1867, Moirs Limited purchased it to construct a dam larger than any previous dam to supply water to the cove.

Moirs Limited hired German engineer Emil Vossnack to construct several dams across the area. When combined, the rock and gravel dams stretched over 500 metres across the pond, redirecting water into a wooden flume that delivered water to the growing industrial complex in Mill Cove. By the 1900s, this complex included factories to create spools and wooden boxes as well as a refining plant and several stores and cottages. A new stone and wooden dam was constructed around 1900 and the wooden flume upgraded to a large iron pipe. Controlled almost entirely by the Moirs family, the river became known as Moirs Mill Brook.

During the first part of the 20th century, a chocolate factory was established as part of the Moirs bakery, emphasizing the need for a reliable source of electricity. In 1930, the Moirs commissioned a dam and hydroelectric facility on the river. This dam was constructed farther downstream where the river narrowed, close to the location of the modern-day dam. The former iron pipe was repurposed to deliver water downstream, where a turbine was installed in a small, one-storey concrete powerhouse and accompanied by a large surge tank to control water flow.

With a new, reliable source of power, the Mill Cove industries operated until the early 1960s, when activity dwindled as other industrial centres opened throughout the region. Around this time, the powerhouse was shut down and decommissioned. Eventually, the Mill Cove industrial complex was replaced by new development; the area is home to several commercial and residential buildings. The dam and powerhouse were the last two obvious reminders of the cove's operations until the early 2010s, when it was decided to replace the aging dam.

ABOUT THE AREA

In 2012, when the lake was drained to replace the Moirs dam, a collection of artifacts, including the foundations of several homes and the Acadian Paper Mill, was exposed. Rock, wood, and concrete structures from the many dams on the former river were also found. Since the construction of the new dam, high water levels have submerged the artifacts until the next lake draining.

But on the shores of the lakes and on its several islands, rock foundations and pieces of concrete and wood are reminders of the lake's fascinating history.

Downstream, more accessible reminders, such as the concrete supports of the former iron pipe (later replaced by a wooden penstock), are in the river. Tracing this downstream brings you to the last intact structure of the Moirs Ltd. industrial complex. The powerhouse stands along the side of the Bedford Highway, now converted into a small tourism office and recognized as a significant historic site. However, with the words *Moirs Limited* engraved in its concrete façade and a curious iron pipe protruding from its side, the history of the powerhouse and the impact of Moirs family on the area will not soon be forgotten.

MOIRS POWERHOUSE: **N 44.714075, W 63.678231**
PAPERMILL LAKE BEACH PARK: **N 44.717781, W 63.685740**

Park near the former powerhouse and walk along the riverside trail for 350 metres. On reaching the road, walk 110 metres and reconnect with the trail system on the right. From here, a short walk leads to the lake and dam.

5. Shubenacadie Canal

Dartmouth to Shubenacadie

Credit for an inland route to connect the Minas Basin with Halifax harbour cannot be awarded to a European settler, but to the Mi'kmaq, who have used the lakes, ponds, and rivers to traverse the Nova Scotia interior for over 4,000 years. After Europeans claimed control over the land, the inland water route was likely lost but, by the late 18th century, the settlers of Halifax harbour dreamed of a new means of transporting people and goods from the harbour to the Bay of Fundy. At that time, the only way to achieve this was to sail around the south coast of Nova Scotia, enduring the rough seas of the North Atlantic. By the end of the century, however, engineers and merchants explored new options to transport goods across the interior.

The first surveys were completed as early as 1796 but little was done until 1824, when a feasibility study commissioned by local governments investigated the possibility of constructing a canal between Halifax harbour and the Bay of Fundy. Engineer Francis Hall, who led the study, concluded that the 114-kilometre route was possible with a 19-lock canal system.

On June 1, 1826, the Shubenaccadie Canal Company was incorporated, with Halifax politician Michael Wallace as president. The company's secretary was long-time project supporter and advocate Charles R. Fairbanks. With government financing shares being sold to local investors, a ceremony was hosted on July 25, 1826, to mark the start of construction.

Hundreds of people were hired to excavate channels, dredge rivers, and construct locks and dams. The project was soon over budget, and many workers were not paid in 1828. While new investors were found, changes to the canal's route and issues with locks that had already been built halted construction in 1831.

In 1847, several years after Fairbanks died, his son Charles W.

Fairbanks reignited hope in the project. Construction restarted in 1854 under the newly established Inland Navigation Company. To cut costs, the company changed the canal's route and decreased the number of locks required by constructing two marine railways to carry ships uphill at Dartmouth and Portobello via a system of pulleys and railway tracks.

The canal was opened in sections, as each was completed. Marine railways in Portobello and Dartmouth opened in 1857 and 1861 respectively. With the opening of the Dartmouth Marine Railway, the canal was complete. On November 23, 1861, the steamship *Avery* became the first ship to complete the crossing, which took two days.

The Shubenacadie Canal contained nine locks and two marine railways and resembled the small, tranquil canals found throughout England and Scotland. Each lock was constructed of cut granite stone and contained dams, weirs, and pipes to raise boats by approximately 3 metres. For many years, the canal shipped cargo, lumber, and equipment to farms, lumber mills, and mines in the interior. The company collected tolls to pay for the canal.

In 1862, the company experienced financial trouble and the system was purchased by the Lake and River Navigation Company. Three years

later, it was transferred to the younger brother of Charles W. Fairbanks, Lewis Piers Fairbanks. Fairbanks hoped that a new tolling system would make the canal profitable, but with new railway lines connecting Halifax and Truro and the loss of several customers along the canal route, it once again fell into financial ruin, shutting down completely in 1871.

ABOUT THE AREA

For years, parts of the canal—such as the marine railway at Dartmouth—were used periodically but gradually deteriorated. In 1986, the Shubenacadie Canal Commission was established to revitalize the canal. Since then, canal sections have been transformed into parks and recreation areas. Recognized as a National Historic Civil Engineering site, many artifacts remain visible along the 114-kilometre canal and can be explored, including its locks, dams, buildings, and bridges.

 DARTMOUTH INCLINED PLANE MARINE RAILWAY: N 44.669428, W 63.563414

 SHUBIE PARK: N 44.702367, W 63.554087

 PORTOBELLO MARINE RAILWAY: N 44.746642, W 63.564418

6. Devils Island

Hartlen Point, Halifax Harbour

At the eastern extremity of Halifax harbour is a low-lying, rocky outcrop covered in windswept grassy fields and bog. But what captures the eye is a small tower protruding high above the rest of the island. Devils Island is the site of an abandoned community, and the tower is the island's former lighthouse, the last standing structure of the 19th-century town. The island appears barren but closer investigation exposes artifacts, foundations, and equipment that tell the story of those who settled here.

The island was first recorded on French maps in 1711 as Isle Verte (Green Island). At some point in the next several decades, the name Devils Island was adopted, believed to be an anglicized version of Deval, Devol, or Deville. Records show that the island was partly forested with several stands of trees near its centre before people settled there.

In the first half of the 19th century, the island's fields were used to raise livestock such as sheep. In 1830, the first permanent settlers arrived. Andrew Henneberry and his family moved to the island from McNabs Island after securing a lease from the family of Jacob Horn. As with the many families that followed them, the Henneberrys raised livestock and fished. Even after Andrew's tragic drowning in 1840, his wife and children remained on the island. Around this time, the forest on Devils Island was burned down. It is not known if the fire was intentional or accidental, but it did clear land that allowed settlers to raise livestock.

The year after Andrew Henneberry's death, his daughter Margaret married Thomas Edwards, who moved to the island and built a house there. This began an era of growth, as more people took advantage of the island's proximity to fishing grounds. By 1850, there were three houses there and a small school was built.

Before 1852, the island had a small beacon and several unofficial markers to help ships navigate around it. In 1849, the *Southhampton* ran aground while attempting to sail into the harbour, an incident that

resulted in the loss of the ship and one crew member. A petition was sent to the government in 1851 by local sailors, mariners, and fishers requesting that a lighthouse be established on the island. Construction began in the summer of 1852.

The lighthouse, a wooden, octagon-shaped tower, supported an oil-powered, fixed red light at its top. At the base of the tower, a one-room wooden dwelling accommodated the lighthouse keeper. Although the tower was a victory for ships passing through the harbour, it did have two problems. The dim red light, chosen to distinguish it from that of other nearby lighthouses, did not provide adequate navigation aid to ships; attempts to brighten the light over the years were unsuccessful.

The small dwelling at its base was too small to permanently house a lighthouse keeper and his family. The first keeper, Edward Bowen, was forced to live in the lightkeeper's house alone, away from his family, until a larger dwelling was built in 1859.

The importance of a lighthouse at Devils Island was underscored by the many ships that ran aground on the island. On January 15, 1974, the lighthouse keeper and five other residents of the island rushed out into a winter storm to help the crew of the schooner *Union* which had run aground nearby. The government provided the island with a large lifeboat for future emergencies. The inadequate, dimly lit lighthouse continued to be criticized.

In the summer of 1877, the government funded a second lighthouse. A new wooden, octagonal tower was installed near the original light but stood much higher, at 11.4 metres. At its top, an iron lantern room housed 13 lamps and a 17-inch reflector which produced a fixed, white light. To complement the new light and to ensure that it would not be confused with nearby lights, the first lighthouse remained in operation but was moved farther east and upgraded to shine a fixed, bright white light. The two distinct lights aided ships in navigating the notorious Thrum Cap Shoal, located at the south end of McNabs Island. The new light was known as Devils Island South East Lighthouse.

The government established a lifeboat station on the island in 1883. Run by local residents, it was an attractive opportunity for the low-income community because the government wage was based on the number of sailors rescued.

In 1890, a new lighthouse keeper's house was built and, in 1892, a breakwater was constructed to protect the island from storms. The population increased; 18 structures were on the island by 1901, and a post office was established in 1913.

During World War II, the government relocated island residents out of fear of a German U-boat attack and to eliminate the potential danger posed by Halifax's numerous coastal defence batteries pointed at the outer harbour. The lifeboat station was decommissioned. Most of the island's residents did not return there after the war, and after the government announced that it would not replace the island's deteriorated breakwater, the community was declared abandoned.

In 1949, the old lighthouse was decommissioned, and a new flashing white light was installed in the newer tower. In 1967, the lighthouse was automated and de-staffed, making Charles McDonald the last keeper stationed on the island. At this time, many of the buildings associated with the lighthouse were removed and 11 years later the lantern room was also removed, leaving only the flashing white light to warn ships of the dangerous water surrounding the island.

In 2009, the tower light was removed because of concern about the structural integrity of the 132-year-old tower. In 2011, the tower was officially decommissioned and abandoned; a replacement light was installed on a square, skeletal tower on the island's southwestern side.

ABOUT THE AREA

Since it was erected in 1877, the lighthouse on Devils Island has helped countless ships pass safely through Halifax harbour. Although it is no longer operational, the white tower is a marker for vessels using the harbour. It is one of the last wooden octagonal lighthouses in the province and the last standing reminder of the community it helped to establish. Years of neglect have left the lighthouse in poor condition. Farther east, the circular foundation of the original 1852 lighthouse is visible: an ominous reminder of what awaits the standing lighthouse if it is not preserved.

The remains of the lighthouse keeper's residence, which blew down in 2012, and that of other structures are still in place. Throughout the grassy fields are many more artifacts: foundations, chimney remnants, and machinery and equipment. On the north side, a rocky beach provides one of the few landing sites on the island. Inland from the beach are a steam motor and winch system that likely belonged to the lifeboat station. Within the confines of this small island are stories from those who lived here, their hardships, and their daring and tragic rescues—stories now embodied in the island's many artifacts, many of which are yet undiscovered.

Despite its location near Halifax, Devils Island is a hidden gem largely because of its inaccessibility. There are only one or two places to safely access the island by boat, and an underwater sandbar connecting the island to the mainland creates unpredictable waves. As the remote island is home to migratory birds and a colony of seagulls, precautions must be taken to avoid disturbing them. Devils Island is perhaps best left unexplored.

 DEVILS ISLAND: N 44.582720, W 63.458704

As no private charters travel to the island, transportation must be arranged. The closest access point to launch a boat is from a trailhead (N44.594265, W63.454803) along Shore Road near the Hartlen Point Forces Golf Club. A short hike to the nearby beach provides one of the few launch points. From here, a dangerous 1-kilometre paddle is required to the north side of the island. Here, a narrow beach provides the easiest access to the rock-lined island.

7. Devils Point Battery

Hartlen Point, Eastern Passage

Construction began on the Devils Point Battery in late 1940 on a small hill near the coast. By April 1941, much of the excavation and construction was nearing completion. The gun emplacement, constructed below the rolling hill, was hidden from passing ships. Behind the battery under cover of the hill, living quarters and barracks were built, along with an observation tower to guide the gun crews. To thwart an attack on the battery, a small complex of buildings was designed to resemble a farm and the observation tower a church similar to those in Sydney. Additionally, a dummy battery equipped with fake buildings and "guns" made of telephone poles was installed on a cliff farther east to misdirect any attack on the battery.

By 1942, the fully operational battery had three 9.2-inch Mark 10 guns watching over the harbour's outer reaches. The battery remained operational throughout the rest of the war. It was one of the largest single defence systems constructed in Halifax during World War II but shut down in the 1950s; its guns and equipment were shipped to Europe as part of Canada's NATO agreements.

Its heavily fortified construction means that most of the battery (at least its concrete components) is still visible at Hartlen Point. The site, however, has been incorporated into the Hartlen Point Forces Golf Club. While incorporating the battery into the golf course limits exploration, doing so also preserves this intriguing harbour defence. For non-golfers, the entrance to the battery's tunnel system can be seen along Shore Drive; it is a sight that captures the attention of all who pass by.

⊕ **DEVILS POINT BATTERY: N 44.596361, W 63.457101**

The entrance to the tunnel system is seen at the intersection of Shore Drive and Caddys Road. The remaining structures can be viewed only with access to the adjacent golf course.

8. Fort Chebucto

Duncans Cove

Guarding the western edge of the outer Halifax harbour, Fort Chebucto was the harbour's first line of ground defence during World War II. Three 6-inch guns were installed on the bluff with a series of support buildings and observation bunkers in front of and behind the three-gun emplacement. The bunkers can still be observed from afar, although they have been architecturally incorporated into the modern houses that now sit on top of them.

As part of the recommendations in Major B.D.C. Treatt's 1936 report on the defensive condition of Canadian ports and harbours, two coastal gun batteries were required in the outer harbour to respond to an attack on Halifax. One was to be built at Hartlen Point; another at Chebucto Head. As at Hartlen Point, where Devils Point Battery was constructed, Fort Chebucto would become the first line of defence and response if attacked by German warships.

Construction of the concrete gun battery began in the winter of 1940; however, problems delayed the installation of the site's three guns until 1942. The guns deployed at the site were 6-inch Mark 24 guns on Mark 5 mounts. The guns' elevated location gave each a range of approximately 22 kilometres. Located just below the guns was a fire control station and closer to the shore were two long-range searchlights in concrete bunkers. The battery remained in operation until 1956, when it was decommissioned, and its guns and equipment were shipped to Portugal as part of a NATO assistance program.

Chebucto Head is on private property and several houses have been constructed on top of the former gun foundations. Although this prevents people from visiting the site, it is still possible to see the former gun emplacements from the nearby Chebucto Head Lighthouse. Below the battery, two small concrete buildings that once housed artillery searchlights can also be seen. Visiting the lighthouse

provides panoramic views of the surrounding area. Nearby are several foundations and a small concrete building that once belonged to a small radar tower that was built on the site.

TRAILHEAD: N 44.507158, W 63.522978

Drive approximately 15 kilometres south of Spryfield to the town of Duncans Cove. Turn left onto Chebucto Head Road and continue for approximately 1.5 kilometres to arrive at the trailhead. Park on the side of the road (do not block access to the gate) and walk the remaining 650 metres to the lighthouse.

9. Connaught Battery
Fergusons Cove

Hidden in the forest near Fergusons Cove on the western side of Halifax harbour is one of Halifax's most significant wartime coastal defence batteries. Connaught Battery was the first such battery built by the Government of Canada and its unique design combined three concrete gun emplacements into a single unified structure, making it one of the largest structures of its kind. The battery has been incorporated into a small community park, and although the bottom half of the battery has been backfilled, the 80-metre-long concrete structure on which three quick-firing guns were once mounted remains.

In the spring of 1906, the last of the British Army, which owned the fortifications built in and around Halifax harbour, departed, and the fortifications were transferred to the Canadian government. Understanding that Halifax would have an important role if war should break out in Europe, the Canadian government constructed a modern gun emplacement to protect approaches to Halifax. Construction began in 1912, but almost immediately there was a problem: the site's hard granite was challenging and costly to excavate. Nevertheless, approximately 200 people worked non-stop to excavate 13,000 cubic metres of solid rock and transport it to the outer side of the hill.

The Connaught Battery was different than other, similarly armed batteries. Instead of creating a separate concrete foundation for each gun, the three emplacement foundations were combined into a single unified battery, approximately 80 metres long, 20 metres wide, and two stories high, with gun mounts on top and ammunition and supply storage below. The battery was located at the crest of the hill, with the gun emplacements flush with the surrounding terrain. Behind the battery, an excavated area offered access to the rooms and storage facilities built under the battery. It also protected the wooden barracks, operations buildings, and other facilities.

Below the battery, several wooden buildings were constructed for the installation of searchlights to monitor the shipping lane at night. During World War I, these searchlights became the first to be manned when they began operation in September 1915. The three QF 4.7-inch quick-firing coastal defence guns were delivered to the site from Fort Clarence (at the Imperial Oil wharves) and Fort Charlotte (on Georges Island) in January 2016. Each gun was designed to fire a 20-kilogram projectile a maximum distance of over 7 kilometres.

In August 1916, each gun was tested and officially put into service. The following month the battery was officially opened in a small ceremony attended by the Duke of Connaught, Prince Arthur,

for whom the battery was named. It was then operated by a 70-person artillery unit from the 1st Halifax Regiment. While the battery was not finished until halfway through World War I, it was in time to respond to the increased number of ships being sunk in Nova Scotia's waters by enemy U-boats.

In 1931, the Department of Defence stopped funding the battery and the following year equipment and ammunition were removed. The three guns were moved to other sites in the region. After several other changes to Halifax's defence structure, including the decision to construct two long-range batteries at the mouth of the harbour, the potential for the Connaught Battery's reuse diminished.

During World War II, the Connaught searchlights operated until 1941, when new searchlights were installed at other locations around the harbour. The battery site was then used as temporary housing for troops and soldiers. Shortly after the war, the battery was abandoned, and in the early 1950s many of the wooden buildings and barracks

were torn down. Over the next decades what remained at the site was subjected to looting and, for a short while, the area was littered with discarded vehicles.

In 1971, the land was obtained by the provincial government, which cleaned up the site and transformed it into a municipal park. The lower half of the gun emplacements were backfilled, leaving only the upper 2 metres exposed. The concrete, since fallen into disrepair, remains an interesting feature of the quiet park. The site is designated a National Historic Site, but its tucked-away location means that it is rarely visited.

 CONNAUGHT BATTERY: N 44.605112, W 63.560604
Travel south for approximately 1.2 kilometres on Purcells Cove Road and then turn right onto Devils Hill Road. Drive 350 metres to the end of the road, and park on the side of the road. A 100-metre hike leads to the battery.

10. Point Pleasant Park
South Halifax Peninsula

At the south end of peninsular Halifax is one of Nova Scotia's best-known parks. Point Pleasant Park, a popular spot for Haligonians, offers readily accessible views of the harbour. But the forested, windswept park was not always as pleasant as it is in 2023. The point's strategic location at the harbour's entrance, close to the main shipping channel, made it an important site for protecting and defending the city.

Fort Ogilvie

In 1793, the French Revolutionary War created concern in Britain of a possible attack on its largest North American naval port, Halifax. Because of this, a fort was constructed in the summer of 1793 overlooking the harbour and capable of protecting its main shipping channel. The fort was built primarily of earth and gravel, with six 24-pound cannons hidden behind a parapet surrounding the fort. Magazines and support buildings were constructed nearby. The fort remained active until the end of the Napoleonic Wars in 1815, when much of the site's equipment was removed.

The fort was reactivated and partially restored in 1852, rearmed with six 24-pound cannons, which were upgraded to 32-pound cannons several years later. As global political relationships eroded in the second half of the 19th century, Britain again feared an attack on Halifax. At the beginning of the American Civil War in 1861, many of the harbour's defences were upgraded, including Fort Ogilvie; redesigned in a V-shape, it was more capable of defending the harbour and main shipping channel. To do this, five 9-inch guns and more modern five 7-inch rifled muzzle-loading guns were installed. Construction was completed in 1870.

In 1900, Fort Ogilvie was rebuilt again. A concrete two-gun emplacement was equipped with ammunition storage, barracks, and an equipment room. Its guns were replaced with two advanced

6-inch Mark 7 breech-loading guns which protected most of the inner harbour. In World War II, the fort was a training facility until it was decommissioned in 1942, becoming the last operating military site in Point Pleasant.

The well-maintained site attracts walkers along the park's trails. Two 7-inch guns are displayed behind the concrete gun emplacements, with a single 10-inch rifled muzzle-loading gun mounted on the emplacement itself. The remnants of former iterations of Fort Ogilvie, such as partially buried foundations and embankments, are also visible.

 FORT OGILVIE: **N 44.623774, W 63.566030**

Cambridge Battery

Cambridge Battery was constructed between 1862 and 1868, part of Britain's efforts to upgrade its defence systems as concern grew about the potential of an American invasion of British North America during the American Civil War. The four-sided stone, brick, and concrete battery originally housed three 7-inch rifled muzzle-loading guns, positioned to guard the entrance to the Northwest Arm and inner harbour shipping channel. In the 1870s, five 10-inch rifled muzzle-loading guns were added to the battery.

The battery was extensively rebuilt during World War I, even though its importance had decreased with newer defences being built around the harbour. The once-powerful battery now contained only two, albeit advanced, 6-inch Mark 7 breech-loading guns. These protected the harbour's shipping channels until the end of the war, when the site was deactivated and its equipment shipped to storage facilities in the province.

The battery is one of the largest military facilities in the park and each summer the large open area behind the gun emplacement becomes an outdoor summer theatre for Shakespeare by the Sea.

 CAMBRIDGE BATTERY: N 44.620434, W 63.568068

Point Pleasant Battery

Point Pleasant Battery, known as both Fieldings Battery and Breastwork Battery, dates to 1762 when tensions were high between the French and English. That year, a large defensive battery was constructed on the shores of Halifax harbour, overlooking the narrow shipping channel. Here, five 24-pound and two 9-pound cannons thwarted any harbour invasion attempt. Tensions faded and the battery was abandoned until the early 19th century, when six 24-pound cannons were reinstalled to become part of the harbour's defences during the War of 1812.

As with all harbour defences, escalating threats of attack at the end of the 19th century resulted in periodic upgrades. Larger guns were installed in 1861 and searchlights and a generating station in the 1890s. The two-gun concrete battery was almost entirely constructed in the early 1900s. Two 12-pounder quick-firing guns defended the harbour's anti-submarine nets and nearby searchlights during World War I. Following the war, the battery was deactivated and most of its equipment was placed in storage.

Since that time, the battery has degraded, with parts of it and nearby searchlight emplacements slowly falling into the sea. Much of the area is fenced off to dissuade people from entering the dangerous ruins, and in January 2023, the City of Halifax considered dismantling the historic site. Although its future remains uncertain, the photogenic battery is one surviving reminder of the strategic importance of Point Pleasant Park.

 POINT PLEASANT BATTERY: N 44.620135, W 63.563825

Chain Rock Battery

In 1762, concerns about a French attack on Halifax grew. To deter unwanted ships from entering the Northwest Arm and the city being flanked, the British government commissioned the installation of a system of timber booms and chains across the arm's entrance. To protect the system, a small three-cannon battery was installed on the shore, and for a while a naval ship was stationed nearby, ready to respond if a ship attempted to enter the arm. While the system was upgraded in 1796, by 1800 the boom and battery were abandoned and declared obsolete because of other defensive fortifications in the area. Little remains of the site, except for iron bolts and anchoring points in rocks and pieces of the concrete foundations of a structure built long after the booms were removed.

 CHAIN ROCK BATTERY: **N 44.620696, W 63.574243**

11. York Redoubt & York Shore Battery

Fergusons Cove

York Redoubt, one of Halifax's oldest fortifications, was constructed around the same time as Fort Charlotte on Georges Island and the Point Pleasant fortifications. The hilltop was first fortified by the military with a blockhouse and Martello tower in the late 18th century. The elevated site overlooked the harbour and the few places an enemy ship could land along the shore.

Originally armed with 32 smooth-bore cannons, York Redoubt was rebuilt between 1863 and 1877 and 11 muzzle-loading guns were installed there along with additional fortifications. The fort's defences were soon outdated; the fort was rebuilt between 1888 and 1893. This time, the site's muzzle-loading weapons were enclosed in concrete and brick emplacements, and two advanced quick-firing breech-loading guns were installed. The fort experienced little activity during World War I except for its use as a troop training facility and living quarters. This was largely due to construction of the Sandwich Battery approximately 1 kilometre south of York Redoubt, which became the new home of the area's primary gun emplacements.

This was not the case during World War II, however, when the fort was selected as the harbour's fire command post, target plotting centre, and an infantry housing base. Fifty temporary huts were built on the grounds to house troops in addition to new barracks, mess halls, and operations buildings. York Redoubt was not armed during World War II except for a nearby anti-aircraft gun. Originally, the Fire Command Post was installed farther south but was later relocated within the fort's walls. The concrete building had clear views of the harbour and was designed to receive the location and movements of targets out at sea. This data was then placed in a fortress plotter, a primitive computer

that could accurately calculate required firepower and trajectory information and relay it to gun emplacements around the harbour. Few defensive positions in Halifax harbour were ever attacked, but during World War II a yacht entering the harbour gave the examination battery on McNabs Island (see Strawberry Battery, page 241 and Fort McNab, page 237) the wrong identification number, causing it to fire a warning shot that exploded just south of York Redoubt. No one was injured, but before the war was over two other similar incidents occurred.

York Redoubt remained an active military site until 1956. It then came under the control of Parks Canada and opened to the public in 1968. The site offers visitors an opportunity to safely explore the complex of underground rooms, tunnels, and buildings. Although most of York Redoubt would not be considered hidden, scattered throughout the area are many forgotten and abandoned structures that were once affiliated with the base.

 YORK REDOUBT ENTRANCE: N 44.597171, W 63.554420

Drive 1.7 kilometres south of Purcells Cove, on Purcells Cove Road. Turn east onto Fergusons Cove Road, drive for 150 metres, and turn south into the parking lot.

PRACTICE BATTERY

Located 0.5 kilometres south of York Redoubt, along one of the many trails that wind along the hillside is a collection of concrete buildings, some of which are enclosed by wooden structures. At first these look like small wooden cabins, but closer inspection reveals them to be an attempt to preserve the interior crumbling concrete buildings which were used to train soldiers to operate searchlights and small coastal defence guns. They are located at the south end of the National Historic Site.

 PRACTICE BATTERY: N 44.591845, W 63.549420

YORK SHORE BATTERY

The trail encircling York Redoubt's walls passes many wartime relics. The first is a concrete building that likely housed naval mines belonging to the harbour's minefields. The well-maintained trail passes old roads, stairs, and walls and eventually leads to York Shore Battery. This World War II battery defended against small, fast-moving boats and protected the harbour's anti-submarine nets.

The concrete battery contained two heavily fortified gun emplacements. At the start of the war, the battery was armed with two 12-pounder guns relocated from Fort Ives (page 226) but were later replaced by two quick-firing 6-pounder Mark 1 guns. The battery also contained a fire observation tower and several storage rooms that housed equipment and ammunition. Although the battery was permanently crewed, no living quarters or barracks were constructed; crews lived in shelters at York Redoubt. Along the shore, to the north, a concrete searchlight structure housed three searchlights that provided lighting for the harbour's anti-submarine nets and examination boats. Following the war, the battery's equipment and guns were removed and the main structure was abandoned.

York Shore Battery is part of the York Redoubt National Historic Site; however, its position next to the waters of the Halifax harbour has caused both it and the searchlight emplacements to deteriorate. Parts of the crumbling battery are gated off to protect visitors, yet the battery is an informative place to explore. Watch for the ammunition storage bunker, which was excavated into a cliff south of the battery.

◉ **YORK SHORE BATTERY: N 44.596896, W 63.551265**
York Shore Battery is accessible via a hiking trail outside the walls of York Redoubt. The trailhead (N 44.597236, W 63.554359) is north of the parking area. Follow the trail for 450 metres, veer left (downhill) and hike for another 550 metres, keeping left at any major intersections. The battery is along the shoreline; searchlight emplacements are farther north.

12. RCAF Station Beaverbank

Beaver Bank

As the Cold War began, Canadian and US governments became concerned about how to detect and respond to Soviet aircraft that might approach North America. In the late 1940s, the two countries established a jointly operated system of early warning radar sites across the country known as the Pinetree Line (pages 111, 282).

One of three sites selected in Nova Scotia was a hilltop near the community of Beaver Bank. Construction began on RCAF Station Beaverbank in 1951; it was fully operational in the fall of 1954. Four advanced radar systems were installed there, including search-finding radar, height-finding radar, and a backup system for each. The fortified operations centre was larger than that at other Pinetree Line sites but, as was the case with other sites, it was designed to be completely self-contained: with its own power, water supply, and accommodations and amenities for base workers. A small town was constructed at the base of the hill approximately 1 kilometre from the radar site, with administration buildings, barracks, base housing, recreation halls, sports fields, and a chapel. The base covered more than 175 hectares and could accommodate up to 300 people.

While the base was financed by the US Air Force, the base and radar were operated by the Canadian 22nd Aircraft Control and Warning Squadron. Crews actively scanned the skies, searching for aircraft approaching the Halifax region. If an aircraft was identified and did not have proper clearance, the radar tracked its height, speed, and direction, information which would be sent to the No. 2 Air Defence Control Centre at RCAF Station St. Margarets in New Brunswick. From there, this would be relayed to intercept fighter jets in Nova Scotia, New Brunswick, Newfoundland, or Maine.

The radar systems were some of the most advanced of their time, but emerging technologies soon made this system redundant. In 1962,

the US Air Force ceded full operational and financial control of the site to the Canadian government. Over the following two years, the Canadian government undertook the expensive task of upgrading the Pinetree Line sites and installing a SAGE (semi-automatic ground environment) system. Fully operational by the beginning of 1964, it could relay information remotely to a NORAD command site at Topsham Air Force Station in Maine. Four months later, Beaverbank was declared redundant, with similar sites in Sydney and at Baccaro Point patrolling the airspace over Halifax. Most of the site's equipment and buildings were removed or demolished.

The former base and all of its lands belong to private developers. A continuing-care facility has been constructed on the south end of the site, and the rest of the base is used periodically for film production.

Two buildings once belonging to the radar station lie at the south end of the site near Ivy Meadows. The same cannot be said for the rest of the site, where deteriorating roads lead through a maze of overgrown foundations. On the hilltop, the concrete operations building remains and was Beaverbank's most popular attraction. The property owners prohibit access to the site, leaving it inaccessible without their permission.

⊕ **RCAF STATION BEAVERBANK: N 44.903769, W 63.709605**
Because the site is now mostly private property, the best place to view the former base is from Beaver Bank Road (NS-354), approximately 13 kilometres north of Lower Sackville.

13. McNabs Island
Halifax Harbour

The dynamic story of McNabs Island, situated on the eastern side of Halifax harbour, is representative of Halifax itself. Its origins can be traced to the Mi'kmaq who used the island as a fishing and hunting outpost. This changed when French settlers established a fishing station there in the late 17th century, naming it Isle de Chibouquetou (later anglicized to Chebucto Island). The ongoing wars between France and England eventually forced the French to surrender their claim to the island, passing it into British hands in 1713. After the establishment of Halifax in 1749, the island was owned by Edward Cornwallis and received a new name, Cornwallis Island. As the population grew, new immigrants began looking for land to settle. One of the key actors in the development of McNabs Island is Scottish immigrant Peter McNab, who acquired land deeds from the Cornwallis family and established a fishing outpost along its shores. The island was renamed McNabs Island, where it remained, at least in part, under the ownership of the McNab family for over 150 years.

But as the social and industrial landscape of Halifax changed, so did the use of McNabs Island. Its isolated location made it the perfect spot to temporarily hold people immigrating to the city and as a quarantine area when disease broke out on ships entering the harbour. It also made it a popular amusement and recreation area for those living in the city. For a period, the island was home to many attractions, hotels, and restaurants, with hundreds of people visiting via an established ferry route. But while these uses reflected Halifax's social and cultural changes, Halifax's industrial and military complex had the greatest effect on the island. For many years, the island was a dumping site for the harbour's aging ships and barges. Eventually, this practice was stopped due to its aesthetic and environmental damage, but as a result the island is littered with dozens of shipwrecks, many of which are visible from shore. But the island's defence fortifications had the longest lasting effect on the island. Since Europeans first visited the harbour, the defensive significance of McNabs Island was realized. This began an almost 150-year military presence on the island, which has been reduced to several abandoned fortifications and buildings.

In 1974, the provincial government acquired the island's northern section and the following year it was transformed into a regional park. On November 4, 2002, the island became part of the McNabs and Lawlor Islands Provincial Park. Each summer, private boat tours operating out of Halifax, Dartmouth, Eastern Passage, and Purcell's Cove transport hundreds of people to the island, where 22 kilometres of maintained hiking trails await. Interpretation signs along the most popular trails tell the story of the people who lived, worked, and served there. Many historic houses are preserved and open for visitors. Surrounding the island are numerous shipwrecks, both beneath and above the water, in Wreck Cove and Ives Cove. The historic military fortifications are perhaps the island's best-known attraction. Fort McNab, now a National Historic Site, and Fort Ives are regularly maintained by park staff, and visitors can wander freely through the many tunnels, rooms, and buildings on each site. Hugonin Battery and Strawberry Battery did not receive the same level of care and have fallen into a state of disrepair.

GETTING THERE

Tour operators safely deliver passengers to the island, and the well-maintained trails make traversing it relatively easy. If you wish to skip the hiking, the island's sandy beaches and protected coves make it an excellent place to spend a quiet day. There are few amenities and no access to fresh water, but vault toilets are placed at regular intervals along the trails. The quiet island holds a collection of sites and stories, including abandoned war fortifications, shipwrecks, and both happy and sad tales of the harbour's development. This secluded oasis hidden within the province's largest city is a must-visit.

Ives Cove Shipwrecks

Northwest McNabs Island

Ives Cove on the north coast of McNabs Island is home to one of the province's largest ship graveyards. McNabs Island's seclusion and proximity to Halifax have made its coves a popular spot to discard ships. Most of the ships now seen in the cove, therefore, have been purposely sunk. The environmental effects of this have likely been devastating to the cove's sea life, but since their abandonment, the wrecks have become an overlooked attraction that embodies the long maritime history of Halifax harbour. In the 1990s, the City of Halifax proposed constructing a sewage treatment plant in the cove, leading to a study of its heritage assets. The study offered details about many of the ships that had been sunk in the area and provided the first insight into what visitors see when exploring the cove.

Along the cove's rocky beach, it is impossible to miss the long pieces of wood held together by large steel bolts and nails. Many more are visible in the shallow waters around the cove. The largest of these is a broken-up rectangular grid of wood and metal seen at low tide several metres from the water's edge. These are likely pieces of three Canadian National Railway barges. Little information exists, but it is believed that these barges were brought to the cove during World War II to be discarded.

The most identifiable remnant is a rusting boiler surrounded by pieces of jagged metal, less than 60 metres from the shoreline, that once belonged to the *Keenan*, a tugboat scuttled in the harbour in the late 1930s. The ship, built in 1907 by D.G. Dobson in Midland, Ontario, measured 28.2 metres long, 6.2 metres wide, and 3.1 metres deep and was originally powered by a 75-horsepower steam engine. Once a mail boat christened the *Winnanna*, the vessel sailed throughout Lake Huron.

On October 19, 1909, the *Winnanna* was moored at Tobermory Harbour, Ontario, when it caught fire and sank close to shore. The following year it was refloated and towed to nearby Wiarton to be restored. The ship was put back into service and sold to Keenan Towing and Wrecking of Owen Sound. Renamed *Keenan*, the tugboat regularly

towed the company's barge, *Proctor*. In 1926, the *Keenan* was refitted and a 37.5-horsepower diesel engine replaced its original steam engine.

In 1936, the ship was sold to dredging company J.P. Porter and Sons Ltd. Headquartered in Montreal, the company owned equipment and ships across North America. Nova Scotia native J.P. Porter, after purchasing the *Keenan*, shipped it to the company's base at the foot of the Angus L. McDonald Bridge in Halifax. The company became known for having many derelict ships that would be scuttled or scrapped. This foreshadowed the fate of the *Keenan*, and in the late 1930s, not long after it had arrived in Halifax, the ship was taken to Ives Cove and sunk, possibly as a breakwater for a wharf in the cove.

Years of constant wave and wind bombardment have caused most of the ship to slip beneath the surface. The pieces that remain above the water, however, spark wonder and curiosity about what else might lie at the bottom of the cove.

Joining the wreck of the *Keenan* are the rusting remains of a tugboat (perhaps named *Togo*), several wrecks with no distinguishing features, and the scattered hull fragments of the *Davis McNab*, a popular ferry that was sunk in the 1930s and detonated for salvaging in 1981. As Ives Cove often falls at the beginning or end of a visitor's adventure on McNabs Island, it is often overlooked or unnoticed. Numerous shipwrecks line the coast of McNabs Island and Nova Scotia in general, but few places in the province have more to offer in this regard than the ship graveyard of Ives Cove.

◎ IVES COVE SHIPWRECKS: N 44.622586, W 63.538876

From Garrison Pier in McNabs Cove, walk north along the island's many well-maintained trails. The cove is located at the end of the trails known as Old Military Road and Garrison Road, approximately 1.5 kilometres north of the pier.

Fort Ives

Ives Cove, Northwest McNabs Island

In the early 1860s, the British feared that an attack or invasion by the US was imminent. This fear was not unfounded, as during this time there had been several confrontations between the two nations as well as a growing worry that Americans were destined to expand their sovereignty and ideologies to the rest of North America and even Europe. These concerns were shared by Haligonians and, as a result, the entire harbour's defences were updated. In 1864, the decision was made to construct a new fort overlooking the harbour's shipping channel and waterfront on the north end of McNabs Island. Yorkshireman John Brookfield, who had built his reputation constructing railways in New Brunswick, was tasked with its construction; it was officially completed in 1870.

The modern fort was designed to protect the inner harbour, working in conjunction with Fort Clarence (formerly near the modern-day Imperial Oil Terminals) and Fort Ogilvie (in modern-day Pleasant Park). Fort Ives represents several significant periods of military defence in Halifax, each of which is represented in the remaining structures at Fort Ives. The fort protected the harbour in two different directions. The first, facing southwest, guarded Maugher Beach and the outer harbour. Here, three 10-inch 20-ton Mark II muzzle-loading guns were installed. The second direction faced west, toward Point Pleasant and the harbour's main shipping channel between McNabs Island and Halifax, and contained five 9-inch 12-ton Mark III muzzle-loading guns. Between the two faces, a 9-inch gun eliminated any remaining blind spots. The guns were placed on top of the fort's brick and stone walls, while underneath a series of rooms and hallways sheltered the fort's ammunition, equipment, and operating crews. Behind the enclosed walls, a well-protected courtyard provided space for training soldiers and to house additional barracks and operations buildings.

In the late 1880s, the fort underwent a series of modifications. Prior to this, its guns fired through narrow holes in the walls known as embrasures; however, in 1888, the walls and embrasures were filled

in, with the guns reconfigured to fire over the fort's parapet instead of through it. The following year, the remaining 9-inch guns were replaced by two more 6-inch breach-loading guns and two 12-pounder naval guns. In 1890, the fort was one of the largest in the harbour.

Two years later, the fort needed to protect a newly installed minefield placed in the harbour's main channel. To provide better detection, a completely new fortification was constructed on top of the west-facing gun emplacements. This modern battery used reinforced concrete instead of masonry and could support two 6-inch breech-loading quick-firing guns. These guns were some of the most modern of their time. In addition to the gun mounts, an observation building overlooked the harbour, and below were several tunnels, ammunition bunkers, and storehouses. To support the longer-range guns, coastal artillery

searchlights were placed along the edge of the water, each encased in its own concrete building. By 1912, four searchlights installed at the fort allowed gun crews to see their targets and provide lighting for the harbour's minefields.

The fort was ready when World War II broke out in Europe. Under threat of attack from German warships and U-boats, anti-submarine nets were installed across the harbour, anchored just north of the fort at Ives Point. As long-range weapons evolved, the nets were moved farther away from land to effectively defend the harbour. As a result, Fort Ives was no longer considered a critical defence fortification, and soon activity there decreased.

After the war, the fort was placed in reserve. In the interwar years, it was used for training but by the time war was declared with Germany in 1939, the fort's usefulness had ended. The searchlights were used at the start of the war, while longer-range defence batteries were constructed farther south on the island. The site was temporarily used as barracks throughout the war but eventually it was decommissioned completely.

ABOUT THE AREA

Fort Ives is the oldest surviving military fortification on McNabs Island. When it was constructed, Fort Ives reassured Haligonians that they were safe. Having been regularly upgraded throughout its operational history, the fort provides a rare opportunity to see and experience the changes in coastal defence between 1865 and 1918. The layout of the fort consists of a large courtyard enclosed by a spiked steel fence. On the east side are several buildings, each representing different construction eras and architecture. Along the side of one building are seven of the fort's original guns, including six 9-inch guns and a third 10-inch gun, now resting on wooden supports.

The original southwest gun emplacements built along the fort's walls mark the first period of construction, clearly defined by its brick and stone block design. Positioned along the wall are two of the three 10-inch muzzle-loading guns, still on their original iron carriage that was placed there between 1865 and 1870. Beneath the wall are closed-off rooms and bunkers where ammunition and equipment were once stored.

On the west side of the complex is the modern concrete gun emplacement and battery constructed over the original six 9-inch gun emplacements. Resembling more modern batteries built during the world wars, this battery has a distinctive observation tower that overlooks the gun emplacements. Adjacent to them are several sealed-off underground rooms and tunnels.

 FORT IVES: N 44.621240, W 63.540668

From Garrison Pier in McNabs Cove, walk north along the island's many well-maintained trails. Fort Ives is located near Ives Cove, at the end of the trails known as Old Military Road and Garrison Road, approximately 1.5 kilometres north of the pier.

Fort Hugonin

Finlay Cove, Northwest McNabs Island

Walking along Garrison Road between McNabs Cove and Ives Point brings you alongside an abandoned concrete building partly hidden by an overgrown forest. The building was once the main operation centre for Fort Hugonin (also referred to as Hugonin Battery), named after James McNab's son-in-law, Captain Roderick Hugonin. Built at the turn of the 20th century, the four-gun battery was built specifically to protect the harbour's minefields and the waters below York Redoubt on the opposite side of the harbour (page 212). The fort's operation building, gun emplacements, and their adjacent storage facilities are overgrown with vegetation; it is one of the few former military installations on the island no longer maintained by park staff.

Built between 1899 and 1900, Fort Hugonin was part of a larger project to upgrade the harbour's security and defences. Part of this expansion included protection for the minefield in the harbour's main channel. The fort and its gun emplacements faced west toward York Redoubt and Fergusons Cove, providing it with a vantage point for defending the minefield and the waters below York Redoubt.

The fort consisted of a two-storey concrete operations building and officers barracks as well as a nearby four-gun battery farther west. The gun emplacements were oriented parallel to the shore and constructed of concrete before being backfilled to provide extra protection and camouflage. The battery was armed with four 12-pounder quick-firing guns mounted on pedestals (later replaced with at least one 4.7-inch quick-firing weapon), capable of a close defence of the harbour's shipping channel. Adjacent to each gun was a series of underground magazines, crew shelters, and machinery rooms.

There was little activity at Fort Hugonin until World War I. Throughout the war, the battery protected the harbour channel but, by war's end, it had become obsolete. After the war, the battery was partly abandoned and, in 1922, two of its guns were moved to Sandwich Point Battery across the harbour to be used for training.

At the outbreak of World War II, Halifax harbour's defences were aging. Until new batteries could be built, Fort Hugonin was temporarily reactivated. Its two remaining guns were operated by the 51st Heavy Battery until May 1940, when the site was again deactivated.

The story of Fort Hugonin did not end there. Early in the war, German magnetic and acoustic mines were becoming a problem for shipping convoys crossing the Atlantic. In 1940, the Royal Canadian Navy hired two professors from Dalhousie University, George Henderson and John Johnston, to investigate underwater acoustics and the demagnetization of ships, a process known as degaussing. The research led to several degaussing ranges being installed across Canada, with a site chosen near Fort Hugonin to become a combined acoustic-magnetic range. Fort Hugonin was taken over by the Royal Canadian Navy, who operated the range as a research facility to study ship acoustics and demagnetization methods. The facility in turn gave the fort, and more specifically the barracks and operations building, the nickname "the range." The research team later established the Naval Research Establishment, which studied ways to combat acoustic and magnetic mines.

The operation was shut down in 1992 after a modern facility was built near Connaught Battery in Fergusons Cove. When it closed, Fort Hugonin was the last active military site on the island. The property remained under the ownership of the Department of Defence for several years but was eventually incorporated into the provincial park. The officers' barracks and operations building are visible from the many trails that pass by the site.

The overgrown four-gun emplacement is approximately 20 metres to the northwest; look for a linear concrete structure. The corresponding underground shelter and magazines have been covered with corrugated metal to bar entry; many smaller storage compartments are visible behind the battery. Fort Hugonin provided critical protection of the inner harbour and ended its service life as an important research facility that saved an unknown number of ships. The closure of the facility marked the end of military presence on McNabs Island, a presence that had existed since the late 18th century.

 FORT HUGONIN: N 44.616215, W 63.538150

From Garrison Pier in McNabs Cove, follow the trail along the coastline along for 1.1 kilometres to the concrete operations building. The gun emplacements are in the forest to the west.

McNabs Island Military Detention Barracks

McNabs Cove, Centre McNabs Island

The war had brought many soldiers to Halifax, and, with them, increased crime. Before World War II, Halifax's military prison was located on Melville Island. In 1935, however, that facility burned down and its prisoners were moved to temporary barracks on McNabs Island. As new military structures were constructed on McNabs Island, the military also established a permanent detention barracks on a hill near the island's centre. While there is some debate over when the McNabs Island detention barracks officially opened, it was likely around 1941.

The barracks was comprised of a central parade square surrounded by several small buildings housing the prisoners. A small concrete

building along the edge of the perimeter housed approximately 20 members of the Canadian Provost Corps, the military police for the Canadian Army. Officially named the Number 69 Military Detention Barracks, it hosted a wide range of soldiers and military prisoners from around the world, all of whom were stationed in or around Halifax at the time of their detention. Many of their crimes were deemed minor, and the prisoners were low-risk.

The average incarceration time was believed to be less than a month, but the prison gained a reputation for its uncomfortable living and working conditions. The barracks, renamed the No. 7 detention barracks in 1946, operated only a short time after the war. In July 1947, it was decommissioned and a new military detention facility built at what is now CFB Shearwater.

The former detention barracks lies on an overgrown hill overlooking McNabs Cove and Garrison Pier. The first indicator of the site, found along the Detention Barrracks Road, is a one-storey concrete building with a large garage door and brick chimney rising from the roof. Several other foundations are visible, including a post for the fence enclosure. As with many other sites on the island, knowledge of the detention barracks is limited. This may be why the barracks is often an overlooked destination.

⊕ MILITARY DETENTION BARRACKS: **N 44.612458, W 63.525217**
From Garrison Pier in McNabs Cove, walk south along Garrison Road trail for 600 metres and turn north onto Detention Barracks Road. Continue along the trail for 500 metres to the site on the west side of the road. The area and trail around the detention site are not as well travelled as others on the island.

Shipwrecks of Wreck Cove

Wreck Cove, Eastern McNabs Island

The quiet Wreck Cove, along the eastern shore of McNabs Island, popular in the summer with boaters, is one of the island's main drop-off points for visitors. Hidden along its shores, and just beneath the waterline, is the source of the cove's name. Dozens of shipwrecks are said to line the sea floor there, with some visible from the surface. For many years, the cove lay outside the harbour's boundary lines, where strict rules made it difficult for shipowners and businesspeople to abandon or scuttle aging ships. Because of this, ships were towed and abandoned, left to sink as they deteriorated in the cove. By the 1950s, nearby residents and other cove users petitioned the government to clean up the rusting hulls lining the shores. The cove still contains dozens of wrecks of tugboats, barges, and cargo ships.

Lucia P. Dow

One of the most well-known and visible remains of a ship in the cove is the steel hull of the *Lucia P. Dow*, an American four-masted cargo schooner that for many years transported cargo to and from the Bay of Fundy. Built in 1919 in Rockland, Maine, for the Atlantic Coast Company of Boston, the 57.6-metre-long, 11.4-metre-wide, and 6.1-metre-deep vessel was christened the SV *Lucia P. Dow* and assigned to transport bulk cargo from ports in the Bay of Fundy. One of these ports was Walton (page 253), where the ship was loaded with gypsum for US markets. For 21 years, the steam- and sail-powered schooner was a well-known sight in the bay.

In 1940, the aging ship was retired as a coal storage barge in Halifax harbour for the Dominion Coal Company. Eventually, it became too expensive to maintain and in the late 1950s was towed to the cove and scuttled. Despite being purposely sunk, the ship remained above the waterline, an eyesore and a navigation hazard. Explosives broke apart what remained of its hull. This left one section of the ship's steel hull, likely the hull visible on the south beach.

Other Wrecks

The *Lucia P. Dow* is one of the few ships that remains above the water's surface. Approximately 70 metres to the northwest of it and just below the waterline are the remains of barges used by the Dominion Coal Company. Although they are difficult to see except by divers, these barges are accompanied by other schooners and tugboats at the bottom of the cove. Another boat that greets visitors to the cove's southern beach is the fishing and pleasure yacht *Taylor Made*. Believed to be beached in the early 2000s, the wooden vessel has since broken apart, with the bow the last visible piece, perched at the edge of the forest that surrounds the cove.

Wreck Cove is a popular drop-off point for visitors and thus their introduction to the island. While many of its secrets now lie below the waves, many stories can be told from the pieces of ships along the cove's shores. Collectively, they tell of a time when ships were freely discarded in the busy harbour.

LUCIA P. DOW: **N 44.602972, W 63.512818**

From Garrison Pier in McNabs Cove, walk south along Garrison Road trail for 1.2 kilometres, then turn east onto a trail leading to the cove. Continuing along Garrison Road for another 750 metres (veering left at major intersections) takes you to the east side of the cove, near the drop-off location for those coming from Eastern Passage.

Fort McNab

Southwestern McNabs Island

Fort McNab is one of the main attractions of McNabs Island. Built at the end of the 19th century, the fort was upgraded regularly to keep up with rapidly changing warfare technology. Because of this, it provides insight into the evolution of coastal defences from 1888 to 1960. It has been designated a National Historic Site; the complex's many underground rooms, buildings, and gun emplacements may be fully explored.

Construction of the fort began in 1888 and finished in 1892. It was to be the outermost battery of Halifax harbour's defences, armed with a new type of gun: a breech-loading gun. Breech-loaded weapons, reloaded through the back of the barrel, could be reloaded much faster than its predecessor, muzzle-loading guns. In 1890, a 10-inch and two smaller, 6-inch breech-loading guns were installed at Fort McNab as part of a fire control system that defended the entire inner harbour. Once completed, the fort contained seven casemates to house ammunition and shelter gun crews and a three-gun emplacement facing the harbour.

Only 10 years later, the fort was deemed outdated. Upgrades between 1903 and 1906 included replacing the 10-inch gun with a

more modern 9.2-inch breech-loading gun and adding two modern 6-inch gun emplacements to the site.

The next major change to Fort McNab came at the start of World War I. The fort was to support inspection ships, which led to the installation of a 6-pounder quick-firing gun and searchlights along the water. The fort was declared the primary counter-bombardment battery that would first respond to a long-range attack by enemy ships in the outer harbour.

In January 1919, the base was placed on standby status, with only basic and necessary maintenance completed on the fort. As technology and weaponry advanced through the 1920s and 1930s, the fort and its weapons became obsolete.

Fort McNab was reactivated at the start of World War II, again providing coverage to the inspection system and reactivated as the harbour's primary counter-bombardment battery until new batteries were built at Hartlen Point (page 199) and Chebucto Head (page 200). Between 1940 and 1941, a battery command post was constructed; it overlooked the harbour and could better direct and control fire from the fort. The concrete building's wide, narrow windows that could be concealed behind metal shutters provided sweeping views of the harbour. The building also controlled searchlight movement and was the primary communications centre for the fort.

In 1942, Fort McNab's 9.2-inch gun was transferred to the newly constructed Devils Point Battery, leaving the 6-inch guns to maintain the examination battery. These guns were shipped to the west coast and replaced with aging 6-inch weapons transferred from Quebec. These were replaced again with more modern 6-inch guns from Sandwich Battery in Fergusons Cove. Before the war ended, new searchlight emplacements were constructed farther south, including a support building and, in 1945, an early radar facility known as a CDX microwave radar was built on the former 9.2-inch gun emplacement.

Following the war, the fort was deactivated, and all remaining equipment and guns were dismantled. As with other fortifications, the fort was reactivated temporarily in 1948 before being decommissioned for the last time in January 1960 and dismantled shortly after that.

In 1965, Fort McNab was designated a National Historic Site. Management and maintenance by Parks Canada allow visitors to openly explore the complex's many underground rooms, buildings, and gun emplacements without the hindrance of gates, fences, or a fee.

 FORT MCNAB: N 44.600388, W 63.514833

From Garrison Pier in McNabs Cove, walk south along Garrison Road trail for 1.5 kilometres, turning onto a secondary trail and following the signs to the nearby fort.

Strawberry Battery

Maugher Beach, Central McNabs Island

At the start of World War II, many of Halifax harbour's fortifications were incapable of defending the city against modern German weapons. Fort Hugonin, on the island's northwest coast, was far enough away from Halifax to stop a ship from firing on the city. As longer-range weapons were used, however, the harbour's anti-submarine nets were pushed farther out into the harbour. A new defence and examination battery was needed.

The new battery, the Strawberry Battery, was constructed north of Fort McNab between 1939 and 1940. The reinforced artillery battery was operational in May 1940; its compact design housed two-gun emplacements, barracks, crew shelters, and an ammunition magazine. Its location on a south-facing hillside afforded clear views of the anti-submarine nets installed across the shipping channel. Strawberry Battery was also selected as an examination battery to provide artillery support for vessels inspecting ships entering the harbour.

To do this, four concrete searchlight emplacements were installed in an arc formation at the base of the hill. The searchlights, critical for crews installing and maintaining anti-submarine nets, were operational before the rest of the battery: it came into service by March 1940. Stationed at Strawberry Battery was the 52nd Heavy Battery, which was later replaced by the 51st Heavy Battery when Fort Hugonin closed. Fort Hugonin's two 12-pounder quick-firing guns were transferred to the site and installed.

The battery had a short service life compared to that of other fortifications on the island. After being shut down at the end of the war, its guns and equipment were removed in late 1947 and early 1948. As the political situation between the US and Russia, as well as Korea, deteriorated, the Department of Defence retracted this decision and reinstalled the battery's guns in September 1948. The battery remained in service until 1956, when it was decided that a future attack on Halifax was unlikely.

Strawberry Battery remains off the beaten path, even for McNabs Island. Located high above a rocky beach surrounded by grassy fields and forest, the battery is in relatively good condition. It resembles a small fortress rather than a typical battery and is enclosed by a concrete wall that conceals a series of stairways, corridors, and buildings. Except for a concrete fire control tower at its centre, the highest point in the complex is the two-gun emplacement at its front. These features combined with its isolated location make the battery one of the highlights of the island.

STRAWBERRY BATTERY: N 44.602928, W 63.523112

From Garrison Pier in McNabs Cove, walk south along Garrison Road trail for 1 kilometre before reaching a fork in the road; keep right, following the trail toward the water. At the fork, continue walking for 400 metres before arriving at a rocky beach. Walk north for another 400 metres to the searchlight emplacement. From there, a short climb to the top of the coastal terrace leads visitors to Strawberry Battery.

Chester

Halifa

Lunenburg

Bridgewater

3

4

5

Liverpool

8

Yarmouth

Shelburne

6

11

9

7.2

7.1

10

1

2

St. Margaret's Bay & the Southern Shore

The ragged coastline of the Southern Shore is dotted with islands and navigation obstacles that have posed a danger to sailors for centuries. But within this dangerous coastline are hundreds of well-protected harbours and inlets close to nearby fishing grounds; the area was settled quickly after European contact, with towns such as Lunenburg, Shelburne, and Yarmouth still reflecting this early history and culture. Inland, forest covers a landscape littered with lakes, ponds, and bogs. Flowing from the interior to the ocean are some of the province's largest and most scenic rivers, which have provided the region with a reliable source of food, power, and electricity.

Fishing has long been the primary source of income for those living on the Southern Shore. But shipbuilding and logging were perhaps more critical to the area's development. The accessibility of the inland forests led to the establishment of saw- and lumber mills, which in turn drove local shipbuilding industries. Over time, the original small mills were replaced by larger pulp and paper mills, which have employed hundreds of year-round employees, helping grow local economies and communities. Fishing and forestry remain active in the region but have been largely replaced by tourism. Each summer, thousands of people drive the famous Lighthouse Route that passes many of the region's heritage districts, prominent lighthouses, and provincial and municipal parks.

Most of the region's population is focused along the shores. Highway 103 provides the quickest access to coastal communities;

however, many prefer to take the longer, more scenic, Lighthouse Route (Highway 3). In the north, St. Margaret's Bay and Mahone Bay are popular locations for sailing, boating, and swimming. Farther south are the historic communities of Lunenburg and Bridgewater, the latter built on the LeHave River, more inland than most other communities on the Southern Shore. Many small side roads provide access to fishing communities along the isolated coast, while larger settlements such as Liverpool, Shelburne, and Port Clyde are located

at the mouths of the region's major rivers. Several highways provide access to the interior and are joined by hundreds of former and active logging roads; this makes the region popular with outdoor enthusiasts and cottage owners. Finally, in the south, is Yarmouth, a historic fishing and shipbuilding community best known for its tourism shops, beautiful architecture, and the terminus of the CAT high-speed ferry that travels to Bar Harbor, Maine.

1. Blandford Whaling Station

New Harbour, Blandford

Whales are not an unusual sight on the coast of Nova Scotia. Each year, thousands pass through the area as they migrate to colder waters in the north, helping support countless whale and sightseeing tours. Seeing these majestic animals makes it difficult to believe that they were once hunted and harvested for their meat, bones, and oil. Unlike its neighbour to the north, Newfoundland and Labrador, Nova Scotia did not develop a prominent whaling industry. Before the mid-20th century, the only recorded whaling operation was a small operation out of Dartmouth by Nantucket whalers between 1785 and 1792. This short-lived endeavour is an all-but-forgotten piece of Nova Scotia history. Beginning in the mid-20th century, however, was Nova Scotia's first major attempt to harvest its whale population, with the establishment of the Blandford Whaling Station.

The Blandford Whaling Station begins with Norwegian native Karl Karlsen. In 1940, Karlsen left his fishing village of Aalesund for Halifax, where he was employed by the Norwegian Shipping and Trade Mission (Nortraship) to oversee Norwegian supply ships travelling in North Atlantic ship convoys. Karlsen came from a long line of sealers and whalers and, in 1948, he purchased a plot of land in New Harbour, a small rocky cove near the community of Blandford. There he established a sealing plant; he hired 35 people and quickly brought economic prosperity to the area. In late winter and early spring, ships left the small harbour and sailed to the Gulf of St. Lawrence, where they hunted seals on the ice floes. Upon the ships' return, the sealskins were harvested and an on-site seal-oil refinery extracted oil from their blubber. The pelts, meat, and oil were sold primarily to Newfoundland and European markets.

The sealing operation operated successfully for many years, but in the early 1960s, Karlsen explored the possibility of whaling from

the same location, having seen and participated in Norway's prominent whaling industry. He converted the *Minna*, a small sealing vessel, and chartered the wooden Norwegian trawler *Haroyfjord* to complete an experimental whale harvest in the summer of 1964. The federal government supported the idea of establishing a whaling industry in Nova Scotia and awarded Karlsen a $6,000 grant to retrofit the ships, including adding 60-millimetre harpoon guns capable of firing a 60-pound, 4-foot-long harpoon.

Within the first few weeks of the experimental fishery, the *Minna* returned with two pothead whales and the *Haroyfjord* with eight bottlenose whales. No upgrades had been made to the plant or facilities to support a whaling endeavour; as the whales could not be lifted onto the wharf, they were processed while the boat was still tied to the wharf. The summer was successful; the *Haroyfjord* captured approximately 50 whales.

In preparation for the next whaling season, the sealing plant was upgraded with new docking facilities, the purchase of a new vessel, and the installation of two 25-ton boilers to extract oil from whale blubber. Whale oil was used in machinery lubricants, oil lanterns, and paints. Whale meat and bone meal provided feed for pets, livestock, and even humans. The products were shipped to markets across the US and Canada. Whale bones were not used and, in the first few years of operation, they were discarded in the waters surrounding the plant.

Over the next several years, the industry flourished, with peak production in 1968, when 361 whales were caught, with a total value of approximately $750,000. Although the government set lower whale quotas for the next four years, out of concern for the sustainability of local whale populations, the plant continued to thrive, likely due to its efficiency in producing whale oil and meat. However, on December 20, 1972, the Canadian government announced an immediate halt on all whaling in Canadian waters due to declining whale populations. This shocked both the company and the community and despite petitions against the ban by local community members and politicians, it has remained in place.

This marked the end of the Blandford Whaling Station. Between 1966 and 1972, over 2,100 whales had been killed and processed there. Part of the plant operated as a fish plant, processing herring, mackerel, salmon, and squid until 1999, when it closed and the facilities abandoned.

Little is left of Nova Scotia's whaling industry. The small port of New Harbour is used by fishing vessels and pleasure craft, but on the harbour's south shore, an empty field, an aging dock, and several deteriorated concrete foundations are the remains of Karlsen's operation. After 1999, unsalvaged buildings were left to deteriorate. The area has been cleaned up and many pass by the site, thinking it nothing more than a grassy field.

BLANDFORD WHALING STATION: **N 44.473061, W 64.090658**

Turn south off Highway 329 in the community of Blandford, travel 2.8 kilometres to New Harbour.

2. Polly's Cove Foundations

Polly's Cove, Peggy's Cove Preservation Area

At the end of the short hiking trail to Polly's Cove in the Peggy's Cove Preservation Area, hikers are often surprised to see extensive concrete foundations perched on the rocky landscape. The structure's origins remain a mystery, but its enormous size suggests that it required considerable time and money to build.

The structure, approximately 24 metres long and 13.5 metres wide, contains what appears to be several concrete walls, many of which have notches for support beams and almost all of which are aligned perpendicular to the length. The structure begins at the top of the hill but is perched over the side of the cliff, giving its ocean-facing side a height of over two stories. At its centre is a square section with two doorways. Surrounding the structure, steel anchors are embedded in the rounded rocks.

Many speculate that the structure may be an unfinished house, because of its strange rectangular shape and scenic location. Its location on the highest point of land facing south-southwest over the Atlantic Ocean has led many to speculate that the foundations are a former radar or transmitter station possibly designed to monitor ships or aircraft flying over the coastal waters. While the foundation's layout, centred around an enclosed square, might suggest the placement of a radar system, little information can be found about its provenance.

The structure is an intriguing place to explore, complemented as it is by the beautiful surrounding landscape and unique rock features that have made the short hike a popular destination for hikers, mountain bikers, and rock climbers.

⌖ **POLLY'S COVE FOUNDATIONS: N 44.489640, W 63.888833**
The trailhead (N 44.493426, W 63.889886) is 2.3 kilometres east of the Peggy's Cove turnoff on Highway 333. An easy 450-metre walk leads to the site.

3. Abandoned Ships of the LeHave River

LeHave River, Bridgewater

Sitting at a wharf on the shores of the LeHave River are three rusting trawlers. This collection of vessels consists of two sister ships, *Hannah Atlantic* and *Ryan Atlantic II*, as well as the trawler *Zarp*. Although residents consider them an eyesore, they remain in place near the historic community of Bridgewater.

Along the outside of the wharf are *Hannah Atlantic* and *Ryan Atlantic II*. Built at the Halifax Shipyard, these trawlers were purchased by National Sea Products for their new fish processing plant in Lunenburg. The almost identical ships measure 40 metres long and 8 metres wide and have a depth of 3.6 metres. Constructed of steel and aluminum, they were capable of handling the rough seas off Nova Scotia. The *Hannah Atlantic*, launched in 1964 and christened the *Cape Ann*, had a 765-horsepower engine. The *Ryan Atlantic II*, launched in 1967 as the *Cape Rouge*, contained a much more powerful 1,200-horsepower engine, allowing it to handle larger loads and rougher seas. For most of their lives, the two ships operated out of Lunenburg. They changed hands several times before being purchased by a private buyer who planned to scrap them for metal. In the early 2000s, both ships were brought to Bridgewater, where they have remained ever since.

Located on the backside of the wharf is the *Zarp*, launched in 1963 from the Davie Shipbuilding yard in Lauzon, Quebec. Originally christened the *Rupert Brand VI*, it was built for British Columbia Packers Ltd. and used as a groundfish trawler off the east coast of Canada. In 1977, it came under the ownership of Fisheries Products Ltd., which changed its name to *Zarp*, and operated along the coast until 1996. Like the *Hannah Atlantic* and *Ryan Atlantic II*, the *Zarp* was purchased by a private buyer who planned to scrap it. In 2002, it was towed to Bridgewater, where it has remained.

Since these ships arrived in Bridgewater, local residents have expressed concern that, if the rusting ships sank, they would damage the river's ecosystem. This fear was warranted when, in March 2014, the *Ryan Atlantic II* sank at the wharf, leaking much of its fuel into the river. The Coast Guard refloated the ship and cleaned up the spilled oil. To prevent future disaster, fuel left in the *Hannah Atlantic* was removed at this time.

For 20 years, these three ships were joined by the HMCS *Cormorant*, a retired Canadian Navy dive support ship that was decommissioned in 1997. In 2000, that ship was moored at the wharf waiting to be scrapped. Almost a year to the day that the *Ryan Atlantic II* sank, so too did the much larger *Cormorant*. Believed to have been caused by ice buildup, the ship sank at the wharf; the Coast Guard refloated the ship and cleaned up the resulting mess. In 2020, the *Cormorant* was scrapped under the Ship-source Oil Pollution Fund.

As of 2023, the *Hannah Atlantic*, *Ryan Atlantic II*, and *Zarp* remain tied to a wharf on the riverbanks.

⌖ THE ABANDONED SHIPS: N 44.370382, W 64.505392

As the wharf is privately owned, the closest viewing point of the three ships is from Tannery Park on the opposite side of the river. The park is on King Street, on the southeast side of Bridgwater.

4. Bridgewater's Public Service Commission Hydroelectric Dam

Petite Rivière, Conquerall Mills

The scenic Conquerall Road runs through the sparsely populated community of Conquerall Mills. But as the forested road approaches the intersection with Crousetown Road, the scenic forest disappears, revealing a large concrete dam and powerhouse metres from the road. The dam runs parallel to the road and disappears into the forest on either side of the concrete structure. At the dam's centre, a large section of missing concrete allows the rushing water of Petite Riviere to freely flow through it.

The dam and adjacent powerhouse were part of a hydroelectric facility operated by the Bridgewater Public Service Commission, established to provide power and water to Bridgewater. Built in 1939, the dam raised the river's water levels to just over 9 metres, redirecting the flow into the 1930s-era powerhouse. Once inside, the water flowed through a short penstock until it reached a turbine. Built by S. Morgan Smith of York, Pennsylvania, the turbine, known as a Kaplan turbine, resembled a ship propeller with adjustable blades. This turbine was more efficient than the more common Francis turbine. A shaft connected the Kaplan turbine to a Westinghouse generator capable of producing 440 kilowatts of power. The plant provided power to surrounding communities until it was made obsolete by larger hydro facilities. In 1971, the dam and powerhouse were decommissioned and abandoned.

Before being dammed, Petite Riviere was a well-known fishing river. To ensure that Atlantic salmon and gaspereau would migrate up the river, a fish ladder was constructed in 1939. It used the waters of the tailrace (the powerplant's discharge) to attract fish through the ladder and over the dam. However, when the dam was shut down, the tailrace stopped and upstream fish populations began to decline. Fish were trucked around the dam and reintroduced into upstream lakes until a better solution was

found: in 1977, a 9-metre section of the dam was removed, allowing the water to flow through and fish to freely swim up it. Efforts were also made to revitalize the barren landscape of the former dam reservoir. A tree planting program followed, which explains the seemingly perfectly laid out forest that stands upstream of the dam.

Over time, the dam and its powerhouse have slowly deteriorated. A private developer purchased the facility and removed most of its equipment and machinery but left it abandoned and vulnerable to vandalism. In 2015, a fire destroyed most of the powerhouse interior.

Although the middle section of the dam has been removed, fish such as the rare Atlantic whitefish struggle to swim through the fast-flowing waters created by the narrow section. The dam is a reminder of the legacy of hydroelectric dams and their continued effects on vulnerable wildlife.

 HYDROELECTRIC DAM: **N 44.308202, W 64.525985**

Drive approximately 8 kilometres south of Bridgewater on Highway 103 and turn east onto Conquerall Road. Drive another 3.6 kilometres to the site.

5. Nova Scotia Wood Pulp & Paper Company Mill

Medway River, Charleston

Before the 1880s, the economy of Charleston revolved around a small gold mine and several sawmills that took advantage of the power of Medway River. Throughout the second half of the 19th century, new technology offered the opportunity for smaller mills to produce groundwood pulp. Looking to introduce a new industry to the town, Halifax politician Alfred G. Jones and medical doctor A.P. Reid promoted the construction of a pulp mill on the banks of the Medway River. The Nova Scotia Wood Pulp and Paper Company was incorporated and in 1881 began construction on a small pulp mill at the site of a former sawmill at Salter's Falls in Charleston. Once completed, the mill was considered to be the first pulp mill in Nova Scotia.

Using local timber reserves, the mill produced large bales of pulp, which were loaded onto carts and towed to nearby Dock Cove by horse and oxen (later replaced by trucks). From there, it was transported via barge to the shipping yard in Port Medway, placed on steamers, and shipped to American markets.

At its peak, the mill produced up to 1,500 tonnes of pulp per day. In 1903, the mill burned to the ground but it was quickly rebuilt. In 1916, a new rock dam was built on the Medway River to provide the mill with more power. Water from the reservoir was channelled through a concrete and stone canal, which flowed into the mill and spun a newly installed 1,600-horsepower generator. In 1927, the mill was sold to the Scott Paper Company.

The mill and its dam became controversial when it was noticed that salmon had drastically declined in the river. Beginning in 1933, extensive studies resulted in fish counting traps being installed in 1933 and 1934. As a result, the mill was ordered to allow a certain amount

of water to always flow into the river to rehabilitate fish stocks. This often left little water to power the mill, forcing it to temporarily shut down during periods of low water. The controversy continued until 1947, when the mill was again destroyed by fire, shutting it down, and putting 50 employees out of work.

Despite the controversy related to fish stocks, the mill was welcomed in Charleston because of the employment it offered. Following its closure, most of the mill's wooden buildings were dismantled, leaving only the concrete hydropower housing and the stone and concrete belonging to the dam and river. Farther upstream from the mill, rock berms and large chunks of concrete outline the former dam's location. Across the river, a concrete intake structure and stone-lined channel

are also visible. The mill considered to be the first pulp mill in Nova Scotia continues to be a monument to this revolutionary industry, but it also serves as a warning to poorly managed watersheds and fish habitats.

⌖ **PULP AND PAPER COMPANY MILL: N 44.174694, W 64.661284**
From Highway 3, near the crossing of the Medway River, turn north onto Port Medway Road. Travel along the road for 1 kilometre to the intersection with Old Highway 3 in Mill Village. Continue straight on Medway River Road for an additional 3.8 kilometres to the Medway River bridge. From the bridge, the mill and hydroelectric facility can be seen on the west side of the river.

6. CFS Shelburne

Shelburne and Government Point

The town of Shelburne in southwestern Nova Scotia has a large ice-free harbour comparable to Halifax harbour in terms of the protection and shelter it provides but also in its potential for the establishment of a large settlement. Unsurprisingly, the Mi'kmaq were the first people to use the land and nearby fishing grounds. Following European colonization, the harbour became a safe haven for British Loyalists and Black slaves fleeing the US, as well as immigrants arriving from England, Scotland, and Ireland. Over time, the settlement and harbour became home to many new communities and industries ranging from fishing and shipbuilding to logging and forestry.

In World War II, the harbour began a new chapter when it attracted the attention of the Canadian military.

HISTORY

By 1941, the Canadian naval facilities in Halifax were overwhelmed with naval and merchant marine ship repairs and retrofits. The Royal Canadian Navy decided to build a second naval repair facility and shipyard at Shelburne: HMCS Shelburne opened in early 1942. Along the water, a 3,000-ton marine railway and shipyard was constructed as well as wharves, machine shops, and storage facilities. Farther inland, ammunition bunkers, fuel storage, and administration buildings were built, and throughout the town, barracks, recreation facilities, and a hospital were established. By the end of the year, almost 2,000 people lived and worked in the once-quiet community.

South of HMCS Shelburne, a small seaplane base was established by the Royal Canadian Air Force. Originally the base was to be owned and operated by the US Army Air Force; but after the base was complete, it no longer interested the US, and the RCAF used it for a short period. The seaplane base closed in 1944 and the site was taken over by HMCS Shelburne.

The establishment of HMCS Shelburne also meant that the harbour became a potential target for enemy ships and U-boats. Because of this, several defensive fortifications were constructed throughout the area, the largest on McNutts Island (page 268) and another south of Shelburne at Government Point. At Government Point, the Canadian Army's 104th Coastal Battery Division built a reinforced concrete battery with two casemated 4.7-inch quick-firing guns and two artillery searchlights. The battery operated in tandem with the McNutts Island Battery and for a short period was the primary examination and inspection battery for the harbour.

The Shelburne facilities closed at the end of 1945. Almost 100 buildings had been constructed there and in the surrounding area related to military operations. Many of these buildings were transferred to private businesses and companies, including the former hospital, which was repurposed into a civilian hospital, and the naval facility, which remained partly an active shipyard and industrial park.

In the early 1950s, growing concern about a Soviet attack again brought Shelburne to the attention of the US and Canadian governments. As part of a collaborative effort between the two countries, the advanced underwater surveillance system SOSUS (Sound Surveillance System) was installed near the Government Point Battery. The jointly operated facility was disguised as an ocean research facility but was actually a top-secret system designed by the US military to detect Soviet submarines passing by the southern reaches of Nova Scotia. For decades, the site monitored the Atlantic Ocean, regularly receiving upgrades and expansions to keep up with emerging technologies.

In 1968, the site was renamed CFS Shelburne. Over time, its technology and need slowly diminished, exacerbated by the collapse of the Soviet Union in 1989, which caused a drastic slowdown in operations. On March 13, 1995, CFS Shelburne was officially decommissioned, ending the region's long and pronounced military history.

Following the closure, the facilities came under the ownership of the Shelburne Park Development Agency and were transformed into the Shelburne Film Production Centre. Opened in July 2000, the repurposed

site experienced a new era of activity with many movies and shows being filmed in its warehouses and buildings. The studio operated for about 10 years before being purchased by a marine contracting company.

ABOUT THE AREA

The former SOSUS base and neighbouring buildings have deteriorated. Most of the area remains under private ownership, with measures in place to keep people out of the crumbling buildings. Because of this, the site can only be viewed from the nearby road. From the entrance of the site, the Government Point Battery can also be seen. Farther north, near the town of Shelburne, remnants of the former naval base are visible, including buildings and foundations, some of which have been repurposed. The area is littered with relics from this era, one of which includes the crumbling remains of the seaplane base, one of the last reminders of the RCAF base.

⊕ **CFS SHELBURNE: N 43.743009, W 65.312813**

⊕ **GOVERNMENT POINT & SOSUS FACILITY: N 43.663373, W 65.258471**

Most of what is left of CFS Shelburne is located along Sandy Point Road at the south end of the town. To reach the facilities at Government Point, drive south from Shelburne on Sandy Point Road for 12.5 kilometres. The facilities are no longer accessible but can be seen from the road.

7. McNutts Island
Shelburne Harbour

Shelburne harbour is sheltered at its mouth by beautiful McNutts Island, a valuable navigation aid, former military base, and home for many of the region's first settlers. The teardrop-shaped island, approximately 5.5 kilometres long and 2.6 kilometres at its widest, protected the harbour from major storms and waves. The low-lying island is covered in trees, bog, and old-age forest; its proximity to the ocean means that much of the year it is blanketed in fog.

Named Razoir by the Acadians, the island later appears on maps by cartographer Joseph Frederick Wallet Des Barres as Roseneath. It became known as McNutts Island after British officer and colonist Colonel Alexander McNutt. In 1760, McNutt acquired large plots of land across Nova Scotia, including the Shelburne harbour area. McNutt hoped to establish a modern "utopian" community for Scottish immigrants there. Although McNutt's ideal town did not materialize, he lived there for many years with his brother. The foundations of their house are visible on the northern tip of the island.

In the 1800s, a small settlement formed on the island. Residents relied heavily on the fishery for subsistence and employment and used the flat, fertile ground to raise livestock, including sheep and cattle. By the end of the 19th century, dozens of families lived there and a school, church, and hotel were built. As Shelburne and other nearby communities grew, the island's population dwindled. By 1940, it was considered abandoned. The island experienced a boom during World War II when a coastal defence battery, as well as support and accommodation buildings, were constructed at its southern tip, but the endeavour was short-lived.

ABOUT THE ISLAND
Several families from nearby communities regularly visit the island where they have built or repurposed older structures as cottages and

houses. On the northwestern coast, the wharf built by the military in World War II is still in use. From the wharf, an ATV path travels south along the water to most of the cottages and private residences. Intersecting this road, a 4-kilometre-long straight road brings visitors to the south coast and the historic Cape Roseway Lighthouse and World War II fortification. Hikers encounter the island's large deer population and unique old-growth yellow birch trees, some of which measure up to 4 to 5 metres in circumference and are deemed to be some of the oldest of their kind in Nova Scotia and even Canada.

As there is no ferry to the island, visitors must secure their own transportation. The old wharf on the northwest coast can be used for landing larger vessels, and nearby sandbars provide a safe place for experienced kayakers and canoeists to land. The nearest launch point for nonmotorized vehicles is the sandy Carleton Village Beach. Tides and weather should constantly be monitored, especially by those in nonmotorized boats.

 MCNUTTS ISLAND WHARF: N 43.656206, W 65.303613
MCNUTTS HOUSE FOUNDATIONS: N 43.658273, W 65.302003

McNutts Island is accessible only by private boat. The closest launch point is Carleton Village Beach (N 43.660592, W 65.328043). To get there, travel approximately 10.5 kilometres south of Birchtown on Shore Road. Turn east onto Carleton Breakwater Road and park at the end. Launching from the beach, a 2-kilometre paddle is required to get to the north end of the island. Several well-established ATV trails guide you across the island.

Cape Roseway Lighthouse
McNutts Island, Shelburne Harbour

The abandoned Cape Roseway Lighthouse sits on a rocky outcrop at the southeastern extremity of McNutts Island. Once a critical navigation aid to the thousands of Loyalist, military, and fishing vessels that used Shelburne harbour, the lighthouse location stretches back to the late 18th century when its predecessor became only the second light station to be built by the British in Nova Scotia. The abandoned light is surrounded by the foundations of a lighthouse keeper's residence, storage sheds, and navigation equipment. Although it spends much of the year under a blanket of fog, the isolated location plus the spectacular scenery that greets its visitors make the area unlike any other in Nova Scotia.

When the American Revolutionary War ended, many US residents who remained loyal to Britain immigrated to the British territory which is now Canada. In the spring of 1783, nearly 5,000 Loyalists arrived in Shelburne and, by 1784, its population had grown to 10,000, making it the fourth-largest town in North America. The Loyalists were encouraged by promises of land and supplies for their loyalty to Britain. As the number of vessels using the harbour increased, so did the need for proper navigation aids at its entrance.

The first lighthouse was built at McNutts Island between 1787 and 1788. The 23.5-metre-tall octagon tower was constructed of granite blocks with a wooden frame, with a 12-burner lantern at its top. A second, three-burner light was placed in a window near the bottom of the tower. This was only the second lighthouse built by the British

and the third ever built in Nova Scotia (after one built on Sambro Island by the British, another by the French in Louisbourg). The first lighthouse keeper, Alexander Cocken, was given a small two-room dwelling. Although the house was small and lacked amenities such as a full kitchen and storehouse, Cocken lived there with his family until he died in 1812. Supplies were delivered to a wharf on the north side of the island. While the government turned down Cocken's requests to improve the residence, when he made the case that a road across the island would make it easier to obtain supplies, both for his family and the lighthouse itself, the government approved the funding.

After Cocken's death, his son (also Alexander Cocken) took over. The younger Cocken fought for ungraded housing, which was granted in 1833. He built a school at the lighthouse which operated as a boy's school nine months of the year between 1836 and 1860.

Almost a dozen lighthouse keepers were stationed at Cape Roseway during its existence. In 1883, a fog-alarm building with a steam fog

whistle and a 24,000-litre water tank was built alongside the lighthouse. In 1919, a rotating light and lens were installed, and the lower light was decommissioned.

Since the first lighthouse was built, Shelburne harbour had been a centre for immigration into British North America and Canada, a military port through several wars, a successful fishing port, and a recreation centre. The lighthouse's end came in 1959, when the tower was struck by lightning. The ensuing fire destroyed the lighthouse's wooden frame and dislodged the tower from its granite foundation.

Two years later, the government contracted Cameron Contracting Ltd. to construct a new lighthouse. This octagon-shaped, concrete tower was 14.6 metres tall and housed a red lantern capable of being seen up to 18.5 kilometres away. Lighthouse keepers were stationed at the site until 1986, when the light inside became fully automated. The lighthouse is operational but the foghorn was decommissioned in 1989.

Years of deterioration and wind and ocean damage are visible, but the intact concrete lighthouse remains standing on the grassy hillside. The Nova Scotia Lighthouse Preservation Society has expressed its concerns about the lighthouse because of its long period of abandonment.

The field surrounding the lighthouse is outlined by an old wooden fence and hidden within it are the remains of at least eight other partial or full foundations of the keeper's residence, storage sheds, fog-alarm building, and storage sheds. The wooden structure of the fog-alarm building is still visible near the lighthouse. Beneath the lighthouse on the cape's smooth rocks are engravings likely belonging, at least in part, to previous lighthouse keepers, residents, or personnel stationed on the island during World War II. Some of these engravings could belong to the Mi'kmaq, who resided on the island long before the first European colonizers arrived.

 CAPE ROSEWAY LIGHTHOUSE: N 43.622635, W 65.263843

From the north end of the island, follow the ATV trails south. At the fork in the trail (N 43.645663, W 65.301543), turn left and continue for 4.1 kilometres to the lighthouse.

Fort McNutt

McNutts Island, Shelburne Harbour

The quiet harbour of Shelburne does not, at first glance, seem in need of military protection. But during World War II, it was the site of a naval repair base to supply, service, and refit convoy and naval ships transporting goods and supplies to Europe. The base was also designated an alternative naval port and assembly point for shipping convoys should Halifax harbour be compromised. Thus, military engineers established several coastal defence batteries to ensure its protection against German U-boats.

The largest of these fortifications, Fort McNutt, at the southern end of McNutts Island, was operational by 1939. The fort, near the Cape Roseway Lighthouse, contained a two-gun concrete battery with self-

contained power and heating systems. Farther inland, a small town was established to house the base's personnel, equipment, and supplies.

Because the south end of the island had few sheltered and accessible locations where supplies could be brought ashore, the military built a large wharf on the northeastern side of the harbour. The establishment of the battery improved the island's roads and infrastructure, which are still regularly used by island residents.

A large, semicircular concrete gun emplacement located near

the water was supported by underground rooms and tunnels which housed the equipment that operated the guns and carriages as well as stored ammunition. The concrete fort was backfilled with gravel and vegetation to camouflage the fort.

For the first few years, the fort was an observation battery. In 1941, the Lend-Lease Agreement between the US and Allied nations led to the delivery of eight long-range counter-bombardment guns to Canadian bases. The guns, originally stationed at Fort Worden, Washington, were transferred to Newfoundland, Quebec, and McNutt Island. In July, two 10-inch M1888 guns arrived at the island and were mounted on M1893 barbette disappearing carriages, which allowed them to be raised above the fort's walls to fire and then retract below cover. As with many of the items delivered under the Lend-Lease Act, the guns were considered outdated. Nonetheless, they were Shelburne harbour's primary defence against an attack from German U-boats or Navy ships. Each gun barrel was 9.3 metres long and could launch an armour-piercing projectile to a maximum of 15 kilometres. The guns were test-fired on March 19, 1942, by the 104th Coast Artillery Battery, which operated the battery. The garrison was made up largely of local gunners from New Brunswick and Nova Scotia.

In October 1943, the battery was decommissioned. Most of the equipment and supplies were removed, including the wooden barracks built farther inland. One of the 10-inch guns was removed and partially dismantled for scrap; the other remains in its carriage.

The battery is a hidden gem. The two 10-inch guns, one still perfectly preserved in its carriage, are some of the last to be found in a Canadian battery that has not been preserved in an historic site. Each represents the animosity between the US and its allies when each nation signed the Lend-Lease Act in 1941. As little effort has been made to preserve the battery, it is slowly being returned to nature. Some of the underground rooms and tunnels are partially filled with water, others are used for storage; all can be accessed. The two-gun emplacements are spaced from one another, and some exploring is required to find them. All the buildings of the inland community that provided the base with housing, storage, and support have been torn down and the area is overgrown with trees.

 FORT MCNUTT: N 43.625039, W 65.265705

From the Cape Roseway Lighthouse, walk 250 metres back the trail and turn north on a narrow path. Continue for 100 metres to the former battery.

8. Indian Fields Airfield

Indian Fields, Shelburne County

Along the lonely Highway 203 between Shelburne and Yarmouth is an abandoned airfield that was built in the 1950s. While information on the location is sparse, it is believed to have been constructed by the military for firefighting. The T-shaped airfield, locally referred to as "the Airport," had two runways: one running east to west for approximately 350 metres; one north to south for approximately 500 metres. On the west side of the airfield were a fuel storage area and an aircraft hangar. Following the airfield's use as a base of operations for firefighting, private planes landed and took off from the site. Little remains of the airfield, but it is a popular place for hunters, fishers, and off-roading enthusiasts.

 INDIAN FIELDS AIRFIELD: N 44.042927, W 65.464475

From Highway 103 in Shelburne, travel north along Highway 203 for 33 kilometres before turning east onto a gravel road.

9. Remains of Clyde River's Forestry Industry

Mill Creek & Clyde River

Located on Mill Creek near the crossing of Highway 103 is one of the few remnants of the area's logging industry. At one time, several sawmills were located along Clyde River and Mill Creek's two rivers, which built the surrounding communities and developed the local shipbuilding industry. On Mill Creek, an aging wooden dam obstructs the flow of the river and serves as a reminder of this time. The dam likely powered machinery in a nearby sawmill and/or aided the river's well-known log drives. For decades, logs were cut in the upstream forest and floated to the mills in Clyde River using a system of dams, sluices, and channels.

Near the dam was once a large sawmill built by the Sutherland family, for many generations a well-known shipbuilding family. To supply shipbuilding yards with lumber, the family operated several sawmills in

the area, the largest by Robert Sutherland, a lumber manufacturer. Little remains of Sutherland's logging operations, with perhaps one of the last reminders being the Mill Creek Dam.

Farther north along Mill Creek and Clyde River are several less obvious relics of the area's logging operations. Where Clyde River splits to form Mill Creek are the remains of a rock-lined dam. Designed to redirect flow from the river into the creek, it was likely built by the Clyde Pulp Company, which established a ground pulp mill on the creek in 1909. For a brief period, the mill hired 25 to 30 people, making it an important industry in the small community.

Relics from logging operations are not abnormal in Nova Scotia. But along the Clyde River and its many branches and tributaries are likely countless lost artifacts originating from these early operations.

CLYDE RIVER'S FORESTRY INDUSTRY: N 43.634456, W 65.469676
The wooden dam can be seen from the side of Highway 3, 300 metres north of the intersection with Cross Road. As the shoulder is narrow, exercise caution when pulling off this well-travelled highway.

10. Barrington Air Station
Baccaro Point

The southerly location of Baccaro Point, a large peninsula that extends into the Atlantic Ocean on Nova Scotia's south coast, on a flat, boggy peninsula interested the Canadian Air Force as an ideal site for a series of radar stations that would make it a critical part of the continent's Cold War defences. In 1943, the primitive American radar system LORAN (long-range navigation) detected potential threats—such as aircraft or U-boats—to shipping convoys. Operations slowed when the war in Europe ended.

As the end of World War II marked the beginning of the Cold War, soon the US and Canadian governments considered locations on which to install a series of early-warning radar systems, later known as the Pinetree Line. Two sites were chosen in Nova Scotia: the first near Sydney and the other near Halifax. Baccaro Point's location made it an obvious selection for one of these sites, and construction began in 1955. Two radar systems that could determine an aircraft's location, direction, and altitude were initially installed. Once recorded, this information was relayed to nearby intercept jet squadrons that were capable of intercepting and responding to potential threats. Over a dozen other buildings and structures provided support. Before long, the barren peninsula resembled a small town.

Financed by the US, the station, which opened on August 1, 1958, was operated by the Royal Canadian Air Force's 672 Aircraft Control & Warning Squadron. The site underwent many upgrades, with the largest in the early 1960s when it was automated with a SAGE (Semi-Automatic Ground Environment) system. Information could now be automatically relayed to a NORAD command centre in Topsham Air Force Station in Brunswick, Maine.

The Royal Canadian Air Force took full control of the site on June 1, 1962, renaming it CFS Barrington. Upgrades continued throughout the

following decades as the Air Force struggled to keep up with advancing technology and changes to Canada's national defence networks. But eventually the system became obsolete, and closed in August 1990.

Many of the site's buildings were torn down, except for several structures, including one of the site's radar towers, that were restored and repurposed for use by the Canadian Coast Guard. The radar tower operates as a transmitter and receiver station. A few empty roads and paths separate concrete foundations. The site feels more like a ghost town than a Cold War radar site, a sense further deepened by the blanket of fog that regularly shrouds the coastline.

 BARRINGTON AIR STATION: N 43.452912, W 65.472917

Leave Highway 309 in the community of Port La Tour, drive south on Port La Tour Road for 6.4 kilometres (the road turns into Baccaro Road after 3.8 kilometres). Turn south onto Lighthouse Road and continue to the site.

11. Hispon Creek Stone Arch

East Pubnico, Yarmouth County

In the community of East Pubnico along Highway 3 is the Hipson Creek stone arch bridge. A bridge has spanned French Lake Brook since the late 1700s, but for most of that time it was made of wood, necessitating constant repairs and upgrading. Because the bridge connected East Pubnico to nearby towns, the community sought a longer-lasting alternative. In 1900, local Irish immigrants were hired to construct a stone bridge; it was completed in the fall of 1901 for less than $1,500.

This stone arch bridge was built with local stone and mortar. Along the railings, sharp decorative rocks embedded along the sides prevented travellers from straying over them. In 1936, the road which passed over the small brook (later named Highway 3) was realigned to the northwest and a new bridge built to handle more traffic. The new road made the stone arch bridge obsolete.

In time, the bridge's historical significance was recognized, and it was transformed into a small day-park area and an informative sign explaining the bridge's past was installed. Adjacent to the bridge is a memorial to those who have been lost at sea. In 2018, it was noticed that the brook had eroded the bridge's foundations; water seeping through its mortar threatened to collapse the structure. After the community hired an engineering firm to complete a rehabilitation strategy, preservation efforts costing approximately $300,000 were undertaken.

◈ **HISPON CREEK STONE ARCH: N 43.674542, W 65.766089**
Travel south on Highway 103, turn onto the Pubnico Connector and drive for 550 metres. Turn east onto Highway 3 toward East Pubnico and drive 4 kilometres to the bridge.

Western Nova Scotia & Lower Annapolis Valley

Western Nova Scotia and the Lower Annapolis Valley span from the southern reaches of Nova Scotia near Yarmouth, north through St. Mary's Bay before entering the Annapolis Valley contained on either side by the North and South Mountains. Historically, the area has provided access to the province's inland forestry reserves and, along its coast, fishers have navigated the strong tides and storms to reach the Bay of Fundy and southern Nova Scotia's fishing grounds. While miles of this coastline are lined by cliffs and rocky shores, it also boasts sheltered harbours and inlets, the most well pronounced of which is the Annapolis Basin, a protected inlet surrounded by rich soil that attracted settlers. Many rivers flow through the area, with most flowing east to west, creating the potential for hydroelectric power as they descend the North Mountain.

The varied landscape has attracted diverse cultures. Mi'kmaq first used the area's abundant rivers for subsistence and travel into the interior. Later the French sought farming opportunities in the Annapolis Valley and wood from the surrounding forest to construct Nova Scotia's first settlements. These amenities also drew disagreement, and the area became an epicentre for some of the worst conflicts between and against the Mi'kmaq, Acadians, and British, who would later control the land. However, the area now boasts many Mi'kmaw and Acadian flags. This is one of the few regions in Nova Scotia in which French is regularly spoken.

While industries such as mining, manufacturing, and power generation are not uncommon, fishing, farming, and forestry have shaped the contemporary landscape. South of Digby, fishing has been the main source of income for people sheltering in the many protected coves and inlets. For others, the region's fertile soils provide a source of food and income; this is especially true in the Annapolis Valley. Numerous saw- and lumber mills were established in the interior forest and used the many rivers and brooks as a power source. These industries remain important, but the charm and culture of communities support a well-established tourism industry, as visitors explore the vineyards, farmers' markets, and charming downtown areas.

The main highway through the area, the Harvest Highway or Highway 101, follows the coast from Yarmouth to Digby and then continues through the Annapolis Valley, passing through Annapolis Royal, Bridgetown, and Greenwood before continuing north. Highway 340 in the south connects to inland communities, while Highways 8 and 10 cut across the interior, connecting the east coast communities to those in the west and providing access to a maze of forestry roads. A scenic alternative to Highway 101, the Evangeline Trail (Highway 1), which follows Highway 101 but takes the more scenic coastal route, passes through many fishing communities and cultural hubs. Digby Neck in the western reaches is one of Nova Scotia's most scenic drives and is accessible via Highway 217, which includes two free provincial ferries: to Long Island and to Brier Island.

1. McMaster Mill
Rockville Notch, Greenwood

The remains of a large lumber mill and hydro-power plant belonging to the philanthropic McMaster family are tucked away along the forested riverbanks of the Fales River, south of the town of Greenwood. The McMaster Mill produced barrels, doors, and windows which were sent to markets across the province and the country. The McMaster family, who founded, owned, and operated the mill for almost 96 years, donated time and money to strengthen the surrounding communities. Although it is a good example of a mid-19th-century mill that helped build the province, the McMaster Mill also represents a successful, long-running family business.

Mills that produced lumber and flour were not unusual; historians believe that almost every stretch of river flowing into the Annapolis Valley had a milling operation associated with it. Hoping to take advantage of this boom, the recently immigrated Scottish brothers Robert, James, and Thomas McMaster purchased the land and water rights to a plot of land above Rockville Notch Falls (later known as McMaster Falls). In 1858, the family built a lumber mill, gristmill, and several workshops, including a blacksmith shop, there. This early lumber mill produced lumber, shingles, and staves for sailing vessels; the gristmill produced flour. A water wheel turned the machinery in these riverside mills.

In 1903, Robert and Edward (James's son) McMaster partnered, took over the successful business, and planned an expansion. In 1907, they built a concrete dam to supply more water to the hydro-powered lumber mill farther downstream. A new lumber mill followed in 1912.

The complex of large wooden buildings was built on concrete foundations along the riverbanks. A small reservoir was created upstream by the Mill Pond dam, which would direct water through a sluice gate. From there, the water flowed through a narrow channel

before dropping over the side of the waterfall. At the bottom of the drop, the water rotated a turbine connected to a series of iron gears and axles that powered the mill's machinery.

When the quantity of products outweighed local sales, these goods were shipped across the region and province via rail. In addition to providing much-needed local employment, the McMaster family regularly provided nearby communities with shelter, food, fuel, and electricity.

In 1923, the business's management was passed to Edward McMaster and his two sons Clifford and Clayton. Several years later their younger brother, Lewis, joined, and the company was renamed E.R. McMaster and Sons. In 1930, tired of waiting for the government to bring electricity to the area, the company installed a gas-powered generator at the mill and placed lights throughout the surrounding community. A short while later, a flume was built beside the water penstock, redirecting water to a second turbine, which created a new source of electricity.

During the Great Depression, the family asked its workers to take a major pay cut instead of being laid off. They agreed. When the lumber markets recovered, operations continued successfully for another 20 years.

The McMaster operations at Rockville Notch were abandoned in 1954 and moved to nearby Kingston, where it remained, family-owned, until 1983.

ABOUT THE AREA

The wooden structures left at Rockville Notch were dismantled after the McMasters' departure. Left behind were pieces of machinery, the foundations, the dam, penstocks, and flume channels. In 2010, the McMaster family gifted the land to the local municipality to develop a park. A short trail system through the mill site and its adjacent dam allows visitors to safely explore and learn the impacts of the operation and the family on the surrounding community. Artifacts are evident throughout the area, accompanied by interpretation signs that highlight the story and success of the McMaster family.

 MCMASTER MILL: N 44.950936, W 64.893624

McMaster Mill Historic Park is south of Greenwood in the community of Rockville Notch. Park near the intersection of Rocknotch Road and Harmony Road; the trailhead is at N 44.950918, W 64.893711.

2. Nictaux River Falls & Hydro Facility

Nictaux Falls

The power of Nictaux Falls has been harnessed since 1911, when a small concrete dam was constructed above the falls, directing water into a wooden penstock and powerplant at its base. This hydro facility supplied power to machinery and buildings at the nearby Torbrook Iron Mines.

Just two years after the plant's completion, though, the nearby iron mines shut down and the facility came under the ownership of the Avon River Power Company. In 1929, this company and its facilities were purchased by the Nova Scotia Light and Power Company. The dam and powerhouse were deemed too small to be economically viable, and between 1954 and 1956 the company demolished the former powerhouse, retired the dam above the falls, and constructed a canal and several dams 8 kilometres upstream. Water was redirected from a dam on the river, through a 5-kilometre-long canal, where it entered a penstock and flowed downhill to a new powerplant built on the site of its predecessor. The penstock was designed to run underneath the 1911 concrete dam. In the mid-2010s, when Nova Scotia Power (who took over the company in 1971) investigated the possibility of removing the dam, it was determined that the dam needed to remain in place to avoid damaging the penstock underneath the reservoir. Because of this, in 2016 Nova Scotia Power constructed a new dam, several metres downstream, submerging the 105-year dam.

WATER CONTROL DAM

Several kilometres upstream, a flow-control dam was constructed in the late 1950s to control water flow on the Nictaux River during penstock and powerplant construction. This concrete dam was approximately 50 metres wide and had two control gates to prevent flooding. A spillway was constructed on the dam's southern half. The large structure, later called the "New Dam," was likely abandoned after construction. The concrete has deteriorated, but New Dam remains a hidden historic wonder on the peaceful river that flows around it.

RAILWAY TRESTLE PIERS

It is hard to miss the towering pillars of concrete that stand in the river at Nictaux Falls; they are a significant monument to its mining history. At the end of the 19th century, the Torbrook Iron Mines were restarted and ore was shipped to the ironworks at Londonderry. Ore was first transported along a spur line that connected the Torbrook Mines to the Windsor and Annapolis Railway. In 1905, two new mines opened farther west, and a new line was surveyed to connect the mines with the Halifax and Southwest Railway near the community of Nictaux. Grading and track-laying were completed in the fall of 1909 and the railway was operational in June 1910. Little remains of the 6.5-kilometre railway, except for the towering concrete piers that supported a trestle over the Nictaux Bridge.

ABOUT THE AREA

Other sites in this area include former drainage tunnels along the riverbanks, the foundations of early mining operations, and other remnants.

 TRESTLE PIERS & WATERFALL: N 44.908359, W 65.030888
WATER CONTROL DAM: N 44.900098, W 65.025326

To get to the Water Control Dam, park along Highway 10 (N 44.905330, W 65.030861), south of the community of Nictaux Falls. Hike south along the South Shore Annapolis Trail for approximately 500 metres and take the trail down to the river. Follow this rough trail for 350 metres to reach the dam.

3. Britex Factory
Bridgetown

Overrun by weeds and grass and encircled by deteriorating roads, it is difficult to imagine that the Britex Factory was once one of the largest employers in the Annapolis Valley. Before it closed in 2004, the textile factory provided hundreds of jobs. The enormous one-storey structure now sits idle on the side of Highway 201, forgotten by its former owners but important to the families who relied on the factory.

HISTORY

Bridgetown Textiles, better known as Britex, established in 1960, manufactured a variety of stretch fabric garments. Originally a branch of the New York-based United Elastic Limited, the factory was founded by two American businesspeople who chose the site after a vacation to the area. From the time it opened its doors, the factory was a major source of employment. The building was expanded over the years, resulting in a 14,000-square-metre factory that produced a variety of textiles that were shipped across Canada and the US to be used in clothing made by Stanfields, Victoria Secret, Playtex, and more.

Between 250 and 300 people likely worked at the factory; these year-round jobs were the first of their kind in the valley, which had long relied on the seasonal agricultural and seafood industry. Many two-income families relied entirely on the factory. There was a reported drop in agriculture output while the factory operated. The factory quickly became important to the town and the area.

Throughout the 1970s, the plant's production declined and many workers experienced problems with management. It had acquired new owners (New York-based J.P. Stevens and Company) who showed little interest in expanding or modernizing the plant's equipment, believing that the plant was too far from markets and suppliers to be viable over a long period.

In 1980, the owners decided that the factory was too remote and too small to continue being economically viable. Believing that output problems could be fixed with changes in management style and production processes, its general manager, Sandy Archibald, and several plant managers, created a plan to control the operation. The group approached the federal government's Department of Regional Economic Expansion, whose mandate was to promote the economic expansion and social adjustment of "disadvantaged regions" in Canada. After presenting their business plan, the managers successfully negotiated a $1.1 million grant to purchase the plant and retain hundreds of jobs.

After only two weeks of downtime, the factory resumed operations in August 1980 under new ownership. For 20 years, the factory prospered, but it faced problems in the late 1990s when imported garments from Asian markets outsold locally made products. More significant was newly created US trade legislation which stated that garments manufactured outside the US would be subject to duties when shipped across the border. The company quickly lost its US-based customers.

As the factory was still the largest employer in the area, the federal government offered grants to make the plant more competitive in other international markets. But the factory's debt piled up, reaching almost $3 million by July 2003. That month a local newspaper reported that about 100 employees had worked two weeks without pay to help the business save money. These endeavours were futile. The company announced that it was in receivership, shutting its doors forever early the following year and leaving some 250 people without jobs. Its assets were sold and the building was placed on the market to settle the owner's debt.

In 2006, Windsor, Nova Scotia-based Nu-Air Ventilation purchased the factory building for manufacturing and commercial rental space. But while this announcement was promising, the building was used merely as a storage facility for material and equipment. Its apparent abandonment left it vulnerable to vandalism and theft and, in 2011, an estimated $100,000 of copper wire was stolen.

Nu-Air Ventilation Systems considered how to offload the building, as it had become an expensive safety and insurance concern. The Annapolis County council voted in favour of placing the building for tax sale to pay off the tax debt accumulating on the property. The building was put up for sale in 2021.

ABOUT THE BUILDING

The brick building continues to be used occasionally for storage, which explains the many no-trespassing signs scattered throughout the property, but it continues to deteriorate. Many windows have been broken or boarded up and its siding and roof deteriorate more each year. After years of vandalism and theft, the building is being watched closely by locals and county officials.

While the one-storey building does not stand out above the surrounding forest, at the back of the property is a tall pedesphere water tower that seems to mark the building's location, seen from miles away.

 BRITEX FACTORY: N 44.816203, W 65.333671

As the factory is private property, permission is needed to access the grounds. However, it can be viewed from the side of Highway 201, approximately 4.5 kilometres south of the community of Bridgetown.

4. Upper Clements Park
Upper Clements

Every year thousands of people visited Upper Clements Park, a seasonal theme park with over 30 attractions, including roller coasters, amusement rides, a water park, and a train that delivered guests to the park's sites, from its creation in 1989 to its closure in 2019. The park has been abandoned and many former amusements have been taken down and sold.

The park was built by the Nova Scotia government in 1989 to attract tourists. After only a few years of operating, it began to struggle and, in 1993, the government sought a new organization to lease and operate the park. A local group attempted to bid on the park, but lost to Amsdale Resources Management, a company comprised of 16 Hong Kong-based investors who were awarded a three-year lease.

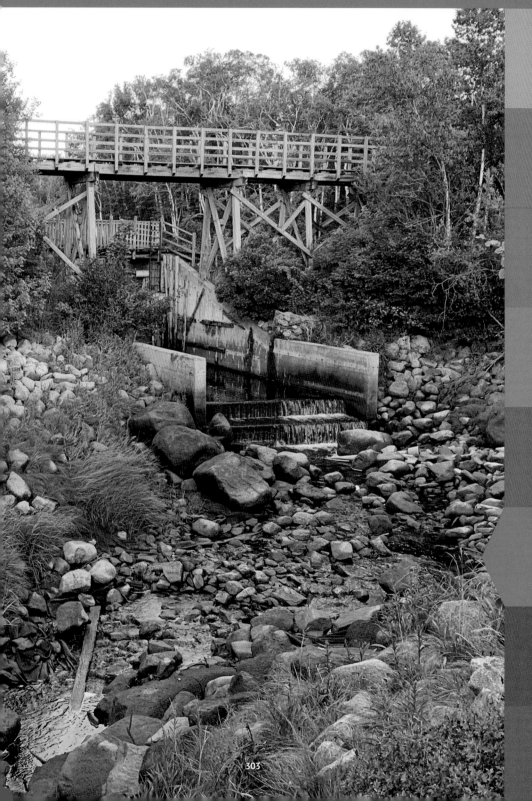

The park's annual visitors decreased from 90,000 to 70,000. This was partly due to the closure of the nearby Canadian Forces Base, CFB Cornwallis, which caused a decline in the local population. (The Royal Canadian Sea Cadets continued to attract some visitors to the park.) During the company's three-year lease, the park's rides and infrastructure declined further and, by the end of the lease, major renovations were required to ensure the safety and comfort of its visitors.

At the end of the lease, the government called for new leasers. The Hanse Society, which had lost its chance to lease the park three years before, was awarded a 10-year lease and received over $1.3 million to complete the necessary repairs and maintenance. The park boomed for several years, receiving another $1 million in upgrades in 2003. By 2006, the park's annual visitors were up to 100,000 and it employed up to 400 people, directly and indirectly. With confidence in the park's success, in 2007 the Hanse Society purchased the park, giving it more control over its operation and income.

As the park had become a major attraction and local employer, the government provided an additional $1 million for improvements. Many new additions were added, including the 2012 transformation of the Wildlife Park into an Adventure Park.

But later in the 2010s, the number of visitors declined again. As the cost to repair and replace infrastructure continued to climb, the park was forced to close after the 2019 summer season, disappointing thousands of Atlantic Canadians.

In March 2020, the local municipality purchased the land, intending to sell it to New Brunswick developer E.A. Farren Limited to construct an elite Scotland-based Gordonstoun boarding school. However, that deal fell through and the developer moved the school to Pictou County.

Throughout 2020 and 2021, some of the park's rides, equipment, and facilities were sold, including the custom-built diesel train. In 2022, the municipality awarded Dexter Construction the contract to demolish the park and clean up the site. As of 2023, most of the park

and its rides are visible along the Evangeline Trail (Highway 1) and the nearby Annapolis County Rail Trail.

UPPER CLEMENTS PARK: N 44.703393, W 65.565338

Although the park is now private property, it is still possible to see many of the former attractions from the side of Highway 1, approximately 6.3 kilometres south of Annapolis Royal. Additionally, accessing the adjacent municipal park (N 44.701643, W 65.567962) and walking the Annapolis County Rail Trail also provide views of the park.

5. Russel Brothers Winch Boat & Forgotten Logging Camps

Medway Lake, Annapolis County

Little is left of the logging operations that once peppered Nova Scotia's interior. In the backcountry of Annapolis County are the remains of several logging camps and a steel-hulled boat that once towed logs and booms across the region's lakes. These relics are slowly being returned to nature, but they do offer insight into an often-overlooked piece of the province's history.

RUSSEL BROTHERS WINCH BOAT

Sitting in the boreal forest of interior Annapolis County is a forgotten winch boat once used for logging. Because of the boat's rusted condition, specific details elude local historians but, by comparing it to similar boats used in the area, its story can be pieced together. It was built by the Russel Brothers in Owen Sound, Ontario, before likely being sold under the trademark Steelcraft to the Bowater Mersey Paper Company Limited. Built between the late 1940s and 1960, the approximately 8-metre-long boat had a strengthened, flat-bottom steel hull which protected it from the booms and logs it was designed to tow.

The boat had a small, central 20- to 30-horsepower engine which powered a small propeller at the stern. Its winch system was installed in the central cabin. Although a 30-horsepower motor is relatively small for towing large loads of logs, the boat was designed to take advantage of the onboard winch to pull itself across lakes, rivers, and even land. From the interior winch, a set of rollers guided a tow line to the front of the boat, where an anchor was attached. The boat anchored itself (typically to the lake bed) before reversing and attaching the load it was set to tow. As the winch wound up, the boat slowly moved along. The winch could move the ship at a maximum speed of 1.5 kilometres per hour, but given

the small lakes and rivers these boats typically operated on, this was sufficient. This system was beneficial for remote logging operations; no additional trucks or cranes were needed to move the ship between lake and river systems.

The boat offers insight into the feats necessary to exploit Nova Scotia's forests. It is also noteworthy as a Russel Brothers vessel. In more than 50 years, this world-renowned company built more than 1,200 boats, from ferries to logging boats and everything in between, including two Maid of the Mist ships used at Niagara Falls and several tugboats and landing craft used in the June 6, 1944, Allied invasion of Normandy.

LOGGING CAMPS

Along the shore of Medway Lake are steel cables, log boom anchors,

and evenly cut timber. Southwest of the tug, along East Branch Medway River, rotting structures and building foundations of a former logging camp are visible in the forest. Farther south on the Medway River, a more recent logging camp containing several structures and bunkhouses that remain in relatively good shape, can be explored.

 BOAT: N 44.552185, W 65.113239

LOGGING CAMP: N 44.526922, W 65.135109

Both sites are located along the interior logging roads northeast of Highway 8. The closest access point is Albany New Road (N 44.426735, W 65.109446) along Highway 8. From there, knowledge of the area is required to traverse the rough road for approximately 15 kilometres before reaching the former logging camp. The tugboat is nearby.

6. Moose River Stone Tunnel
Clementsport

At the mouth of the Moose River along the shores of the Annapolis Basin is a beautiful stone-lined tunnel. Now sealed, the tunnel is a remnant of nearby 19th-century ironworks. The story begins with the discovery of red hematite, a common iron-bearing rock, along the banks of Moose River. In 1825, Moses Shaw of Clementsport petitioned the provincial government to establish a company to mine and process the Moose River ore. As little iron had been found in the British colonies, the government responded enthusiastically, and the Annapolis Iron Mining Company was formed. Investors were sought and shares sold to fund the project. By the following year, enough funds were raised and the company was officially incorporated.

The Annapolis Iron Mining Company purchased the land, as well as mineral and timber rights to the area, and mined two iron seams located 5 kilometres upstream of the mouth of the river. To process the ore, a wood and brick complex was constructed near the river mouth with a blast furnace, foundry, and storage facilities for coal, iron, and equipment, and a makeshift railway using maple rails allowed railcars towed by horses to deliver iron from the mine to the plant.

The facility processed the iron from Moose River mines as well as a mine owned by the company near Nictaux Falls. The ore was smelted into iron in the brick blast furnace and cast in the adjacent foundry to produce stoves, pots, kettles, and other tableware products.

To power the ironworks at Moose River, a small dam was built at the mouth of the river in 1828, at the site of the modern-day Evangeline Trail. A small wooden bridge on the river, built around 1800, was demolished in building the dam and replaced by a stone tunnel that acted as a control structure for the dam and the water in its reservoir. The tunnel was funded partly by the Annapolis Iron Mining Company and the Nova Scotia government. The new river crossing was well

received; unlike many wooden bridges built during this time, it seemed less susceptible to deterioration.

The Moose River mine and ironworks were not in operation long before the company experienced trouble. American investors expected the iron to be smelted into pig iron at the Moose River furnace before being shipped to the US, where it would be cast into sellable products and sold back to Canadian markets. This differed from the vision of local shareholders, who wanted to promote and help the local economy. The disagreement escalated and, seemingly overnight, the Moose River mine and ironworks were abandoned in 1833. All facilities and equipment were abandoned, including warehouse and storage facilities, which were reportedly full of coal, charcoal, and iron. The dam along the mouth of Moose River slowly returned to nature. Attempts to restart the operations in 1857 and the 1870s were short-lived and, eventually, the facilities were scrapped and torn down.

The mine was one of the first iron mines in Nova Scotia, believed to be second to the Nictaux Falls mine. While the endeavour did not dramatically impact the surrounding communities, word of its closure disappointed the small town. The Evangeline Trail, the main road through the area, now tracks over the former dam and few signs of the dam exist. Along the road, however, drivers can glimpse the stone tunnel as they drive toward it. The stone-lined tunnel, marked with its building date followed by AIMC (Annapolis Iron Mining Company), has been sealed. Around 1900, a second bridge was built to the north of the tunnel; it has been replaced by a concrete culvert immediately adjacent to the tunnel.

Nearby, a monument of the ironwork's trip hammer, used for crushing ore, is the operation's last surviving relic. But the tunnel equally represents the Annapolis Iron Mining Company's endeavours and is a reminder of the once-hopeful industry.

⊕ MOOSE RIVER STONE TUNNEL: N 44.660983, W 65.604089

The culvert is south of Clementsport at the crossing of Highway 1 over Moose River. Parking is available here (N 44.660631, W 65.604509) and, during low tide, a trail leads to the water.

7. Peter Island Lighthouse
Westport, Brier Island

Peter Island is in the middle of Grand Passage, between Brier Island and Long Island. The grass-covered island is flat and barren except for a tall wooden lighthouse overlooking the passage's southern entrance. The building is now faded and covered in lichen; on the east and west side of the lighthouse are two modern markers that replaced the lighthouse as the island's primary navigation aid in 2014.

In the 1840s, Westport residents petitioned the government for a lighthouse to mark the southern entrance to Grand Passage. In 1850, the Nova Scotia government funded five lighthouses, including the Peter Island Lighthouse. In 1851, a square 4.5-metre-tall wooden lighthouse was built, with a small dwelling attached to the white tower as a lighthouse keeper's residence. At the tower's top, two fixed white lights were placed on the eastern and western sides, allowing the light to be seen for up to 16 kilometres. The attached dwelling was later expanded but little else was done to improve the lighthouse, which operated until 1909.

In 1909, a new light was funded by the Nova Scotia government. W. Brooks of Digby was in charge of building the light, and by the end of the year a new 13.4-metre-tall octagonal wooden lighthouse stood at the southern edge of the island. The circular lantern room contained a gas-powered fixed light; a circular walkway wrapped around the lantern room allowed the lighthouse keeper to see in all directions. A new one-and-a-half-storey keeper's residence was also constructed.

In the early 1960s, an electric light and foghorn installed at the lighthouse were powered by a submarine electricity cable from Brier Island. The small harbour and passage were becoming more popular with fishing vessels that were based out of the harbour and using it as a passage between the Bay of Fundy and St. Mary's Bay.

In 1972, Peter Welch became the last lighthouse keeper at the Peter

Island Lighthouse. In 1984, the automation of the light eliminated his job. The light shone until December 11, 2014, when it was reported by local sailors to be no longer working. The owners of the lighthouse, the Canadian Coast Guard, investigated; mould in the tower's interior made it unsafe for workers to repair it. The lighthouse was decommissioned and two temporary navigation lights were installed nearby. In September 2016, the Coast Guard installed a more permanent structure equipped with a flashing green light installed at the top of a skeletal tower embedded in a concrete foundation.

Peter Island is currently owned by the Nova Scotia Nature Trust, which protects the populations of cormorants, terns, and seagulls that call the island home by prohibiting access to the island during their nesting season between April and October. In December 2021, the lighthouse was designated a heritage structure under the federal government's Heritage Lighthouse Protection Act.

 LOOKOUT: N 44.256036, W 66.341862

The best viewpoint of Peter Island Lighthouse is from the lookout at Southern Point (N 44.255993, W 66.341886) in the community of Westport on Brier Island.

8. Town of New France, the Electric City

Digby County

New France is an off-the-beaten-path ghost town. Once home to a successful logging operation owned by the Stehelin family, the town became known as the Electric City when a generator installed at the mill provided electricity for the town's lights—30 years before the electrification of nearby, more established, towns.

In 1892, Jean-Jacques Stehelin arrived in Nova Scotia from France. Financed by his father, industrialist Émile Stehelin, Jean Jacques purchased the timber rights around Silver River between Little Tusket Lake and Langford Lake. He and his workers constructed a small cabin, sawmill, and a series of roads and paths along the river. A system of dams, flumes, and control gates was built to direct water into the mill, where it rotated three turbines that powered the mill's machinery. The Stehelins built a wharf in nearby Weymouth to ship the mill's products.

Workers, many of whom were Acadians, lived in bunkhouses and harvested the region's diverse trees. Maple, oak, birch, and beech were highly desired for decorative items, which the sawmill transformed into doors, window frames, flooring, mouldings, and shingles.

In 1894, Jean-Jacques's older brother, Émile-Jean, and two younger brothers, Roger and Paul, arrived from France to join the operation. Land was cleared to accommodate the growing number of workers and soon a town, given the unofficial name New France by residents, took shape. By 1895, the town had a forge, cookhouse, offices, and living quarters. Later that summer, Émile arrived to inspect the operation; he was so impressed that he sold his assets in France and moved, with his wife, Marie Thérèse, to New France.

The family-oriented community continued to grow, with new offices, a small casino, and housing added. Two dams were built: one

adjacent to the mill, the other at Little Tusket Lake. The Little Tusket Lake dam controlled water elevation on Silver River to allow logs to be transported to the mill. This water passed through a dynamo, which produced electricity. This innovative technology was still very new. In New France, electricity powered a series of lights and streetlights placed throughout the town, earning the town the nickname Electric City. Nearby towns such as Weymouth would not acquire this technology until 1926.

Lumber from the town was originally transported to Weymouth by horse and ox, but in 1895 after years of unsuccessfully petitioning the government to build a road to the site, Émile decided to construct a railway line. The railway, designed by Robb Engineering Co. of Amherst, had wooden pole tracks with lightweight locomotives, flatbed railcars, and, later, a passenger car. The locomotives, named Mouche a Feu (Firefly, 1985) and Maria Thérèse (1987), used wood-burning steam engines to transport lumber and passengers up to a maximum speed of 16 kilometres per hour.

With the addition of the railway and passenger cars, thriving New France became a popular spot for local tourism. By 1897, the sawmill produced 15,000 feet of lumber a day.

Operations continued to thrive with the outbreak of World War I

in 1914, due to a high demand for lumber products. After the war, however, lumber prices fell, and the town declined, as many workers moved to other industries. By 1919, the town's operations, including the sawmill, generation site, and substantial timber rights, were sold.

The forest around New France was logged by several companies after that, but the community did not recover. In the last 30 years, the land was logged by J.D. Irving Limited, which, in partnership with the New France Historical Society, preserved the remaining foundations and equipment. In the early 2010s, the land was returned to the Nova Scotia government.

Most of the area has been slowly reclaimed by nature except a few stone foundations, roads, and pieces of equipment found throughout the forest. For a short time, part of the area around Langford Lake was used as a day-use park; the forest around the old town site was cleared, making it easy to walk through.

NEW FRANCE, THE ELECTRIC CITY: N 44.317650, W 65.766697

Travel south of the community of Southville along Langford Road, drive on the gravel road for approximately 5.4 kilometres, turn northeast and continue for another 4.4 kilometres. From here, a 600-metre ATV path takes you to the vicinity of New France.

9. Église Sainte-Marie
Church Point

With its 56-metre-tall steeple and location alongside the Evangeline Trail, Église Sainte-Marie (St. Mary's Church) is hard to miss. The church has held on to its French origins because of the many Acadians that settled in the surrounding communities. It is believed that Église Sainte-Marie was, at one time, the largest and tallest wooden structure in North America. Declining visitation and increasing costs of repair and maintenance have jeopardized the structure's future.

Église Sainte-Marie was the third church at Church Point. The first, built in 1774 on the coast, remained open until 1829, when a new church was constructed farther inland, near the parish cemetery. At the end of the 19th century, the aging church was too small for the number of visitors wishing to attend each service. In 1899, Pierre-Marie Dagnaud, head of Collège Sainte-Anne, became the parish priest. Dagnaud announced the need for a new, larger church and hired French architect Arthur Regnault to design the new structure and master carpenter Léo Melanson to lead its construction. Regnault designed the church to resemble the stone churches found in Dagnaud's hometown of Bains-sur-Oust, France.

The wooden church had a cruciform (cross-shaped) layout. At the front of the building, a 61-metre-high central spire with two rounded turrets along its sides and four additional turrets closer to its peak distinguished it from other buildings or topographic features in the area. The main rectangular structure had a nave or central section length of 58 metres and a width, at its transepts, of 41 metres.

Construction began with a ceremonial blessing of the cornerstone at 10 a.m., June 19, 1903. Melanson coordinated the approximately 1,500 volunteers and parishioners who helped with the construction. One challenge: high winds threatened to blow down the tall steeple. To fix this, 40 tonnes of ballast rock were placed at the steeple's base to

secure it to its foundations and better support the steeple and the three French-made bronze bells that were to be placed in the tower.

Construction was completed in 1905. Inside the 900-capacity church, 21-metre Norwegian red spruce pillars supported a large painted vaulted ceiling. Surrounding the pews were 41 stained glass windows. The building became a beacon for those living in the community and for those travelling along the coast. Although the new church was farther from St. Mary's Bay, the enormous steeple could be seen for miles.

In 1914, lightning struck the tower, catching it on fire. Although rain extinguished the fire, the steeple needed to be rebuilt, resulting in the loss of 4.6 metres: the steeple was now 56.4 metres high, with an additional 1.7 metres added by a cross at its peak.

For the next 114 years, the church served those in the community and beyond. By the end of the 20th century, attendance had dwindled and, with the increasing costs of upkeep and maintenance, the church was closed. The last service was held on December 24, 2019.

By then, the roof had numerous leaks. Buckets were placed on the floor to catch dripping water, plywood was installed over broken windows, and the shingles were damaged by years of relentless ocean gusts. Repairs were estimated to cost about $3 million, but this did not deter local volunteers from forming the Société Édifice Sainte-Marie de la Pointe to raise the funds needed to save the iconic church. The Archdiocese of Halifax-Yarmouth gave the society until September 2021 to raise the funds before deciding the church's fate. The group fought tirelessly to save the structure but, even after being given a one-year extension, were unable to raise the restoration cost. As of 2023, the fate of the church has yet to be decided by the Archdiocese, but with restoration costs now believed to be closer to $11 million, the church's days may be few.

The parish established a small museum inside the church in 1969, which was expanded in 2000 to encompass the entire church. Many artifacts, informative panels, and a souvenir shop reconnect people with the building and its significance to Church Point.

ÉGLISE SAINTE-MARIE: **N 44.333979, W 66.115559**

The church is located in the community of Church Point, along Highway 1.
Parking is available at the church.

10. Bangor Sawmill

Meteghan River, Bangor

Historically, sawmills have never been a strange sight on the banks of the Meteghan River. For centuries, settlers harnessed the river's power to produce lumber. One of these was Joe Maillet, who constructed a water-powered sawmill on the riverbank in 1870. Maillet built a dam across the river, directing water through a water wheel (known as "Little Giant") that powered the sawmill's machinery. Maillet operated the mill for 10 years before selling it to the Parker Eakins Company.

The sawmill was profitable, for the company and the surrounding communities, as it employed up to 30 people. In 1889, it constructed a 650-metre-long spur line from the Dominion Atlantic Railway line to the sawmill. From here, the lumber was transported to Yarmouth, loaded onto ships, and sent to market.

The final owner of the sawmill, Thomas Comeau, purchased it from Parker Eakins Company, likely around 1950. Comeau replaced the water wheel and dam with a diesel engine, but kept both systems in operating condition. The sawmill operated until the 1980s, when it was shut down.

The Bangor Sawmill was likely the last operating water-powered sawmill in Canada. A group of concerned citizens started a not-for-profit organization to preserve the mill by turning it into a museum and historic site. After renovating and repairing the building, equipment, and dam, the sawmill was opened to the public as a museum in 2001.

In 2010, a flood severely damaged the sawmill's dam and turbine but was fixed by its owners. While it reopened for a short period of time following this, it was forced to shut down again in 2018 due to funding complications. As of 2023, the site is expected to reopen.

 BANGOR SAWMILL: N 44.217218, W 66.088624

The Bangor Sawmill is in the community of Bangor along Maza Road at its crossing with the Meteghan River. Parking is available at the sawmill.

East Annapolis Valley to the Shubenacadie River

This region extends from the eastern reaches of the Annapolis Valley through the town of Windsor and to the Shubenacadie River. Within this diverse landscape are some of Nova Scotia's best kept geologic, historic, and cultural secrets. The Annapolis Valley, hemmed in by mountains on the north and south sides, has long been the agricultural centre of Nova Scotia. The mountains help produce a warm, long growing season; its geology has produced rich, fertile soils. In contrast to the low-lying hills and flat farmland of most of the valley, at the Bay of Fundy side of the valley's North Mountain are steep jagged cliffs, including Cape Split, a large peninsula that protrudes into the Bay of Fundy, marking the beginning of the Minas Basin. East of the Annapolis Valley is Southern Bight, a large inlet that provides access to the towns of Kingsport, Hantsport, and Windsor. The shallow bay is surrounded by sedimentary rocks and unusual geologic formations. The same processes that formed these sedimentary rocks also produced large quantities of gypsum. The landscape changes east of Windsor, where the forest contains ponds, wetlands, and tightly packed trees. While logging communities can be found through the area, most people continue to live along the coast. Where the shallow mud flats of Southern Bight are transformed into dark, jagged cliffs—marking the southern shore of the Minas Basin— the world's highest tides have been recorded.

The Mi'kmaq regularly used waterways such as the Shubenacadie River and Panuke Lake to travel across the province's interior. European settlers immediately recognized the region's agricultural potential. The Acadians first settled there in the late 17th century and established large farms, many of which used a system of dykes to reclaim salt marshes as productive farmland. Conflicts between the French and English eventually led to the Acadian Expulsion, effectively removing any competition from English land claims. Population growth was concentrated in the Annapolis Valley, where crops and livestock fed the growing city of Halifax.

The modern history of this region is much different than that of western Nova Scotia and the southern Annapolis Valley. To the south, farming is the primary industry, thanks to the long growing season and fertile soils of the Annapolis Valley. The shallow waters and incredible tides of the Minas Basin encouraged the shipbuilding industry and helped establish crucial seafaring communities such as Hantsport. Mining was prevalent in this region as well, largely due to the enormous gypsum reserves in the Windsor area. Farther east, the towns of Walton and Renfrew mined barite, gold, copper, manganese, and other minerals. Tourism is also a major industry in this region.

The region encompassed from East Annapolis Valley to the Shubenacadie River is accessible by three highways. Harvest Highway (Highway 101) from Halifax to Windsor continues south through the Annapolis Valley. Once in the valley, roads are generally grid-shaped, with major highways travelling east to west. North of Windsor, the Glooscap Trail traces the scenic coastline of the Minas Basin, ending at Truro. Smaller backcountry highways provide access to the region's interior forest and small logging-based communities. At the southern end of the region, Highway 102 connects the Halifax area to the TCH in Truro.

1. Baxters Harbour & Black Hole Falls

Baxters Harbour

Among the strangest of Nova Scotia's diverse landscapes is the shoreline near the community of Baxters Harbour; it differs vastly from the shorelines 10 kilometres away in Medford. Instead of coastal terraces and sea stacks, arches, and caves, the coastlines near the community of Baxters Harbour is characterized by jagged cliffs, dark basaltic rock features, and plunging waterfalls.

To the south, the Annapolis Valley is underlain by weak sedimentary rocks, which are susceptible to erosion and leave behind a flat, fertile landscape. In contrast, North Mountain formed from a massive upwelling of basaltic magma from beneath the Earth's crust; this igneous rock layer is resistant to erosion. This process happened approximately 200 million years ago, leaving a coastline defined by steep, jagged dark cliffs.

Rivers draining from the upper highlands creating spectacular waterfalls backdropped by the dark cliffs. During high tide, the water flowing over some of these coastal falls descends into the ocean. Near Baxters Harbour, Baxters Harbour Falls and Black Hole Falls demonstrate these qualities. Black Hole Falls, at the end of a steep-sided inlet, is a popular destination for experienced kayakers and boaters.

At the entrance to Black Hole Falls inlet is another natural wonder: columnar basalts. When thick layers of basalt, such as those along this coastline, cool, they often crack and break into hexagonal patterns. This is evident in the famous Giant's Causeway formations in Ireland and, closer to home, Balancing Rock in Digby Neck. Near Black Hole Falls, large columnar basalts have created a maze of narrow canyons and passages. These passages, often filled with seaweed or rounded rocks, resemble the hallways of a complex building, making them difficult to navigate but exciting to explore.

Multiple sea caves and arches are carved into nearby cliffs. As always when exploring the Bay of Fundy, take appropriate precautions. Coastal features can be difficult to traverse and with few locations from which to egress the area, planning around high tides and quickly changing ocean conditions are a must.

BAXTERS HARBOUR FALLS: N 45.230192, W 64.512867

BLACK HOLE FALLS: N 45.234066, W 64.493805

From the community of Baxters Harbour, drive east on Old Baxter Mill Road for 1.6 kilometres to the trailhead (N 45.232187, W 64.495097). Park along the gravel road and follow the ATV path for 1.1 kilometres to Caroline Beach. From here, during low tide, walk along the shoreline for approximately 1 kilometre, where you pass through the area's unique rock formations (N 45.237099, W 64.492358) and arrive at the Black Hole Falls gorge; the falls is located at the far end. Caution should be taken to avoid becoming trapped by the area's high tides.

2. Paddys Island & the Medford Rock Formations

North Medford, Minas Basin

Twice each day the 15-metre tide rushes into the Bay of Fundy, carving the bay's rocky shoreline into sea stacks, arches, and caves. In Nova Scotia, one of the best ways to experience this is to visit the North Medford shoreline of the Minas Basin. The town and surrounding area sit on top of the Blomidon rock formation, a weak and easily erodible layer of red sandstone that has been moulded into some of the bay's most extraordinary sea stacks and arches.

The shoreline between North Medford and Kingsport is defined by vertical cliffs of layered sandstone with regular headlands reaching out into the basin. Each of these points of land is engraved with caves and arches carved by the rushing tide and waves. Near North Medford, these headlands show erosion. As the waves crash around the headlands, they first erode along the sides, not the tip. Over time, this creates a cave which eventually breaks through the headland, forming an arch. If you walk along the seabed during low tide, it is possible to see numerous arches and caves in both early and late stages of development.

After hundreds if not thousands of years of relentless wearing down, a collapsing arch forms a sea stack or an isolated island—such as Paddys Island, located about 300 metres offshore, which was once connected to the mainland. Photographs exist that show the island as having a flat top with short vegetation growing on it: hard to believe given the small and eroded island currently visible.

Contained within these 200-million-year-old rocks are numerous fossils; footprints and even the remains of a 30-centimetre-long reptile, Hypsognathus, have been found.

The coastal rock formations offer an unforgettable hiking experience. At low tide, the water recedes almost 2 kilometres offshore, providing

the chance to get close to the cliff face and arches. The water's receded distance can provide a false sense of safety when exploring; the speed at which the tide comes in—and the limited number of places you can ascend the cliff faces—make careful planning a necessity.

ISLAND & ROCK FORMATIONS: N 45.197320, W 64.359427

North Medford is located 16 kilometres north of Port Williams. From the settlement, travel to the eastern end of North Medford Road and park at the end of the road. No trail exists. Head east to a small stream, which provides the only gradual descent over the cliffs. While this is the most used route to the site, it crosses private property and permission should be obtained before venturing there. Caution should be taken to avoid becoming trapped by the area's high tides.

3. Nova Scotia Textile Limited Mill
Windsor

Along the Harvest Highway in the community of Windsor is the Nova Scotia Textile Limited Mill, a relic from the town's era of industrialization. Built in 1880 as a cotton manufacturing mill, part of the mill continues to be one of the town's largest buildings. But the mill's significance is more than just a community icon; the textile industry exemplifies Canada's industrial progress in the 19th century. Large mills and factories using power-driven machinery modernized the industry and introduced a new means of employment.

HISTORY

The Windsor Cotton Mill Company began construction on the factory in 1881 near the tidal-influenced shores of the St. Croix River. The brick building, which was three stories tall and supported by heavy wooden columns and beams, was completed in 1884, after delays in shipping the equipment and machinery from England. Most of the factory's management and workers were also from England, due to the lack of required skills and experience in manufacturing cotton in the region. In 1891, the company experienced financial trouble and sold the mill to the Dominion Cotton Mills Company, which upgraded the equipment; soon the mill produced a variety of textiles and fabrics.

In 1897, a fire destroyed Windsor and almost destroyed the mill. In the aftermath, fire precautions stipulated that all future additions to the factory would use steel. The wood columns and beams of the original building remained in place until the original section was torn down.

By the beginning of the 20th century, the market value of fabric and textiles declined, forcing the owners to shut down the operation in 1908. In 1916, the mill was purchased by the Nova Scotia Underwear Company (the former Eureka Woolen Manufacturing Company) after its factory in Pictou County burned down.

In the early 1920s, the reorganized company changed its name to Nova Scotia Textiles. For decades, the mill provided jobs for many in the Windsor region. All additions to the building mimicked the original architecture except that steel columns and beams were used instead of timbers.

In the 1990s, Nova Scotia Textiles lost a major contract with Roots Canada. Several years later, the struggling company merged with Stanfields, which operated a similar mill in Truro.

In 2005, the 76,000-square-foot plant closed permanently and was put up for sale. Originally, the building was promoted as an opportunity for a mixed-use development such as a condominium and retail space. Many developers expressed interest—one even replaced the windows in preparation—but little progress was made. Listed for $3.1 million, the price dropped in 2015 to $2.1 million, and was eventually sold to a developer in 2017 for $1 million.

Yet the building remained vacant. After a partial collapse of the roof in February 2021 and the risks posed to onlookers and visitors, in December 2021 a demolition permit was granted for the building's older sections. Approximately a quarter of the building was saved, to be developed in the future.

That remaining section, built in 1947, is the only reminder of this iconic industry and building. It stands vacant beside the Harvest Highway, awaiting redevelopment.

⌖ **NOVA SCOTIA TEXTILE LIMITED MILL: N 44.999531, W 64.132826** From Highway 101, take Exit 6 and drive on Colonial Road, which takes you to the closest viewing point of the former factory. As the premises are private property, permission must be obtained to enter.

4. Windsor & Hantsport Railway
Windsor

Many relics of Nova Scotia's abandoned railway lines are located around the province, including railway bridges, stone tunnels, and, in some cases, the rails themselves. Few are ever accompanied by locomotives and railcars—but this is the case for the Windsor and Hantsport Railway. The surviving trains and rail lines have been placed in reserve, with no signs of being revitalized. Forgotten locomotives, ore cars, and passenger cars line the side of the Harvest Highway on privately owned land.

The Windsor and Hantsport Railway, a 90-kilometre railway line from Windsor Junction to New Minas, was constructed in 1894 as part of the Dominion Atlantic Railway (later a subsidiary of the Canadian Pacific Railway). It transported supplies, cargo, and passengers across the Annapolis Valley until large sections of the line were shut down in the late 1980s.

In 1993, a section of line between Hantsport and the Mantua gypsum mines was sold to Iron Road Railways and the Windsor and Hantsport Railway Company Limited was incorporated. Reuse of the old line made it Nova Scotia's second short-line railway (after the Cape Breton and Central Nova Scotia Railway was established the year before). The company began operations in August 1994, transporting gypsum from the Fundy Gypsum Company-owned quarries in Wentworth and Millers Creek to Hantsport. The Hantsport loading facility is one of the fastest loading facilities in the world, a requirement for ore being loaded onto ships before the tide recedes. The ships delivered the gypsum to US drywall (plasterboard) manufacturing plants. The line was not solely used for moving gypsum; in the summers between 1997 and 2003, the service known as the Evangeline Express transported passengers from Windsor to Wolfville.

As a result of the recession in 2008 and 2009, a sharp decrease in drywall and gypsum demand forced the United States Gypsum

Corporation (parent company to the Fundy Gypsum Company) to shut down its gypsum quarries in 2011. After sending a final load of gypsum to Hantsport in November 2011, the railway was shut down. The Wentworth and Millers Creek gypsum quarries are estimated to be economically viable for another 50 years; optimistic that the quarry would reopen, the owners have maintained the railway line. The line has not reopened as of 2023, but there are signs of hope: in 2020, as part of the provincial government's project to twin Highway 101 near Windsor, a 98-metre-long, $4.3 million rail tunnel was added to allow future railway operations to continue.

As part of the project to twin Highway 101, a section of tracks near the Upper Water Street overpass was removed, and a caboose and a small engine belonging to the railway were moved 400 metres to the east, where a facility belonging to the railway (the Windsor Shop) was being used for storage. The Windsor Shop, a rectangular building with two lines of tracks running through it, provides maintenance and repairs to the railway's locomotives and railcars.

Surrounding the facility, several locomotives, railcars, a wedge plow, passenger cars, speeders, and lines of gypsum ore cars wait for the railway's reopening. The most eye-catching is perhaps the Windsor and Hantsport Railway Caboose, which was previously on display as a reminder of the railway's impact on the community in its almost 120-year service. Although the overgrown tracks and deteriorating condition of the railcars suggest otherwise, optimism remains high for the return of the Windsor and Hantsport Railway.

⊕ **WINDSOR AND HANTSPORT RAILWAY: N 44.997983, W 64.133048**
The location is private property; the closest viewpoint is from Upper Water Street, near the overpass with Highway 101. The site can be seen to the east. Be cautious of fast-moving traffic.

5. Falmouth Station's Apple Warehouse & Greenhouses

Falmouth

The Annapolis Valley and Windsor region's fertile lands are due to underlying sedimentary rock that has produced sandy, nutrient-rich soils. Those who have visited "The Valley" are left with images of fields of crops, rows of fruit trees, and historic homes once owned by prominent farmers. In the small town of Falmouth along the former Dominion Atlantic Railway, two historic structures represent two commonly overlooked stories from the early days of farming.

E.E. ARMSTRONG'S FRUIT WAREHOUSE

An aging brick warehouse parallel to the former railway line contains two distinct parts: a small west section and a larger east section. The west side was built by an early investor in the region's apple industry, Edward E. Armstrong.

Nova Scotia's apple industry began in 1862 when British politicians and businesspeople attending the Crystal Palace Fruit Show discovered Nova Scotia's potential to supply Britain with apples. The success of Britain's ongoing Industrial Revolution depended on maintaining workers in factories and manufacturing plants. With the need to keep wages low came a high demand for low-cost, readily available food items to support them. With new markets thus secured, hundreds of people began growing and harvesting apples throughout the Annapolis Valley.

This quickly expanding industry encouraged the construction of the Windsor and Annapolis Railway to expedite the shipment of goods to the ports of Halifax and Dartmouth.

Instead of cultivating apples, Armstrong focused on shipping them to market. In 1906, he built a brick warehouse along the railway in

Falmouth and purchased two 11-metre-long railway cars, each capable of transporting 27 tonnes, to move apples and other produce from his storage warehouse to market.

Privately owned businesses such as Armstrong's were not the only organizations overseeing the shipping and selling of produce. Looking to keep the money earned from their Annapolis Valley products, many farmer-led co-operatives were created, giving farmers better control over their products and earnings. One of these was the Falmouth Fruit Company, established in 1912, which constructed several large warehouses near Armstrong's at Falmouth Station. Wanting to expand its storage capacity, in

1927 the company purchased the small brick warehouse from Armstrong and built a large addition, now the structure's east section.

The apple industry declined through the late 1930s and 1940s, and many of the region's businesses and co-operatives went out of business. The Falmouth Fruit Company warehouse was abandoned but later became a warehouse for commercial and private storage. The structure is one of the area's last reminders of its connection to the once-prominent apple industry. It is partly used by the Avon Valley Floral Company, which owned and operated several large greenhouses in the community and province.

FALMOUTH STATION GREENHOUSES

On the south side of the railway tracks west of E.E. Armstrong's Fruit Warehouse are several large rectangular foundations. The concrete foundations are easy to miss but on the north side of the complex a brick chimney is visible from the highway. The chimney and foundations are the remains of a greenhouse business.

Nova Scotia's greenhouse industry began at the end of the 19th century. Many believe that Handley Loomer started the first such business in the region. Located in Falmouth, Loomer's business operated for 40 years, until his death in 1939. His estate, including greenhouses and equipment, was purchased from Loomer's children and, in 1941, H. Loomer Greenhouses Limited was established. Loomer's children eventually took over the company (with the exception of one son who, in 1935, organized and established Avon Valley Greenhouses).

Other businesses entered the booming greenhouse industry in the 1940s and 1950s. One of these new greenhouses was constructed along the Dominion Atlantic Railway and is believed to have been first owned by the McLellans, a Falmouth family. The operation was later purchased by the Franks, who operated it through the 1970s. While many farmers focused on growing fruits and vegetables, others discovered a high demand for cut and potted flowers, an industry that continues in the town.

In 1977, H. Loomer Greenhouses ceased operations, and Falmouth Station closed its greenhouses in the early 1980s. The Falmouth Station foundations and chimney are not the only remnants of this industry; the nearby Avon Valley Greenhouses sells plants, flowers, bouquets, and supplies to people across the province and Canada.

 FALMOUTH STATION: N 44.997607, W 64.154790

Along Highway 1 in the community of Falmouth, turn onto Station Lane and continue to the end of the road. From here, the former E.E. Armstrong Warehouse can be seen across the railway tracks and the greenhouse foundations and chimney to the west.

6. Bramber Flower Pot Rock

Mutton Cove, Bramber

Along the Glooscap Trail near the community of Bramber is one of Nova Scotia's most striking rock formations, Flower Pot Rock. The narrow, steep-sided feature appears to be its own little island accompanied by a surviving small forest at its top. This vegetation, together with the rock's shape, makes it resemble a flowerpot. The feature is a sea stack carved by coastal erosion over thousands of years. A hole has since been carved through the small island, large enough for a person to fit through it.

The sea stack was carved from the sedimentary rock layer known as the Horton Bluff Formation. Formed between 375 and 300 million years ago, the layer consists of deposits of sandstone, siltstone, shale, and conglomerates. The island was once attached to the surrounding cliffs, but over time the Minas Basin's powerful waves, storms, and tides eroded the cliff's isolated face, first forming a cave that likely transitioned into an arch before finally collapsing to a pillar of rock. The trees and vegetation continue to thrive.

Flower Pot Rock can be viewed only at low tide. As always when exploring near the Bay of Fundy, be careful not to get trapped by the quickly advancing and receding tides, which can reach up to 14 metres at the sea stack. With proper preparations, however, the trip is worthwhile, as the rock formation is one of the most beautiful in the area. Additionally, the coastal landform is a perfect showcase of the staggering power found in the Minas Basin.

BRAMBER FLOWER POT ROCK: N 45.191165, W 64.165380

Along the Glooscap Trail (Highway 215), travel approximately 3.3 kilometres north of the community of Cheverie before turning onto Ocean Beach Road. Continue 1.9 kilometres to the end of the road. Park here and hike 500 metres west, following the coast during low tide to reach the sea stack.

7. Walton Gypsum & Barite Mine
Walton, East Hants

On the southern shore of the Minas Basin is the small town of Walton. Formerly known as Petite Riviere, the Europeans who first settled there made their living by shipbuilding and logging. But in the early 19th century, the town underwent massive transformations when gypsum, barite, and other minerals were discovered. The small community grew into a booming mining town and was recognized around the world for the products and ore that were shipped from its small harbour. The mining industry is no longer active, but the area is dotted with remnants of the town's glory days.

GYPSUM MINING

The mining of gypsum at Walton has been overshadowed by the important barite mine that opened in the community in the 1940s. However, the region's gypsum reserves first put Walton on the map and began the first of its several mining booms.

Gypsum has been extracted and shipped from Walton since 1807, when rock was primitively extracted from cliffs and exposed outcrops, hand-loaded onto ships along the Walton River, and shipped to market. Before being shipped, the ore was crushed into a fine powder, producing a quick-setting plaster known as plaster of Paris, popular among Canadian and US markets. The mining operation expanded in 1820 when businessperson Francis Parker extracted gypsum from South Mountain Quarry.

The greyish white and blue gypsum mined at Walton was ideal because it contained few impurities and was buried by only a small layer of overburden, making for easy extraction. In 1836, Parker partnered with new investors to form the Petite Plaster and Mills Company. Parker's operation changed little, except for opening a new quarry on North Mountain. By the mid-1870s, almost 4,500 tonnes of ore were being shipped from Walton each year.

Major changes came in 1889 when Senator Ezra Churchill, owner of Churchill & Sons Shipyard in Hantsport, took over the gypsum operations at Walton. Churchill constructed a new shipping pier and breakwater in Walton harbour. Although ore was still mined primarily by hand, it was now loaded onto horse-drawn carts and transported to the shipping facility, instantly increasing the mine's productivity.

In 1908, after his son died, Churchill established the George W. Churchill Estate Company to continue operating the mine and appointed Albert Parsons to oversee its operations. As the mine was producing approximately 36,000 tonnes of ore each year, Parsons looked for ways to expand this. In 1912, Parsons approached New York-based Rock Plaster Manufacturing Company to invest in the Walton operations. The company agreed and a new era of expansions began.

The first expansion under this new partnership was the 1913 construction of a 2-kilometre-long, narrow-gauge railway from the quarry site to the shipping facilities. Two steam locomotives, which arrived in July from a closed quarry in Amherst, carried 4-ton ore cars, an increase in carrying capacity over the previous method of using carts or trucks. As well, a new gypsum processing plant was constructed along the harbour. The plant crushed gypsum into 3-inch pieces, which were transported to storage sheds, then loaded onto ships via conveyor belts. As this system could load 270 tonnes per hour, a 2,500-tonne-capacity ship could be loaded between low tides, eliminating its dependence on the tides.

The crushed gypsum was shipped to a plant in Staten Island, New York, and distributed to markets across the eastern seaboard. Business was good and the Walton mines employed about 35 people.

In the 1920s, Atlantic Gypsum Products Company purchased the Rock Plaster Manufacturing Company shares and took over all operations. The storage facilities and mill were upgraded again and powered by electricity delivered to the community by a new transmission line that ran along Walton Woods Road. Between 1929 and 1937, the railway was removed in phases. The entire railway line was scrapped, along with the ore cars, in 1937.

The Walton gypsum mine had evolved into one of the most modern of its time. Steam shovels and drills removed overburden and ore in the quarries, and the upgraded mill was run by electricity. A change in ownership occurred again in the early 1940s, when the National Gypsum Company purchased the operation. The mine produced up to 180,000 tonnes of gypsum each year, which it shipped to Virginia, New Hampshire, New Jersey, Maine, and elsewhere.

The company added several quarries—Fry's Mountain Quarry, Finnice Mountain Quarry, and Stevens Quarry—which were mined periodically throughout the 1950s and 1960s. The Walton gypsum mines were plagued by the timing of tides and the harbour's limitations on the size of ships capable of entering it and, when the National Gypsum Company consolidated its Nova Scotia operations in 1972, it ended its Walton operations. Albert Parsons and his sons had managed the mine for more than 70 years.

BARITE MINE

The gypsum industry in the Walton area is often overlooked because of the barite found in the area. Barite was first noted there in 1874

by geologist Hugh Fletcher, but no further exploration was done until the mineral's potential use in extracting underground oil and gas was realized in the 1930s. In 1940, under the leadership of Carl J. Springer, a group of prospectors arrived in the area, rediscovered the barite ore body, and sent samples to be tested for grade and quality.

The findings: high-grade barite in potentially the largest barite ore body in the world, containing 5 to 8 million tonnes of ore. In 1941, Springer Sturgeon Gold Mines established the subsidiary Canadian Industrial Minerals to excavate an open pit mine 3.5 kilometres south of Walton. A barite processing mill and shipping facility were constructed at the mouth of the Walton river, near the gypsum processing facilities.

The mining operation began quickly. In 1941, the mine produced approximately 12,000 tonnes of ore; this had doubled by 1943. This explained the many upgrades the operation went through in 1943-44; the mill was enlarged and new storage sheds and two concrete silos were constructed. The 26.5-metre-tall, 10.6-metre-diameter silos could store 2,200 tonnes of processed barite powder before it was loaded onto ships.

Canadian Industrial Minerals operated between 1940 and 1955, when the Magnet Cove Barium Corporation took over Magnet Cove Barium Corporation continued mining the 100-metre-deep open pit. But because of problems in stabilizing the pit and its depth, the company dug vertical shafts to access the ore body. Over time, the shaft was excavated to a depth of 290 metres with drifts (horizontal tunnels) extending into the steeply dipping ore body. The vertical shaft was likely excavated to a depth of 518 metres.

Miners used explosives and hand tools to extract the ore before loading it onto carts, where it was brought to an elevator in the main shaft. The mill crushed the ore into a fine powder, which was bagged and shipped to oil fields in the Gulf of Mexico.

The end began in 1970 when a planned explosion caused water to seep into the underground workings. The water was salt water seeping in from the Minas Basin, giving little hope that it would stop or dry out. The mine operated at a lower capacity until 1976, when operations began to phase out, shutting down completely in February 1978. All equipment and buildings were removed from the site, except for the processing mill, which burned down in 1979.

Some small-scale mining for lead, silver, zinc, and copper continued periodically but no major mining operation has returned to the area. Approximately 4.2 million tonnes of ore were excavated from the mine and, at its peak, it hired around 150 people. This number had dropped to 50 by the time the mine shut down.

CONCLUSION

Walton is a quiet coastal community best known for its historic lighthouse and scenic tide-influenced river and wetlands. Since the early 19th century, mining has shaped Walton and, while it is difficult to imagine the scale of the mining operations, scattered throughout the area are dozens of remnants from this time.

⊕ **WALTON GYPSUM & BARITE MINE: N 45.230529, W 64.007457**
From the north side of Walton Harbour along the Glooscap Trail (Highway 215), keep left on Hibbert Weir Road for 150 metres before reaching the former Walton wharves and loading facilities.

8. South Maitland Railway Bridge
South Maitland

Towering pillars protruding from the tidal-dominated waters of the Shubenacadie River are all that remain of the Midland Railway's South Maitland Bridge. One hundred and twenty-three years after their construction, the pillars resist forces of the tides and river, a credit to their design and construction. But construction of the South Maitland Bridge proved to be one of the most difficult railway infrastructure projects in the province, one which would take the lives of several workers.

The construction of the railway line between Truro and Windsor began in 1896, the same year the Midland Railway Company was founded. Several routes were considered for the line—several of which connected with existing railways farther south—but, with the backing of wealthy investors, most of whom were based in Montreal, it was decided to build the line through South Maitland.

This route allowed the railway to remain independent of other lines and while most of the railway line would be relatively straightforward, constructing a bridge across the Shubenacadie River was not. Located near the mouth of the river along the Minas Basin, the semi-diurnal tides can fluctuate by over 15 metres in height, twice daily. This, in addition to the normal flow of the river, creates extremely powerful currents that change depending on the time of day. Lastly, the stretch of river where the railway would cross was over 360 metres wide at high tide, with steep riverbanks on each side.

In 1899, the New York-based Engineering Contract Company began constructing the bridge piers and abutments. A cement plant was installed nearby plus a cableway over the river capable of carrying cement, materials, and workers to each pier's location. Supported by two 22-metre-tall towers located on either side of the river, the cableway itself was considered an incredible effort. As the river's bottom was comprised mostly of sand, loose rock, and silt, in order to secure the bridge the piers

had to be secured to the underlying bedrock.

To provide the necessary dry working conditions, large wood caissons were constructed nearby and then floated into the position of each pier. Next, the water was pumped out of the caisson before workers were delivered via cableway to prepare the groundwork. Finally, concrete was poured to support the future bridge. One and a half years later, the bridge's five piers, its lift bridge supports, and the two abutments were complete.

For the bridge's superstructure, Montreal-based Dominion Bridge Company was hired and work began in the fall of 1900. The bridge's five steel trestle spans were prefabricated and assembled along the riverbanks before being placed on barges. At high tide, each 67-metre-long section was floated and then lifted into place. Once the bridge's superstructure was completed, a single railway line was laid across it. The bridge was completed in 1901, and in the two years of construction, 300 people likely worked on the project. Tragically, the project claimed the lives of five people in two separate construction accidents.

The bridge was recognized as an engineering marvel. In 1912, the western abutment lift section and associated piers were demolished and replaced by a 40-metre girder swing stage. This included the

construction of a pivot pier for which the span could rotate around and two support piers for the span to rest on once it was rotated. Still visible, these can be fully explored during low tide.

The bridge operated until 1983, when the railway line was shut down. In 1986, demolition began. The piers, deemed too difficult to remove because of the surrounding currents, were left in place. The piers are much smaller than they once were, having been subject to over 100 years of erosion.

In 1979, when engineers designed a new road bridge to run parallel to the former railway bridge, they used lessons learned during its construction. For example, the road bridge uses fewer piers than its predecessor, taking advantage of large arched spans to traverse the river. A lookout built from the western abutment to the first pier allows visitors to view the famous currents and tidal bores that form along the river. This also provides a safe way to witness the remains of the bridge.

⊕ **SOUTH MAITLAND RAILWAY BRIDGE: N 45.251213, W 63.456205**
Along Highway 236, the trailhead is approximately 1.4 kilometres east of the community of South Maitland on the east side of Shubenacadie River (N 45.250531, W 63.459479). A short and easy walk leads to the lookout.

Cumberland & Colchester Counties

From the northern reaches of the Bay of Fundy to the south shore of the Northumberland Strait, the counties of Cumberland and Colchester contain a wealth of hidden wonders.

Beginning in the south, along the shores of the Bay of Fundy and Minas Basin are many significant sites that have shaped how geologists and paleontologists understand the evolution of life on Earth. These include the 200-million-year-old dinosaur fossils at Wasson Bluff, the oldest ever discovered in Canada. The region's intriguing geologic history has produced diverse landscapes: from the sinkhole-dominated area around the town of Oxford, to the coal beds of Joggins and Springhill, to the erosive landforms created along the coast and by glaciers that once covered the area. The coastline holds some of the most dramatic scenery that Nova Scotia has to offer, with sea stacks, arches, and caves. Many of the region's communities are located along the coastal terrace backdropped by the Cobequid Hills to the north.

The hiking opportunities created by the coastline and surrounding mountains have made this area a top destination for outdoor lovers. In the region's interior, rolling hills and vast forests, seemingly devoid of lakes and ponds, established the area's forestry industry. In the north, the scenery flattens out until it reaches the shores of Northumberland Strait. In the east, the shoreline contains some of Nova Scotia's most popular beaches, while, to the west, flat rocky shores and saltwater marshes dominate the landscape.

The earliest evidence of people in the region dates to 13,500 years ago and was discovered near the community of Debert. These first people lived there before the last ice age was over and are believed to be the descendants of Nova Scotia's Mi'kmaq. The land remained with the Mi'kmaq until colonization. Beginning in the early 17th century, the Acadians settled and developed farmland along the shores of the Minas Basin near Truro. Around the same time, the first coal was taken out of the ground near Joggins by French settlers. By the late 18th century, the land had come under British ownership, who slowly populated the area and took advantage of its proximity to fishing grounds and forests.

The diverse landscape also gave rise to diverse industries. In the north, fishing, especially lobster fishing, in the warm waters of the Northumberland Strait was a major industry; farther inland and along the southern coast forestry was the primary means of income.

After coal was discovered in the community of Joggins, coal mining became a major industry in the region, stretching as far inland as the community of Springhill, where a major mine operated from the mid-19th century and lasted until the second half of the 20th century. The region also was home to the province's largest iron mines, in the community of Londonderry. As the region is the only connected land route to the rest of Canada, the construction of transportation networks such as railway lines and later road networks connected Nova Scotia with the rest of the country as well as established many of the region's settlements. Unlike the rest of Nova Scotia, the militarization of Cumberland and Colchester counties was almost nonexistent—until World War II, when the small community of Debert became home to a large Air Force and Army training facility, which had widespread effects on the province.

The TCH (Highway 104) is the main route across the region. In the south, Highway 2 travels the scenic route along the north shore of the Minas Basin to the historic town of Parrsboro, where it continues north to the communities of Springhill and Amherst. From Parrsboro, continuing west along Highway 209 continues the scenic coastal drive

and passes by Nova Scotia's largest provincial park, Cape Chignecto Provincial Park. Highway 209 then continues north to Joggins and on to nearby Amherst on the border with New Brunswick. In the north, the Sunrise Trail follows the shores of the Northumberland Strait and passes through the popular tourism communities of Tatamagouche and Pugwash, among others. Connecting these primarily east-to-west running roads is a network of paved and unpaved roads that provide access to the interior's beautiful rolling hills.

1. Londonderry Iron Mines
Londonderry

Before the middle of the 19th century, Londonderry was a small, quaint settlement based around logging and agriculture. But after the discovery of iron ore in 1844, it boomed, with a population of around 5,000 people by the century's end. Within the town were several large manufacturing plants centred around the steel plant and coke ovens built alongside modern-day Rockland Brook. The iron ore mine and its associated steel and processing plant were one of the largest and most advanced of its time.

HISTORY

Londonderry was first settled in 1762 after waterfront property along the Minas Basin became difficult to find. The first European settlers logged the area's abundant forests and grew crops on its flat terrain. As more people used the land, the area's mineral potential, specifically its iron ore reserves, became known. The most widely accepted story about the local discovery of iron ore is that in 1844 Charles Vance and John Philips discovered an iron ore seam near their sawmill on Great Village River. Prospectors and geologists flooded the region to confirm the findings and determine the potential for a mine. At the time, most iron used by the British colonies was imported from Sweden or Siberia. When news broke that the area contained large quantities of high-quality ore, both the Nova Scotia and British governments were enthusiastic.

In 1847, Charles Dickson Archibald, the representative of Colchester County, established a joint stock company under the name Londonderry Mining Company. The following year, the company purchased large plots of land in the vicinity of Great Village River and began mining in 1849. The iron-bearing ore was known as ankerite, a form of iron-rich rock known as dolomite, and siderite. As ore was extracted from underground shafts located near the river, it became clear that 70 per cent of the rocks was comprised of iron. Ore was extracted from shafts and underground

workings and towed by horse- and ox-drawn wagons to a port facility in the town of Great Village (also known as the Port of Londonderry).

Unlike many mines, which shipped raw ore to be processed elsewhere, the company established several mills and forges to allow the ore to be processed on site and shipped to market. Six Catalan forges and a puddling furnace were installed nearby. The ore was first crushed to the appropriate size, mixed with charcoal, and placed in the forges. An air blower, powered by the adjacent river, pumped air into the furnace to heat it enough to melt the iron. An iron bar was then placed in the forge, causing the iron in the ore to slowly adhere to it. This slow process was eventually determined not to be economically viable.

In 1851, the company reorganized. The newly named Acadian Iron Mining Company abandoned the forges in 1852 and installed a 10.7-metre-tall charcoal blast furnace to increase productivity. While the

new furnace was better than its predecessor at heating and extracting iron, only three years later the mine's output was still considered low, and new management took over. This was the beginning of a series of management and name changes: Acadian Iron and Steel Company in 1855, Acadian Iron Company in 1856, Acadian Charcoal Iron Company Limited in 1857, and Londonderry Iron Company in 1858.

Londonderry Iron Company constructed a railway line from the mines to the port, which increased the amount of ore that could be delivered to the shipping facilities and thus eliminating the need for slow-moving horse- or ox-pulled carts. In 1870, a steel plant with two smelting furnaces, three reheating furnaces, and two steam hammers was built. By this time, the Londonderry mines and processing facilities were among the most advanced in Canada.

In 1873, the mine was prospering, when the Intercolonial Railway

between Truro and Amherst was completed. The railway added a small branch line to Londonderry Station, opening the mine to new markets and sources of shipment. This attracted new businesses, including a large production facility to manufacture railcar wheels.

In 1874, the Londonderry mines, processing facilities, and all of the Londonderry Iron Company's assets were purchased by the newly incorporated Steel Company of Canada (not to be confused with the Steel Company of Canada [Stelco] which operates a steel mill in Hamilton, Ontario). As the iron mines and steel plants expanded, so did the community of Londonderry. The operations employed nearly 1,000 and enormous amounts of time and money were invested in upgrading and modernizing the steel plant.

Between 1874 and 1875, Dr. Williams Siemans conducted experiments at Londonderry to determine a more efficient method of making steel from molten iron. Although his findings would never directly benefit the Londonderry steel plant, he would use this information to develop an open-hearth converter known as the Siemens

Open Hearth process, a great leap in the process of manufacturing steel and one used around the world for decades.

To this point, the steel plants used coal and charcoal to produce the heat required to extract iron from ore and transform it into steel. But in the summer of 1876, 67 beehive-shaped brick coke ovens were installed in a single building on the east side of the steel plant. These 3.4-metre-diameter experimental ovens transformed coal into coke, a more efficient fuel that contains a higher water content and smaller carbon content than coal. The coke ovens were aligned in a battery linear pattern; a small railway system ran over the top of the ovens. Coal-carrying railway cars dumped coal (primarily from the coal mine in Springhill) into each oven through a small "charging hole" in the roof of the dome-shaped structures. After 40 hours of heating, the coal turned into coke.

In 1877, adjustments were made to the plant to use coke instead of coal. A 19.2-metre-tall blast furnace capable of melting the iron using coke and concentrated air was added. The addition of lime allowed the iron to flow into moulds, where it was cooled and readied for market. The hot material left in the furnace, known as slag, was transferred into railcars while it was still hot and dumped along the nearby Rockland Brook. When the glowing hot waste was dumped, the glow from the superheated mix could reportedly be seen for miles. The piles of slag eventually cooled and make up the strange rock formations visible along the river.

By 1878, with upgrades complete, Londonderry was once again one of the most modern mining and steel processing facilities on the continent. Nearly 1,200 people were hired by the plant itself and soon even more manufacturing plants were established, including a wire mill to produce steel fencing in 1887 and a pipe foundry in 1888. The population of Londonderry had grown to approximately 5,000 people.

Iron ore was being mined from open quarries, horizontal tunnels known as adits, and vertical mineshafts. The mines were concentrated in three distinct sites: Old Mountain Mine, East Mines, and West Mines.

Old Mountain Mines, some of the first mining locations in Londonderry, were located near the steel plants and modern-day Rockland Brook. East Mines, formerly known as Folly Mountain Mines, were located along Slack Brook, north of the town of Debert, and have been mined since 1875. West Mines, located between Cumberland Brook and Martin Brook, were the most productive and extensive: numerous vertical shafts led to extensive underground tunnels, in some cases up to 90 metres below the surface.

In 1887, a reorganized Steel Company of Canada formed the subsidiary company Londonderry Iron and Steel Company to oversee its operations at Londonderry. Mining was slowly coming to an end, however. In 1891, due to dwindling ore supplies in the area, the company imported iron ore from Torbrook in the Annapolis Valley to process at its steel plant. This lower-quality ore threatened the reputation of Londonderry ore. As high-grade ores were discovered in northern Ontario, and export costs continued to rise, the company ceased plant operations in 1898.

The operations lay dormant until the newly established Londonderry Iron and Mining Company purchased the mines and all its assets in 1902. After several small upgrades, all facilities were revitalized in 1904, except for the rolling mills and several workshops destroyed in a 1902 fire. In March 1908, however, the plant and all of its associated mines were shut down for the last time. Between 1849 and 1908, it is estimated that 1.8 million tonnes of ore were mined and processed in Londonderry.

This was the final blow for those living in the town. Many families moved away and soon Londonderry was almost a ghost town. In late May 1920, a house fire spread quickly due to dry conditions and high winds. Soon the entire town and any remaining structures at the steel plant were engulfed: 47 buildings, including four churches and a high school, were destroyed. For the few people living in the area, this was a reason to leave.

Since the fire, the town has been reclaimed by nature and the area is overgrown, with few remaining reminders of the town's past.

ABOUT THE AREA

Given the scale of operations at Londonderry, little remains of the boom town and steel plant. Londonderry Provincial Park, on Station Road, holds several mining artifacts: a mine cart, boiler, and flywheel. Along the road, several houses surrounded by large empty fields delineate the former townsite.

The steel plant and coke ovens were located near where Rockland Brook passes under Mines Bass River Road. From the road, it is difficult to miss the barren hills and strange rock formations along the east side of the river. White porous rocks are intermixed with thin black and rust-coloured layers. If the rock does not seem natural, that is because the hillside was formed from years of slag being dumped into the river. ATV trails wind through the area, taking advantage of the lifeless ground.

Trees and vegetation cover most of the area where the steel plant was located, with the only remnants being elongated mounds that likely supported railway lines and foundations. As you travel farther east, the beehive brick coke ovens are visible from Base Line Road. Now overgrown, they line the eastern side of the property and are unique to the province. Many have collapsed, but some remain in surprisingly good shape.

While most of the mines have been filled in or have collapsed over the past 114 years, open-pit quarries, former roads, and even the occasional tunnel entrance are still visible.

LONDONDERRY PROVINCIAL PARK: N 45.471783, W 63.596331
COKE OVENS: N 45.477184, W 63.601301
SLAG PIT: N 45.477872, W 63.608665

Travel 8.1 kilometres north of the TCH along Highway 104, turn onto Base Line Road, and continue for approximately 6.4 kilometres to the former ironworks site north of the road.

2. Berlin Wall

Cobequid Trail, Bible Hill

Hidden behind Dalhousie University's agricultural campus in Bible Hill are six concrete sections of the Berlin Wall. Erected in 1961 by the German Democratic Republic, the Berlin Wall split East and West Berlin, forcing the separation of families, countries, and differing political ideologies. For almost 30 years, it was a symbol of the Cold War. But in November 1989, after growing pressure from Germans and the deterioration of the Soviet Union, the wall was torn down, broken into pieces, and discarded.

Following its collapse, pieces were purchased and shipped around the world as monuments symbolizing this turbulent part of human history and the struggles faced by those living under communism. When Nova Scotian Martin Young had the opportunity to buy pieces of the wall while on a trip to Germany, he did so and shipped the sections to Truro in 2000, where they were displayed on Prince Street. Each section is 3.7 metres tall and 1.2 metres wide.

Some considered the wall an eyesore, and eventually the town decided to move the sections to the nearby agricultural campus where they could be seen by those walking along the Cobequid Trail, a former railway line turned recreation trail. The sections' new location is behind the campus's Haley Institute. A short path off the main trail leads to them and a small interpretive sign explains their significance. These six pieces of the Berlin Wall in Bible Hill are one of the largest single collections of the wall in the world.

 BERLIN WALL: N 45.370695, W 63.260339
Parking is available at N 45.371201, W 63.267550. Walk south along the Cobequid Trail for 550 metres to arrive at the site.

3. CFS Debert & the Diefenbunker
Debert

Nova Scotia played a critical role in World War II. Across the province were defensive fortifications, naval bases, and Air Force bases—the largest of which was in the small town of Debert. From 1938 to 1998, Debert's protected inland location along the national railway made it the ideal spot for a bustling military town. Operating first as an Air Force base and Army training site, it was at one time the last line of defence to ensure the region's continuity of government in the case of nuclear attack.

While Debert has returned to the quiet town it was before World War II, its landscape is riddled with remnants from this period, each with its own story.

PRE-WAR

Debert's military history begins with the innovations of air travel in the 1920s and 1930s. Air travel was in its infancy and, as more aircraft were put in service, the need for emergency landing sites grew. In the mid- to late 1930s, the Department of Transport and the Trans-Canada Air Lines chose Debert as an alternative landing site, and a small grass and gravel airstrip was constructed in the location of the modern-day airfield. Debert, located along the Intercolonial Railway, had a population of between 500 and 600; mining and farming were the primary sources of employment.

RCAF

This all changed in 1938 when the Royal Canadian Air Force (RCAF) chose the town as a site for a new ammunition storage facility. Its strategic inland location along the province's main railway line made Debert an ideal site from which to distribute ammunition and explosives throughout Atlantic Canada. The site's brick buildings, in place by the start of World War II, were enclosed by earthen berms capable of containing a blast if an accident were to occur. With the outbreak of war, the area bustled, as ammunition was received, inspected, and distributed. Several years later, the facility became known as the No. 16 X Depot.

In 1940, the RCAF paved over the original runway to create a triangular-shaped airfield consisting of three 1,500-metre-long runways. Renamed RCAF Debert, the airfield was home to a Commonwealth Air Training Plan facility run by the British Royal Air Force's No. 31 Operational Training Unit. Flight crews and pilots were trained on the latest aircraft, including the Lockheed Hudson, Avro Anson, and de Haviland Mosquito. The facility operated throughout the war, training pilots to patrol and protect Atlantic shipping convoys. In 1944, the unit was redesignated as the No. 7 Operational Training Unit.

CAMP DEBERT

But the largest change to Debert during World War II was the establishment of Camp Debert, a training facility and holding camp for soldiers heading to Europe. By mid-1940, thousands of troops were being transported overseas via Halifax. With space at a premium in the city, Debert's spacious location along the railway made it an ideal location for a marshalling area and training facility. On August 9, 1940, the 6th Field Company Canadian Engineers selected an area of land adjacent to the RCAF airfield.

The project employed more than 10,000, both civilian and military, to clear the land and construct roads, buildings, warehouses, mess halls, and a hospital. The quiet town of Debert became a bustling town capable of accommodating 20,000 soldiers and employing thousands of civilians for the remainder of the war. Restaurants, bars, theatres, and other modern amenities provided an economic boom for the entire region. Camp Debert and its adjacent RCAF base became Nova Scotia's largest military facility.

WAR'S END

At the end of the war in 1945, military operations at Debert were downsized. RCAF Debert and its ammunition storage facility were declared inactive but remained maintained in case it was required. Camp

Debert was used as a marshalling area for troops returning from the war. A small storage facility was constructed to handle the distribution of ammunition from fortifications across Nova Scotia to other sites in the Atlantic provinces, but most of Debert's facilities were decommissioned. The former base found a new, short-lived purpose in 1946 when buildings of the Nova Scotia Agricultural College caught fire and the facility was temporarily relocated to the former base's hospital.

REACTIVATION

As political tensions around the world rose again during the Cold War, the Debert facilities were reactivated. Camp Debert resumed operations as a training facility until the mid-1950s, when it phased out operations. After the opening of Camp Gagetown in New Brunswick, Camp Debert was officially shut down in 1960. Many of the town's buildings, barracks, and warehouses were demolished.

In the late 1940s, the RCAF airfield was reactivated for aircraft refuelling, training, and maintenance. The short-lived endeavour was phased out in 1954. In 1960, the Canadian Navy took over the airfield from the RCAF to be used as a training facility for aircraft carrier landings. Upgrades included sectioning off a portion of one of the runways to reflect the deck of an aircraft carrier. This new facility shut down in 1968, the same year Canada's last aircraft carrier, the HMCS *Bonaventure*, was retired.

DIEFENBUNKER: RENEWED LIFE

The closure of RCAF Debert and Camp Debert halted military operations in Debert. But escalating tensions between the US and the Soviet Union in the 1950s introduced the next and longest era in Debert's military history. In the late 1950s, the Canadian government's Emergency Measures Organization explored ways to ensure government continuity in the event of a nuclear war. Debert was selected as one of six strategic locations across Canada to construct a large underground complex that would protect government officials and act as a national communication centre. As much of Debert was still owned by the military, it remained a safe distance from high-value targets such as Saint John and Halifax. As well, Debert's location on the windward side of the area's prevailing winds meant that radioactive fallout would be minimal. Officially these complexes were named the Regional Emergency Government Headquarters but were later known as the "Diefenbunkers" after Prime Minister John Diefenbaker, who first established them.

Construction began in 1960 on the former Camp Debert site. Except for several support structures at the surface, the complex

consisted of a 6,000-square-metre, two-storey bunker able to support up to 350 people for 30 days. Designed to be completely self-contained, the facility had power-generation facilities, freshwater reserves, and an air filtration system capable of protecting its occupants against radioactive, biological, and chemical contaminants. The bunker also housed a CBC studio with pre-recorded emergency announcements, an operation centre for the Army's Eastern Command Centre and RCMP coordination, and the Provincial Warning Centre. The facility, capable of withstanding a nuclear blast from fewer than 3 kilometres away, was operated by the Canadian Corps of Signals.

But technology evolved quickly through the Cold War and by the time the bunker opened in 1964, it was already deemed ineffective against modern missile technology. The site did not sit idle, however, and operated as the provincial warning system and as a military communications centre staffed by the 720 Communications Squadron. As the operations centre for the radio transmitter and receiver stations built in Masstown and Great Village, it provided critical communication support to the Canadian Armed Forces.

In 1969, the Royal Canadian Navy, Canadian Army, and Royal Canadian Air Force merged to form the Canadian Armed Forces and Debert's remaining facilities were renamed Canadian Forces Base Debert. In the mid-1970s, bunker activity diminished as new technology made its facilities obsolete once again.

CFS DEBERT DEEMED SURPLUS

In 1971, the Department of Defence declared all facilities at CFS Debert as surplus. Much of Camp Debert was redeveloped into the Debert Air Industrial Park as several companies used the remaining military structures as warehouses, garages, and training facilities. The airfield was maintained and operated as a small municipal airfield.

CLOSURE

An exception, the Debert Diefenbunker remained the last of CFS Debert under military control until the mid-1990s. Between 1971 and its official decommissioning in 1998, the facility was a storage and training facility for a militia reserves unit and a relay station for a satellite communications station near Folly Mountain. Its decommissioning marked the end of CFS Debert. All facilities were transferred to the

development authority Colchester Park for redevelopment.

Debert is again a quiet town. Most of what remains Camp Debert is operated as an industrial park, except for some of the base's former barracks and housing, which have been repurposed for a variety of uses. The airfield is home to several private aircraft and the Debert Flight Centre. Beginning in 1985, it was used as a Cadet glider flying training centre, where Royal Canadian Air Cadets could train to fly glider aircraft and earn their Transport Canada Glider Pilot License. This last connection to its RCAF past ended as a result of downsizing the nationwide program in 2022.

In December 2008, the Colchester Regional Development Association sold the Debert Diefenbunker to a private firm which wanted to use it for computer data storage and a security centre. The restored bunker remains under private ownership and hosts birthday parties, corporate retreats, and data storage servers. Tours are available.

⌖ CFS DEBERT & THE DIEFENBUNKER: **N 45.422924, W 63.449329**
From the TCH (Highway 104), take Exit 13 and travel north on MacElmon Road for 3.7 kilometres. Turn onto Ventura Drive, which passes through the former base before reaching the airfield.

4. Economy's Bombing Observation Tower

Economy

During World War II, convoys of ships transporting troops, supplies, and weapons to Europe were under constant attack by German U-boats. Although they were escorted by heavily armed naval ships, the Air Force was also assigned to protect the convoys as far out as modern aircraft could fly. These assignments meant that new pilots and flight crews had to be trained, leading to the establishment of the British Royal Air Force's No. 31 Operational Training Unit at Debert and No. 36 Operational Training Unit in Greenwood. Crews were trained for anti-submarine patrols and participated in live bombing training over Cobequid Bay.

To observe and monitor the flight crews' progress, two 9-metre-tall wooden towers were built along the shores of the Minas Basin: one along the south shore of the basin, another along the shore in the community of Economy. The towers operated both as a monitoring station and training centre for observers that would direct aircraft pilots to designated targets.

The towers were abandoned at the end of the war. The observation tower on the basin's south side was moved to the Greenwood Military Aviation Museum, where it remains. The Economy tower remained in place, but over time, coastal erosion caused its foundations to tilt at a steep angle for several years. Eventually, residents transported the tower to the side of the Glooscap Trail (Trunk 2), where it was restored and transformed into a visitors' centre for the Cliffs of Fundy UNESCO Global Geopark.

 OBSERVATION TOWER: N 45.384523, W 63.916241

The building, now part of the Cliffs of Fundy Geopark Welcome Centre, is located in the community of Economy along Highway 2.

5. Tunnels of Wentworth Valley

Wentworth Valley

INTRODUCTION

In the mid-19th century, railway fever spread across North America. Railways moved people, goods, and services farther and quicker than any other previous transportation method, and as the population and economies of Upper and Lower Canada grew, so did the importance of connecting them to the east coast. The railway line was also important to military activities and trade, particularly in winter, when ships could not access the St. Lawrence River.

The first survey for the Intercolonial Railway was completed in 1846, but no construction followed. In 1858, completed sections of the Nova Scotia Railway included a railway line from Halifax to Truro.

The remaining section of the Intercolonial Railway, from Truro to Moncton, did not begin for another decade. The route would be fairly inexpensive due to generally flat, forested landscape—except for the Cobequid Mountains. In 1865, engineer Sandford Fleming, who was hired to survey possible routes over the mountains, focused on the Wentworth Valley.

In 1872, Fleming was appointed chief engineer of the Intercolonial Railway construction, and work began on the Wentworth Valley section. The International Contract Company was hired to oversee the project.

TUNNEL BROOK

After departing Truro, the railway passed through Debert before reaching the Folly River Valley at Folly Mountain. A steel bridge would traverse the valley but, to build its western abutment, a small river named McElmon Brook had to be filled in. Fleming had a reputation for designing beautifully crafted stone culverts to allow the passage of water. But the location of the river at the bottom of a deep gorge, combined with a tight budget, forced Fleming to be creative.

Instead of building an expensive culvert, a tunnel was excavated through the solid rock of the gorge's eastern wall to divert the river eastward and into Folly River. As railway construction continued, workers excavated a 24-metre tunnel through the sandstone and conglomerate rocks. Over the years, erosion has left smooth, rounded walls.

The tunnel still redirects water from the railway line's embankment 30 metres above it. The bridge, tunnel, and amount of backfill needed to fill in McElmon Book were engineering marvels, but the most challenging section of the railway line was yet to come.

⊕ TUNNEL BROOK: N 45.447156, W 63.526337

The tunnel is best seen from the east side of Highway 4, near the crossing of McElmon Brook (commonly called Tunnel Brook), approximately 3.9 kilometres north of Exit 11 on the TCH (Highway 104). Parking is available along the road and caution should be exercised when walking on the shoulder.

After the bridge over the Folly River Valley, the railway line continued farther west to access the Londonderry iron mines and ironworks (page 366). From there, the line turned north before reaching Folly Lake and the Wentworth Valley. This stretch of railway, or Section 7, travelled along the west side of the valley, near the top of the mountains. It was the most challenging and expensive section to construct because of the many deep river gullies it had to cross.

Four large embankments were needed to traverse the river valleys. To lower construction cost and allow the free passage of water, a tunnel was excavated through the bedrock beneath each embankment. The tunnels reached lengths of more than 100 metres. The tunnels were incredible accomplishments of their time.

HIGGINS BROOK TUNNEL & WENTWORTH FALLS

Coming from the south, the first and most accessible tunnel in the area was Higgins Brook Tunnel. Carved through solid bedrock similar to that around Tunnel Brook, the 3-metre-wide tunnel is more than 130 metres long. Once the water flows through the tunnel, it cascades over Wentworth Falls. Above the tunnel and waterfall, a large, backfilled embankment supports the railway high on the hill.

Along the railway, private property and difficult terrain make most of the Wentworth Valley Tunnels inaccessible or very difficult to access. Higgins Brook Tunnel and Wentworth Falls are an exception and have become a desired short hike. The waterfall offers a popular spot for photographs and picnics.

 TUNNEL & FALLS: N 45.587931, W 63.563469

The trailhead (N 45.588473, W 63.561003) is approximately 20 kilometres north of the TCH (Highway 104), on the west side of Highway 4. With little room to park a car along Highway 4, use caution to ensure the safety of all travellers. From the trailhead, an easy 200-metre walk leads to the base of the falls.

SMITH BROOK TUNNEL

The greatest challenge for engineers of the Intercolonial Railway through the Wentworth Valley was crossing Smith Brook valley, which

was larger than others traversed by the railway. Smith Brook often transformed into a raging torrent, described by engineers as a "miniature Niagara." A feasibility study determined the cost and effectiveness of a bridge over the valley; an embankment was deemed the most cost effective. Work began in June 1870 and took two years to complete. The final embankment was 335 metres long and 32 metres high and was composed of approximately 360,000 tonnes of backfill.

As for the river, a 108-metre-long, 3-metre-wide tunnel was excavated beneath the embankment, through hard diorite bedrock. This embankment and tunnel are considered by many historians and engineers as the most impressive construction done in British North America to that time. Historian Jay Underwood says that the Smith Brook project deserves national recognition for its engineering accomplishment. This is undisputed by all who witness this isolated section of railway and tunnel.

The rounded tunnel is backdropped by the towering embankment. As water flows out of the tunnel, it descends over a waterfall into a small gorge. After two or three more drops, the water flows into the valley. The area is now private property. The Smith Brook Tunnel and embankment remain an engineering marvel that overcame one of the greatest challenges in constructing the Intercolonial Railway through Nova Scotia.

 SMITH BROOK TUNNEL: **N 45.595456, W 63.569384**

OTHER NOTABLE TUNNELS

As the railway turned west again, leaving the Wentworth Valley, it crossed another tunnel and embankment, constructed on Wheatstone Brook and resembling other tunnels on the line. At the next tunnel, at Caldwell Brook, a 91-metre-long tunnel was excavated through weak limestone and brittle granite; a 64-metre-long section near its centre required the addition of 18-inch brick columns for structural support. This was the only tunnel in the valley that needed additional support.

An estimated 750,000 cubic metres of overburden and over 30,000 cubic metres of rock were excavated for the construction of the line through the Wentworth Valley.

On October 11, 1872, the Wentworth Valley section of the railway was officially opened; the entire Intercolonial Railway officially opened on July 1, 1876. In 1915, the Intercolonial Railway was integrated into the Canadian Government Railway before finally being owned by the Canadian National Railway in 1923.

Thousands of people drive through the scenic Wentworth Valley each year, admiring its rolling hills and thick forests. The railway is set back from the highway; its tunnels are overlooked relics of the historic railway and a reminder of the incredible effort required to connect Nova Scotia with the rest of Canada.

6. Waterfalls of the Cobequid Hills
Economy to Parrsboro

The Glooscap Trail (Highway 2) is a scenic drive between the communities of Great Village and Parrsboro. Following the northern shores of the Minas Basin, the road travels along the flat coastal terrace at the base of the Cobequid Hills. Because it is encompassed within the Cliffs of Fundy UNESCO Global Geopark, it is no surprise that the area contains globally significant geologic wonders. But while many of these sites are marked and advertised, many more are either unknown or too far off the beaten path to gain the recognition that they deserve. This is especially true for the region's many inland waterfalls that cascade over the Cobequid Hills.

The Cobequid Hills parallel the shoreline, roughly following the Cobequid-Chebucto Fault Zone which marks the boundary between two former microcontinents. Composed of sedimentary and igneous rocks, the hills were likely once much taller before being eroded by glaciers during the last ice age. As the glaciers receded, a system of south-flowing rivers was left to drain the inland lakes and bogs before descending the steep hills and flowing into the bay, leaving dramatic river valleys and spectacular waterfalls. The landscape is difficult to traverse, but those willing to explore will be rewarded.

HARRINGTON FALLS

A short but challenging hike leads to Harrington Falls. Formed at the confluence of the west branch of Harrington River and Harrington River itself, the tributary plunges over a ragged 10-metre cliff into a pool of dark water. Confined to a narrow valley, hidden under a thick canopy of trees, the falls and surrounding land are locally known as the "Garden of Eden," reflecting the site's tranquil and peaceful nature. Except for yellow reflector tape, the trail is well hidden. Hurricane Fiona (2022) left fallen trees, adding to the difficulty of accessing the site. Near the falls, visitors can explore a small cave carved into the cliff and possibly glimpse a second waterfall above Harrington Falls.

 HARRINGTON FALLS: N 45.456932, W 64.119757

The trailhead (N 45.453494, W 64.112935) is on Lynn Road, 4.3 kilometres north of Highway 2. A difficult 900-metre hike is required to reach the falls.

EAST MOOSE RIVER FALLS

East Moose River Falls is believed to be the highest waterfall on mainland Nova Scotia. The waterfall's location at the bottom of a narrow, steep gorge makes it difficult to access. Before plunging over a 40-metre cliff, the river is confined within a narrow gorge. But at the cliff edge, it spreads out into a fan-shaped flow as it falls. For most of the year, the river's water levels are high, especially so during spring runoff and after heavy rainfalls. During these times, the mist produced by the plunging water encompasses the narrow gorge. The result: a wet, moss-covered environment that enhances the site's beauty and potential danger, especially during the cold winter months when ice accumulates on the riverbanks and surrounding trees.

Following heavy rains, a second waterfall forms on the adjacent, larger cliff face. While this waterfall does not discharge nearly the same amount of water, it dwarfs East Moose River Falls, plunging from almost 155 metres above sea level to just 50 metres before it reaches the river. The steep trail has few handholds, especially as you approach the river approximately 120 metres below the trailhead.

 EAST MOOSE RIVER FALLS: N 45.441057, W 64.176636

Travel along Highway 2, turn north onto a gravel road (N 45.419484, W 64.193036) near the crossing of Moose River. Continue on the rough road for 4.5 kilometres before turning east. Continue another 3.2 kilometres to the trailhead (N 45.440829, W 64.181562). A difficult 500-metre hike is required to reach the base of the falls.

OTHER FALLS

Many of the other falls are similar to the two listed above: they are found in narrow valleys carved over thousands of years. This also makes them difficult to access. Farther east is North River Falls, for many years a popular destination for avid hikers. This changed after land disputes with a property owner discouraged visitors. Nonetheless, many make the dangerous trek following the course of the river.

 NORTH RIVER FALLS: N 45.434977, W 64.081234

7. Parrsboro Dam

New Prospect

West of Parrsboro in a narrow valley is the picturesque 19th-century Parrsboro Dam, a moss-covered stone dam and perhaps one of the most scenic waterfalls in Nova Scotia. While just a short hike from the nearest highway, many pass by this hidden wonder.

The first Europeans to settle in the Parrsboro area were believed to be the Acadians who arrived in the late 17th century. Following the Acadians' expulsion from Nova Scotia, the land was granted to settlers from New England. The area's population grew slowly, until the establishment of shipbuilding in the 19th century on the tidal shores of Parrsboro. This raised the demand for a reliable source of fresh water for drinking, cooking, and fire-fighting. A site was selected west of Parrsboro, approximately 65 metres above the nearest road. This elevation allowed the water to be gravity-fed to the town, and the narrow valley in which the river was situated meant that a dam would not have to be wide to create a reservoir.

The dam was constructed of rectangular stone held in place by cement. The stones were carted up the hill by horse or ox and lowered into place by makeshift crane and pulley systems. At the centre of the beautifully crafted 5-metre-tall, 25-metre-wide dam, a spillway allowed water to flow over it, cascading over the staircase-like structure, a design which prevented unwanted erosion of its foundation. On the dam's east side was an intake structure, along with a small housing which allowed access to the control valve. From there, an iron pipe transported water down the hill to the surrounding community.

The water supply was likely used until the 1970s, when personal wells eliminated the need for it. It is also likely that the dam was nearing the end of its service life. The structure had begun to show its age and, over the century that the river had been dammed, large deposits of sediment had reduced the amount of water that the reservoir could

hold. Despite this, the dam remains a popular destination for hikers. This forgotten piece of Parrsboro history is best seen in the spring when water levels are high. Later in the summer or during dry periods, the water level in the reservoir lowers, eliminating the water falling over it. Lower water levels provide a view of the back side of the dam and the former water intake. The forested hike also offers a glimpse of scenic Prospect Falls, a series of waterfalls confined to narrow canyons along the way to the dam.

 PARRSBORO DAM: N 45.433457, W 64.268866
Approximately 5 kilometres east of Parrsboro, turn onto Prospect Road and the trailhead (N 45.426721, W 64.272933). A 900-metre hike along an ATV trail leads to the dam.

8. MV *Kipawo*
Parrsboro, Cumberland County

Ferries and coastal boats have transported people and cargo across the Minas Basin since the mid-18th century, when they were first built by Acadian settlers. For many years, ferry services were the only means of travelling to and from the region. Over time, railway lines and road networks changed the ferry's primary use. Once the only means of delivering food and supplies to isolated communities, they soon became a vital link between communities on the northern and southern shores of the Minas Basin and Nova Scotia's Bay of Fundy.

Since its establishment in 1764, over 33 ferries have serviced the route, with the last being the *Kipawo*. After serving the communities of Kingsport, Parrsboro, and Wolfville for 16 years, the ferry had several owners until it ran aground on Newfoundland's east coast. The *Kipawo*'s significance to the communities of the Minas Basin inspired a group of passionate volunteers to save the ship, eventually having it towed to Parrsboro where it was incorporated into the exterior deck of Ship's Company Theatre—making for a curious sight.

THE STORY

The *Kipawo* was constructed in 1925 by the Saint John Drydock & Shipbuilding Company in Saint John, New Brunswick. The 37-metre-long, 8-metre-wide steel hull vessel had two four-cylinder 240-horsepower diesel engines. It was one of the first all-steel, diesel-powered ships constructed at the shipyard. The ship was designed to carry more than 120 passengers and up to eight vehicles, which were loaded by a sling and cradle system that lifted vehicles onto the deck.

The ship's owners, Dominion Atlantic Railway, commissioned the ship on April 1, 1926, and named it MV *Kipawo*. The name is a portmanteau of the first two letters of the three ports it was to service: Kingsport, Parrsboro, and Wolfville. The *Kipawo* was requisitioned by the Dominion

Atlantic Railway to replace Prince Albert on the Kingsport-Parrsboro-Wolfville route, operating from April 1 to December 31 each year. During the winter, the ship was moored in Digby, where it could be safely stored, away from the higher tides experienced in the Minas Basin.

The *Kipawo*, commonly referred to as *The Kip*, expedited the journey of train passengers travelling primarily between Wolfville and Parrsboro. Instead of the long trip around the basin via Truro, the ferry offered a more direct route. However, because of the wide fluctuations

in tides in the basin, the ferry's schedule (and as a consequence the local passenger train schedule) regularly fluctuated as well. The ferry service opened new forms of tourism to areas such as Parrsboro, with large influxes of people in the summer visiting friends, family, and cottages on the other side of the bay. The ferry became an important source of revenue for businesses and families.

The *Kipawo* operated on the Minas Basin for 16 years before it was called into service by the Royal Canadian Navy on April 23, 1941. The ship was sent to Montreal, where it was retrofitted to become a tender for maintaining and servicing anti-submarine nets. Next, it was ordered to Bell Island, Newfoundland, where it serviced the anti-submarine nets placed around the iron ore shipping port. Following the war, the ship was returned to its owners but improved transportation networks around the Minas Basin made the former ferry route redundant.

As a result, in 1946 the Dominion Atlantic Railway auctioned the ship. Recognizing the ferry's significance—the last of 33 ferries to serve the basin over 177 years—the Town of Parrsboro was eager to purchase the *Kipawo* and transform it into a monument or museum. It was outbid by a small amount. The *Kipawo*'s new owners were the Newfoundland-based company Crosbie and Company Ltd., which took possession on September 20, 1946, and used it as a ferry between Bell Island and Portugal Cove in Newfoundland. In 1952, the ship changed owners again; under the Terra Nova Transportation Company, it continued to operate as a ferry between Bell Island and Portugal Cove.

In 1974, the ferry was purchased by Fogo Transport Ltd. to transport passengers and supplies to Fogo Island on Newfoundland's north coast. The endeavour was short-lived, and the ferry was sold in 1975 to Bonavista Boat Tours, who converted it into a ferry to operate in Terra Nova National Park.

In 1977, the ferry took refuge from a storm in the community of Bonavista. That night the storm broke its moorings, pushing it aground in the harbour. The ship was abandoned there for four years, slowly rusting and enduring constant beating from waves and sea ice.

News of the condition of the *Kipawo* reached Nova Scotia, where a group of volunteers led by Jack Sheriff fundraised to return it to the Minas Basin. The concerned citizens formed the *Kipawo* Heritage Society of Wolfville and dreamed of transforming the ship into a permanent museum or cultural centre or restoring it completely so that it could again traverse the Bay of Fundy. A feasibility study led to the decision to transform or incorporate the ship into a museum once the funds could be raised. The group gained enough support to move forward, in large

part thanks to the Canadian Coast Guard's agreeing to tow the ship from Newfoundland to Nova Scotia once it was suited for travel.

Repairs were made to the *Kipawo* in 1981 and 1982 and later that year it was towed from Bonavista to Dartmouth and later delivered to Parrsboro. The Town of Parrsboro planned to turn the ship into a museum. After this idea fell through, it was given to the Ship's Theatre Company. A drydock was excavated at its current location and the ship was floated to its final resting place. Over time, its hull was buried and, in 2004, the theatre expanded its facilities, sheltering the ship and assimilating it into an open deck and stage.

The preservation of the *Kipawo* was first dreamed of 76 years ago, but it took a group of volunteers who recognized its significance and were ready to dedicate time and money to bring it home. Thanks to their hard work, the last of the Minas Basin ferries rests along the shores of the Bay of Fundy, a memorial to the former ferry service.

 MV *KIPAWO*: N 45.400928, W 64.328836

The ship can be seen at the Ship's Company Theatre on Main Street in the community of Parrsboro.

9. Wards Falls & the Diligent River Slot Canyon

Yorke Settlement/Wharton

The Wards Falls hiking trail winds through a narrow V-shaped valley, roughly following the Diligent River banks. The easy 3.5-kilometre-long trail crosses the river several times before the valley abruptly ends at a vertical rock face. Near its base is the 3- to 4-metre-high Wards Falls. The water tumbles from the base of a narrow slot in the cliff that continues as high as you can see. Although the falls are worth the hike, the slot canyon behind them is even more impressive.

Slot canyons are formed from the gradual erosion of a river on bedrock. Most of the area's rock is comprised of 500-million-year-old metamorphosized sedimentary rocks, which is very susceptible to erosion. In the case of the Diligent River Slot Canyon, the river, once located above the cliff, possibly produced several waterfalls as it descended the valley. The river broke down the rock beneath it, eventually creating a canyon.

The canyon is easily missed, even by those hiking to Wards Falls. Although the falls are easy to view and photograph, above them the canyon quickly disappears from sight. Those who make the perilous climb above the falls will find that the narrow canyon continues for 300 to 400 metres and is filled with multiple waterfalls and deep pools.

Other notable canyons are Prospect Falls (page 399), a series of falls confined to several short slot canyons, and the George Fraser Slot Canyon found farther west along the George Fraser Brook.

 FALLS & CANYON: N 45.447436, W 64.419467

Approximately 7.1 kilometres west of the community of Parrsboro, turn onto a small road (N 45.418412, W 64.427727) and continue for 630 metres to the trailhead (N 45.423297, W 64.424500).

10. Eatonville

Cape Chignecto Provincial Park

Cape Chignecto's vast old-age forest has long attracted people interested in its logging and shipbuilding potential. For a period of time, these industries created one community on the western side of Cape Chignecto but located in two areas: one part of the community was on a harbour, the other inland among the forest. As Eatonville was a logging town, many of its buildings and infrastructure were built of wood, but little remains. Among the beautiful inland landscape and coastal area are reminders of this once-thriving community.

HISTORY

Daniel Nicholas is believed to have operated the first sawmill out of the tidal estuary at the mouth of Eatonville Brook. A new road to the region attracted people such as Henry A. Eaton to the area. In 1848, Eaton purchased land away from the coastline, at the confluence of several small brooks, including Eatonville Brook. Eaton established a small sawmill on the river that would become Eatonville's first building.

Seeing the area's logging potential on a visit in 1864, two of Eaton's cousins, David R. Eaton and Charles F. Eaton, purchased the land surrounding the estuary in 1870 and established a sawmill there. The Eatons' large seaside sawmill worked in tandem with Henry Eaton's farther inland. The Eatons built cottages and housing for the workers and their families in addition to a store, school, and church. By 1873, 200 people were employed by the operation, which by this time also included shipbuilding, with the tidal-influenced estuary making the perfect drydock.

Eatonville harbour was the location of a large steam-powered sawmill, several stores, a blacksmith shop, and housing for approximately 100 people. Several kilometres inland, on Eatonville Brook, was Eatonville village, also known as "Old Town," with another sawmill, a school, a church, a post office, and housing for 250 people. The town

steadily attracted more people and businesses from the surrounding area, helping it to grow into the late 19th century.

The large sawmill along the water received logs from Eatonville village and the interior through two methods. During times of high water, such as in the spring and early summer, logs were driven down Eatonville Brook using dams, sluices, and flumes. To combat lower water levels throughout the year, in 1893 a tramway with wooden poles as rails was constructed. It connected both two parts of the community and allowed horses to tow carts of cut lumber along it, eliminating dependence on the nearby river.

The Eatons' operation boomed: lumber was shipped to markets across Canada and the US and the local shipyard produced world-class ships. Despite this, however, the Eatons sold the operation and all of its assets in 1897 to A.C. and C.W. Elderkin of Parrsboro. Following this, the sawmill operation was owned by J. Newton Pugsley of Parrsboro in 1907, James W. Kirkpatrick in 1912, and Hunt and Draper of Maine in 1919. With each change of owners, the mill experienced upgrades and expansions to keep pace with modern technology. One of the largest of these projects was the construction of a brick chimney in 1910 during upgrades to the Eatonville harbour sawmill. Similarly, as the number of ships using the harbour increased, so too did the demand for a navigation aid to guide ships in and out of the dangerous harbour. Following a series of accidents and ships running aground, a lighthouse was built at the government wharf in 1909.

Eatonville's end came in 1920 when depleting forestry reserves and a drastic decline in the demand for wooden ships forced the owners to terminate operations. The area's forest was used by several companies following the abandonment of the sawmill and settlement, but instead of using the forest for timber, it now produced pulpwood by the Minas Basin Pulp and Power Company, Hollingsworth and Whitney, Scott Paper Limited, and other companies.

Logging ended in the early 1980s, and, in 1989, the Nova Scotia government purchased the land and officially designated it Cape

Chignecto Provincial Park in 1998. While the park is focused on the Three Sister Rock Formations and nearby geologic sites, a hiking trail that partly follows the old tramway helps visitors to explore the area.

ABOUT THE AREA

Because most of the buildings and structures associated with Eatonville were built of wood, little remains. Following the end of sawmill operations, many of the houses, buildings, and equipment were removed, especially those in Eatonville village. Near the harbour, however, are the former stone-lined road and wooden bridge, which likely belonged to the tramway which connected the two sections of the community. The sawmill, located on the south side of the harbour, was accessible only by traversing Eatonville Brook during low tide. There, foundations are partly visible with the remnants of the wharves that once lined the harbour. Caution should be taken when exploring the area; at high tide, the harbour is almost completely flooded, preventing access or escape to those who do not plan ahead.

To the north of Eatonville harbour is the Three Sisters, a series of sea stacks best seen from the water and several geologically significant sites. To the north, near the parking area for the provincial park is a small interpretation centre that describes many of the region's historic and natural wonders.

 EATONVILLE: **N 45.420006, W 64.918228**

From the community of Eatonville, drive along Apple River Road for 11.3 kilometres. Follow the signs to the Three Sisters, turn east and continue for 1.3 kilometres to the parking lot and trailhead (N 45.423218, W 64.910209). A short, well-maintained trail leads to the viewpoint.

11. Chignecto Marine Transport Railway

Fort Lawrence to Tidnish

Despite never being completed, the Chignecto Marine Transport Railway was an engineering marvel. Created by civil engineer Henry Ketchum, the project was the closest Nova Scotia came to transporting ships across the 27-kilometre-wide isthmus that separates the Bay of Fundy and Northumberland Strait. After more than three years of construction, the project was nearly 80 per cent complete when political and financial troubles halted it. The project has been recognized as a National Civil Engineering Site and many remnants lie along the former railway line, including pieces of drydocks, engine and machinery housing, and a spectacular stone culvert.

HISTORY

The dream of crossing the narrow Chignecto isthmus by ship had long been on the minds of businesspeople and sailors. Since the late 17th century, the possibility of constructing a canal across the gap to make shipping around Nova Scotia more efficient had been considered, but it stalled due to the challenges of building a canal that could accommodate the differences in tidal height and timing between the Bay of Fundy and the Northumberland Strait. Despite numerous studies, and the establishment of a company to build the canal, such a project always seemed to be both too challenging and too expensive.

This changed when Ketchum drafted designs for a potential marine railway to carry wooden ships from one body of water to another. Ketchum proposed to use a drydock and hoist system to lift ships out of the water, where they would be placed on specially designed railcars. Two locomotives, each on their own designated track, would tow the ships across the 27-kilometre stretch of land, lower them into the water, again by a drydock and hoist system. Known as a marine railway, the system would be much cheaper than excavating a canal.

Working almost entirely on his own, Ketchum produced proposals, detailed designs, and promotional content to start the project. As a testament to his commitment, when, two years after creating the material, much of it was lost in the Great Saint John Fire of 1877, Ketchum recreated the lost documents. In 1881, he sought federal government approval and funding. In 1882, the Chignecto Marine Transport Railway Company was established, with Ketchum as the project's managing director. While waiting for project approval, Ketchum approached private investors in London, who agreed to finance the project. With the help of former Nova Scotia premier and then Minister of Railway and Canals Charles Tupper, the project was approved and the government committed to an annual subsidiary for the railway's operation.

In 1887, the Montreal-based John G. Meiggs & Co. was hired to begin construction. Over the next three and a half years, between 4,000 and 5,000 people were employed to construct the two drydocks, hoist and engine buildings, a large stone culvert over the Tidnish River, and the 27-kilometre-long railway line. Work progressed efficiently, with 80 per cent of the project done by July 1891, including 25 kilometres of groundwork completed, 21 kilometres of track laid, and the Fort Lawrence drydock constructed. The remaining railway line and the Tidnish drydock were expected to be completed in 1892.

In 1891, however, the project halted due to financing troubles. The London-based investors Ketchum had secured could no longer fund the project. In addition, Ketchum had lost federal government support due to the increased efficiency of rail travel to transport goods across the country and the increasing popularity of steel ships, which would be too heavy for a marine railway. In 1892, a House of Commons vote ended the project. Ketchum did not lose hope, however, but after spending the next four years attempting to rebuild support and investment, he died suddenly on September 8, 1896.

ABOUT THE AREA

Nova Scotia's industrial history has had no shortage of megaprojects that promised to change the way people moved across the province. But Ketchum's dream of building a marine railway across the Chignecto isthmus was one of the most ambitious, especially considering that it was the brainchild of one person: Henry Ketchum. Over time, people learned to appreciate not only Ketchum's effort but that of thousands of workers. In 1989, the project was designated a National Historic Civil Engineering Site and, since then, much of the railway line has been transformed into public parks and recreation areas that preserve what little survives for future generations.

RAILWAY LINE

The double railway line that would have transported ships across the 27-kilometre stretch of bog and wetland was challenging. Many kilometres of unsuitable ground had to be excavated and replaced with rock because of the threat of subsidence over time. In one location, an 18-metre-deep hole was excavated and replaced with ballast rock to prevent the railway line from sinking. Once the groundwork was complete, dual standard-gauge railway lines were installed, spaced 5.5 metres apart.

FORT LAWRENCE AND TIDNISH DRYDOCKS

At Fort Lawrence and Tidnish, stone drydocks were constructed along the shores of the Bay of Fundy and Northumberland Strait respectively. Each drydock housed a 72- by 19-metre steel frame that could be raised and lowered by 10 hoists. In addition to the drydocks, a large building contained the engines and machinery needed to power the hoist. The

hoist system was designed to lift ships weighing up to 1,800 tonnes. Construction of the Fort Lawrence drydock was especially difficult due to its location at the mouth of two tidal-influenced rivers. Along the river's muddy shores, a 15-metre pit was excavated to construct the stone drydock.

The Fort Lawrence drydock has been reclaimed by the river and tides, leaving a muddy pit. Nearby, many of the stones that once made up the drydock are piled along the banks of the Missaguash River. Adjacent to the former drydock are the foundations and chimney of the hoist engine building and other artifacts of the project. Looking northward, it is still possible to see the former railway bed, which continues in a straight line to Tidnish.

While even less remains of the Tidnish drydock, the area has since been turned into the Tidnish Dock Provincial Park. Several plaques denote the project's significance, and along the waterfront are the remains of former wharves and stone. It is believed that most of the stone of the Tidnish drydock was later used during renovations to the ferry terminal at Cape Tormentine.

TINDISH DOCK PROVINCIAL PARK: **N 45.996399, W 64.009003**
FORT LAWRENCE DRYDOCK: **N 45.837379, W 64.273087**
Travel approximately 4 kilometres west of Amherst on the TCH; take Exit 1 and continue south for 1.8 kilometres to the trailhead (N 45.840268, W 64.267442). Walk south to the site and the shores of the Bay of Fundy. Do not trespass.

TIDNISH RIVER STONE CULVERT

The relatively flat landscape of the Chignecto isthmus meant that there were few obstructions or rivers that had to be crossed—except the Tidnish River, near the railway's northern terminus. Because of the width and weight of the locomotives, it was decided that a stone culvert be built for the river to pass through. The railway was to cross at a curve in the river, allowing designers to construct the culvert through a nearby riverbank. This eliminated the difficult task of building the culvert over the flowing river and, instead, once the culvert was completed, the river would be filled in during the construction of the railway, creating an earthen dam that would redirect the river through the culvert.

Stonemasons from Scotland were hired to construct the culvert. The cut rocks were quarried and prepared in Scotland, shipped to Tidnish, and assembled. Despite being designed and prepared overseas, the stone culvert was reportedly constructed with almost perfect precision. Adding to this accomplishment was the fact that the stone tunnel was constructed by hand with the help of temporary wooden cranes built on the site. The magnificent stone culvert is now found below the Henry Ketchum Trail, which follows the former railway line. While traces of the stone culvert can be seen from the trail, several small, unmaintained

trails exist along its sides that provide access to the top of the culvert. Nearby a suspension bridge crosses the original path of the river that was to be filled in before work on the project was halted.

 CULVERT: N 45.976274, W 64.043630

From Highway 366 in the community of Tidnish, turn onto Ketchum Drive and continue for 300 metres to the trailhead (N 45.975169, W 64.045516). Hike along the trail for approximately 200 metres to the culvert. Continue for another 100 metres to the Tidnish Suspension Bridge.

FALLS & CANYON: N 45.447436, W 64.419467

Approximately 7.1 kilometres west of the community of Parrsboro, turn onto a small road (N 45.418412, W 64.427727) and continue for 630 metres to the trailhead (N 45.423297, W 64.424500). A 3.3-kilometre hike leads to the falls.

12. Slade Lake & Oxford's Karst Topography

Oxford

Nova Scotia has more than its share of caves, sinkholes, and other landforms known as karst topography. But near the small town of Oxford, a corridor of karst features stands out from all others in the province. While much remains to be learned about the region's geology, here weak carbonate rocks make contact with an overlying layer of sandstone and conglomerate to produce some of Nova Scotia's most obscure and dangerous features.

SLADE LAKE

The strangest of these formations is Slade Lake, located approximately 2.5 kilometres southwest of Oxford and 150 metres from the TCH (Route 104). During a normal year, the 1,600-metre-long, 220-metre-wide lake is unremarkable, but in the summer of 2020, the water in the lake vanished. Follow-up investigations revealed that 783,000 cubic metres had drained out of the lake, dropping the water level in places by 11.5 metres.

But while this water level drop was one of the largest ever recorded, long-time residents of the area were not completely surprised. The lake has become known as Dry Lake because it periodically empties and fills back up. Aerial images shows that the lake drained in 1939 and more significantly in the 1970s, but neither of these times was as dramatic as that of 2020. The exact reason for this is unknown, but it is believed that the lake's water slowly erodes the weak gypsum rock underlying the lake, eventually reaching the underground cave systems believed to occur throughout the area. After the water is drained, the holes may become clogged with sediment, allowing the lake to refill.

While the drainage of Slade Lake remains a mystery, investigation into the area's geology has resulted in a better understanding of why

the area is prone to these occurrences. Like many areas prone to caves and sinkholes in Nova Scotia, the area is underlain by the carbonate Windsor Group. Formed from the evaporation of an ancient sea, these rocks usually consist of gypsum, salt, anhydrites, and/or limestone. A mixture of these rocks likely occurs in the area, but nearby outcrops suggest that gypsum dominates.

It is believed that beneath the lake, groundwater and subterranean flowing water have carved a large cave system that periodically collapses, forming a sinkhole and a new point through which the water can flow. In the case of Slade Lake, geologists believe that a series of sinkholes caused its drainage, one of which is a perfectly circular pond located in the former lake bed and a second along the eastern rim.

When Slade Lake drained, it left a barren landscape. The event was catastrophic to the fish, plants, and freshwater mussels that used the lake as a habitat, but the lake has since become a unique habitat for new and old species. Because of this, the area has been protected under the Nova Scotia Special Places Protection Act and designated the Slade Lake Nature Reserve.

OTHER AREAS OF INTEREST

To the northeast, the town of Oxford has a history of dealing with sinkholes with the most notable happening in the summer of 2018. In late July, a small hole was noticed in a grassy field adjacent to the Oxford Lions Club. The hole, which began as no more than 1 metre wide and 60 centimetres deep, enlarged over the next month to 32 metres by 38 metres and was estimated to be 10 metres deep. As it formed, the hole filled with salt water and swallowed nearby trees, picnic benches, and parts of a nearby parking lot. The area was considered unstable, and the Lions Club decided to sell the property. A resident purchased the land and, after depositing 700 truckloads of fill, the sinkhole was filled in.

Throughout the Oxford area are reports of potholes that quickly reappear after being filled in, and several locations are monitored for subsidence. In September 2019, the Government of Nova Scotia

investigated the risk to the TCH, including a detailed lidar survey. The findings showed a defined corridor with hundreds of sinkholes. In addition to these, aerial surveys taken before the highway was built in the 1960s show that the current highway route traverses a possible sinkhole that was presumably filled in during construction. After further investigation, the risk to the highway was deemed low but officials continue to monitor the area very closely, as almost 10,000 vehicles pass through it each day.

The last natural wonder of the area is Black Lake, an inconspicuous 1-kilometre long, 500-metre-wide lake surrounded by cabins and thick forest. But beneath the surface of the lake a series of interconnected sinkholes give the lake a depth of over 70 metres, making it the deepest lake in Nova Scotia. Most of the lake is contained within private property.

 SLADE LAKE: N 45.715050, W 63.913120

Slade Lake is surrounded by forest, bog, and small lakes and ponds which owe their development to the region's karst topography. As no direct trails lead to the lake, visitors should have proper knowledge of the area before visiting and exercise caution when exploring the fragile landscape.

Index of Places

Acknowledgements

First and foremost, I must thank my best friend and life partner, Lindsay Batt, who encouraged and supported me throughout this journey. She never hesitated in saying yes when I approached her with the idea to uproot our lives and move across three provinces and never left my side when times got tough. This project would not have been possible without her optimistic and adventurous outlook on life.

I am very fortunate to have many parent figures in my life whose support and excitement have helped me see this project through. I would like to thank Tanya Stuckless, Greg Osmond, Bev and Tom McIsaac, Mary Batt and Derrick Baldwin, and my nan, Blanche Osmond. Thanks go to all my siblings for their encouragement: my sisters Ebony and Logan, who are technically far apart but always just a quick message away; and my sister Katie and her partner, Tom, who came to visit at exactly the right time. I would also like to thank all my family and friends who helped us along the way. There are too many to name, but just know that if we grabbed a beer, had a chat, tossed a frisbee, or connected online over the past year, I'm glad to have had you along for the ride.

For helping me experience, understand, and see the many wonderful places Nova Scotia has to offer, I must thank: my cousins Tanya, Dion, and Bethany Antle, who suggested many places to visit and provided great food and a dry place to stay on more than one occasion; my friend Adam Daniels, who served as an excellent tour guide through the Annapolis Valley; my friends Meagan Campbell and Asher Wells, for sharing stories about picturesque Cape Breton over great coffee; and friends Colleen Keagan and Nick Townsend, for their unwavering support and assistance through both books. A special thanks to my many friends and colleagues across Ontario who supported this endeavour and helped us during our transition back to the east coast. As this book was researched and written in several locations across Nova Scotia, I wish to thank the staff at the Halifax Central Library for guiding me through their collection of Nova Scotia literature and, after a long day at the library, the support continued with the friendly staff at Nine Locks Brewing Taproom on Spring Garden Road.

A big thank you to the hard work of my editor, Stephanie Porter; copy editor, Iona Bulgin; designer, Tanya Montini; publicist, Glenn Day; publisher, Gavin Will; and the entire Boulder Books team, who helped make this idea of mine into now two big, beautiful books.

It was only just over a year from the time the idea of *Hidden Nova Scotia* was conceived to the time it was complete. This never would have been possible without the kind hearts and helpful nature shown to me by the people of Nova Scotia. I thank everyone across this beautiful province who provided me with guidance and knowledge of some of Nova Scotia's most spectacular hidden places. I hope that you enjoy this book as much as I've enjoyed exploring your province, and I hope that I've captured it in a way that shows everyone else exactly why they should visit.

430

About the Author

Urban exploration enthusiast Scott Osmond has travelled extensively through Atlantic Canada, visiting and recording lost and hidden sites. Scott grew up in Corner Brook and moved to St. John's to complete degrees in Civil Engineering and Geography at Memorial University of Newfoundland and Labrador. In 2014 he established HiddenNewfoundland.ca as a place to share the Newfoundland's hidden places, lost stories, and natural wonders in hopes that it would bring awareness of its history and provide others with an opportunity for adventure. In 2021, Boulder Books published *Hidden Newfoundland*, Scott's bestselling first book.